The 46 Presidents of America

Stories, Achievements and Legacies - From George Washington to Joe Biden (U.S.A. Biography Book)

By Student Book Shelf

Table of contents

Introduction

Meet the 46 presidents of the U.S.A.

Welcome to the World Leaders series. This book introduces you to all 46 Presidents of the U.S.A. This book features the inspirational biographies of all the brave men that dared to rule America!

This book will teach you everything about the American presidents, including their stories and achievements, from George Washington to Joe Biden. You'll also learn some little-known facts about them!

The 46 Presidents of the USA is a factual and informative book that shows readers some of the most important traits of the American presidents and their decision to run for office.

Get to know more about Dwight Eisenhower, the 36th US President. "Dwight D. Eisenhower became America's youngest president after supplying our troops with food and weapons during World War II. Always unassuming, President Eisenhower didn't want to live in one of Washington's mansions or give too many speeches from his "Elbow." After a lifetime spent making friends at West Point, General Headquarters in Europe, Supreme Allied Command (Normandy) Headquarters in England, he campaigned as an Old Soldier and pledged "I Like Ike!"

You'll love learning about these brave men who dared to be president of America.

Books from the World Leaders feature:

- Fascinating biographies-Read about the lives of the 46 American presidents:
- Vivid portraits-Bring these American presidents to life in your imagination with the help of stimulating illustrations.

About the series: These World Leaders **series** feature fresh perspectives on the U.S. presidents that will inspire young readers to consider their place in society and learn about politics and its history.

The 46 Presidents of America goes beyond other Royal biography books to highlight topics and people from around the world and across time. Who is your favorite American president?

1. George Washington (1789-1797)

Unaffiliated party | Vice President: John Adams

"It is better to be alone than in bad company."

George Washington (Westmoreland County (Virginia), February 22, 1732 - Mount Vernon (Virginia), December 14, 1799) was a general, commander-in-chief of the colonies in the American War of Independence, slaveholder, and the first president of the United States from 1789 to 1797.

Colonial time

George Washington was born in 1732 into a wealthy family of English descent. His great-grandfather, John Washington, had emigrated from England to Westmoreland County (then part of British America) around 1657. George Washingtons father died when George was 11 years old and shortly thereafter he moved to Mount Vernon. Trained as a surveyor, Washington helped plan the town of Belhaven, now called

Alexandria. In 1752, his half-brother Lawrence died and Washington inherited the Mount Vernon estate.

In the 1750s, rivalries between England and France over colonial aspirations in North America slowly reached a climax. In 1753, Washington volunteered unsuccessfully to deliver an ultimatum to the French commander in what is now Ohio. After returning, Washington was promoted to lieutenant colonel in the Virginia militia. He led a mission to the Ohio River and built Fort Necessity in response to the forts the French had already built in the area. After a brief battle and surrounded by French troops, Washington surrendered and marched his troops back to Virginia's capital, Richmond.

Shortly thereafter, the French and Indian War broke out and he accompanied General Edward Braddock on his expedition to conquer Ohio from the French. Although this expedition ended in failure, Washington demonstrated his leadership by remaining cool-headed and withdrawing his troops under enemy fire. In 1755, Washington was promoted to colonel and commander-in-chief of the Virginia Militia.

After securing Virginia's borders from French attack, Washington retired from the militia to devote himself more to his estate. In 1759, he married the wealthy widow Martha Dandridge Custis and became actively involved in politics. He became a member of the Virginia House of Representatives where he gradually began to turn away from British policies in the colonies.

American Revolution

In 1774, as tensions in the colonies continued to rise, Washington was elected as a delegate from Virginia to the first Continental Congress. He was also a delegate to the second Continental Congress, and there he was unanimously elected commander-in-chief of the colonial forces in 1775.

Washington assumed command of the troops around Boston and began training the army of citizen soldiers. In March of 1776 he drove the British out of Boston, but his defense of New York went hopelessly wrong. However, most of the colonial troops managed to get to safety thanks to Washington, but the battles seemed to be going in favor of the British at this stage of the Revolution.

Last phase of the revolution

On Christmas Eve 1776, Washington attacked the Hessians at Trenton and won a victory that did much to boost the morale of the colonial troops. The Revolution dragged on after this with varying degrees of success until slowly but surely the tide began to turn in favor of the colonial troops.

In 1780, French troops began to get more and more involved in the battle after France openly sided with the colonials and declared war on the British. In October of 1781, Washington's army and French troops surrounded British General Charles Cornwallis at Yorktown, Virginia. The battle of Yorktown, which went in favor of the Americans and French, proved decisive, and Cornwallis' surrender marked the de facto end of British resistance to the Revolution.

After the British recognition of American independence in 1783, Washington left the army and again devoted himself to his beloved estate at Mount Vernon.

Battle for the constitution and the presidency

After the Revolution, Washington wanted nothing more than to resume his old lifestyle. Although he was very well-known and had an almost royal following, he felt nothing for a position of importance. However, in 1787, when it became clear that the country's current administrative organization was not efficient and decisive enough (via the *Articles of Confederation*), Washington was delegated to the *Constitutional Convention* in Philadelphia.

The convention in Philadelphia became the scene of fierce discussions between supporters and opponents of strong government. Washington's influence there was significant, although he rarely took an active part in the deliberations. In general, he supported the creation of a vigorous federal government, and his support won over many doubters. After the states of the Union approved the new constitution, Washington was unanimously elected the first president of the United States.

First term

On April 30, 1789, Washington was inaugurated as president in New York with John Adams as his vice president. On modern-day Wallstreet he took the oath of office, on the steps of Federal Hall. He was well aware that his actions as president would set a great precedent for all future presidents. Although he did not formally represent party interests - he hoped that American politics would remain partyless - he had more in common with the Federalists, led by *Secretary* of the Treasury Alexander Hamilton, than with the Democratic Republicans of Thomas Jefferson.

As the first president, Washington was the only one who could appoint the entire Supreme Court. In 1791, Washington led the selection and planning for the federal capital on the Potomac River, later Washington.

Second term and farewell to Washington

In 1792, Washington was again elected, unanimously, as president. One of the major problems early in his second term was the renewed tensions between Britain and France. His sympathies in this impending war were more with the British than with his old French allies, partly because he detested the chaos created in France by the French Revolution. However, he managed to keep his country neutral, to the annoyance of the pro-French sentiments of part of the country.

In the final phase of his presidency, the United States concluded a treaty with Great Britain (Jay's Treaty) that finally governed the withdrawal of all British troops from the U.S. Upon leaving active politics, Washington addressed his people with a letter published in a newspaper that would become one of the most important presidential "speeches." In it, Washington warned against, among other things, too close alliances with other countries. After handing over the presidency to the newly elected John Adams, Washington retired to his beloved Mount Vernon.

George Washington did not run for re-election after two terms in office, but re-election remained legally unrestricted. In practice, subsequent presidents were usually elected only twice. A major exception was F.D. Roosevelt. He was elected four times: in 1932, 1936, 1940, and 1944. Thereafter, the Constitution limited the number of terms of office to two.

Retirement and posthumous honors

Washington devoted himself to the Mount Vernon estate after leaving national politics, although he did reluctantly assume command of the army when war with France threatened in 1798. That war, however, did not materialize. In late 1799, laryngitis proved fatal to Washington. Washington died at the age of 67 at his estate. He was buried there in the family plot.

Shortly after his death, Harry Lee, who served with Washington in the Revolution, characterized the "father of the fatherland" of the United

States in the words, *"a citizen, first in war, first in peace, and first in the hearts of his countrymen."* In 1976, Congress passed a law that posthumously and retroactively promoted Washington to the highest rank of the U.S. Army, that of *General of the Armed Forces* (*General of the Armies*) as of July 4, 1776, the date of the U.S. Declaration of Independence.

The many precedents he set during his presidency continue to be followed. Named after him are the state of Washington, the federal capital Washington D.C., several cities, and other geographical locations. Many monuments have also been erected to him including the Washington Monument in Washington D.C., and the triumphal arch in Washington Square Park at the beginning of Fifth Avenue in New York City. His portrait graces the *quarter* (25-cent coin) and the $1 bill. Also, he is one of the four presidents depicted on Mount Rushmore.

Washington was one of the Cincinnati thanks to his efforts in the American War of Liberty. His diamond-studded eagle of this company is worn by the president of the Cincinnati because Washington left no descendants.

A private university bearing Washington's name has been founded in the US capital. The George Washington University was established by the US Congress more than two decades after his death, after Washington had promoted and supported the idea for years by including a bequest in his will.

Historical significance

Washington is widely regarded by historians as one of the most important and best presidents in American history. In a survey by Arthur M. Schlesinger Sr. conducted by the historian in 1948, and a follow-up survey in 1962 in which Schlesinger asked 75 historians for their opinions, only Abraham Lincoln was rated higher. A survey of nearly 50 historians in 1982, conducted by the newspaper the *Chicago Tribune*, named Washington the third-best president. Other surveys also regularly named Washington among the first three.

By today's standards, however, some argue against him that he manifested himself as a slaveholder with his Mount Vernon estate (as did several presidents after him). Others see in this position an expression of non-professional "place attachment. Before 1775 Washington had no objection to slavery; after this, however, he seemed slowly to be influenced by abolitionism. In closed circles he regularly spoke out against slavery and its reprehensibility. In public, however, he remained silent on this sensitive subject. He was afraid that broaching this subject would split the newborn country in two (which is what happened a few decades later in the American Civil War). The U.S. had only just been founded and he recognized that it would not do his position as leader of the entire country any good if he started a public debate on the subject. So he himself did keep several hundred slaves. This was also regularly blamed on him by the abolitionists. He took relatively good care of his slaves and mostly released older slaves. Washington made sure that the young slaves were educated. His will stated that his slaves would all be free after the death of his wife. A year before her death, Martha voluntarily let the slaves go.

Personality traits

Washington was regularly described as a charismatic and powerful person. His outward display was imposing; he was tall, broad, and physically strong. He could dance well and had a great fondness for horses. Appearance was of utmost importance to him as a new president. Whenever he drove through small villages as president, he would get out of his wagon and ride his white horse. People loved to see him as a great leader and he realized the importance of this. In his letters he was very modest, more than once stating that he was completely unqualified for the presidency, which eventually fell to him.

Because of his special personality and important influences on the U.S. and the presidency, Washington is considered the example to which presidents should aspire.

Religious background

President George Washington was initiated into a Masonic Lodge in Fredericksburg on November 4, 1752. At a Masonic ceremony on September 18, 1793, he laid the foundation stone of the Capitol in Washington. Dressed in Masonic robes, he marched to the construction site where members of a number of lodges were waiting for him.

In 1788 Washington became master of the Alexandria Lodge in Alexandria, Virginia, just outside Washington D.C., on the southwest side, which until the 1840s was part of District of Columbia. For this lodge, the *George Washington Masonic Memorial* was built in the 1920s to 1970s. The model for this 100-foot-tall monument was Pharos, the ancient lighthouse of Alexandria in antiquity. Although

Washington regularly attended church with his wife, he did not take the sacrament. There are reasons to suspect that he was a deist, but it is not certain. In any case, he was an advocate of religious tolerance.

2. John Adams (1797-1801)

Federalist Party | Vice President: Thomas Jefferson

"Everything in life should be done with reflection."

John Adams (Quincy (Massachusetts), October 30, 1735 - there, July 4, 1826) was an American politician of the Federalist Party. He was the 2nd president of the United States from 1797 to 1801.

Adams, a lawyer by profession, as a member of the Continental Congress, was one of the most important figures in the drafting and preparation of the American Declaration of Independence. As a top diplomat, he was the first U.S. ambassador to the Republic of the Seven United Provinces from 1782 to 1788, in addition he also served as the first ambassador to the Kingdom of Great Britain from 1785 to 1788. During the U.S. presidential election of 1789, Adams was defeated by former Commander-in-Chief of the War of Independence George Washington and was subsequently appointed as the 1st Vice President of the United States under President Washington and served from 1789 to 1797. For the US presidential election of 1796, Adams was the candidate on behalf of the Federalist Party and defeated the Democratic-Republican Party candidate Thomas Jefferson who then became vice president under Adams. During U.S. presidential elections of 1800, Adams was defeated for a second term by his vice president Thomas Jefferson.

His son John Quincy Adams was the 6th president of the United States from 1825 to 1829, the only father-son combination until George H.W. Bush and his son George W. Bush were both elected president. Adams' son-in-law William Stephens Smith was a member of the House of Representatives.

John Adams died on July 4, 1826, exactly fifty years after the American Declaration of Independence at the age of 90. On the same day, successor and former political rival Thomas Jefferson died at the age of 83.

Biography

The farmer's son Adams initially became a teacher and school principal, and then a lawyer in Boston. In 1764 he married Abigail Smith. He played a leading role in the pre-history of American independence as an advisor to the 13 states. He helped draft their constitutions. In 1774 he became a Massachusetts delegate to the Continental Congress, which declared independence on July 4, 1776.

In 1778 Adams joined the American embassy in Paris, which was headed by Benjamin Franklin. Partly because of the awkward cooperation, Adams went to Amsterdam in 1780 to seek financial support for the rebellion and to Johan Luzac, the publisher of the *Gazette de Leyde* to inform it of the debates on the American constitution. From 1782 he was the official envoy at The Hague; from 1785 also in London.

His work *"Defense of the Constitutions of the Government of the United States of America"* was written in 1787 and had a great influence on the creation of the U.S. Constitution that same year. According to many, with his presidency, democracy began in the US. But during his presidency, France ignored the U.S. desire to remain neutral in the war against Britain. Because Adams barely responded to this, he lost all his credit. During the presidential election of 1800, he was barely voted for. He would later say of the presidency, "No one who ever holds the office of president will ever wish this office upon a friend."

Dutch period

Adams went to Amsterdam in the summer of 1780 to find political and financial support in the Republic of the United Netherlands for the American revolt against the British. His sons John Quincy (13), Charles (10) and Robert (8) accompanied him.

Initially, Adams gained little foothold in Holland, and in any case the bankers did not dare to make a loan without sanction from the States General. They were, however, sympathetic to the endeavor, while the stadholder was English-minded. Adams understood little of Dutch relations. He no longer saw the Dutch as an "example to the world," but everywhere he discerned "smallness" stemming from "the preoccupation with nickels and dimes that pervades the whole people. To his minister John Jay he wrote: "The deliberations of this people are the most inscrutable I have ever witnessed."

When the tide seemed to be turning in favor of the insurgents, the Republic was willing to establish diplomatic ties with the United States as the second state after France. Thus, on April 19, 1782, Adams was accredited as an envoy to the US. In June he succeeded in obtaining a loan from Amsterdam merchants and bankers worth five million guilders, a considerable sum at the time. (A syndicate was formed between the Staphorsts, the Willinks and De la Lande & Fijnje to organize a loan to the United States.) It was the first foreign loan to the US. In October 1782, Adams signed a treaty of friendship and commerce between his country and the Republic on behalf of the US.

After the signing of the peace between the U.S. and England at Versailles in 1783, at which he was present, Adams became the first envoy to London (1785), with The Hague as a secondary post. In 1788 he returned to the US.

Presidency

Adams was a candidate in the presidential elections of 1789, 1792, 1796 and 1800 and was elected president in 1796 with his political rival Thomas Jefferson as his vice president and sworn in on March 4, 1797. His presidency was marked in part by a war between Britain and France in which Adams' sympathies lay with the English while Jefferson's Democratic Republicans favored the French. During this period, tensions with France ran high partly because the French were obstructing American shipping.

Of greater significance, however, was the so-called X-Y-Z affair. The French government under Talleyrand refused to receive diplomats sent by Adams unless they handed over a substantial sum of money to

France. Adams sent a letter to the U.S. Congress about this undiplomatic treatment by France, and soon this turned into a call to war in which Adams' popularity grew. Some skirmishing at sea followed with the young U.S. Navy coming to the aid of the merchant marine but negotiation prevented outright war.

Shortly before the 1800 election, Adams was the first to move into the White House in the new capital city of Washington, D.C. However, Adams narrowly lost the election that year to Jefferson and Aaron Burr, and Adams retired to his farm in Braintree where he engaged in a long correspondence with his longtime rival, and friend, Thomas Jefferson.

Death

On July 4, 1826, exactly 50 years after the *American Declaration of Independence*, Adams died at the age of 90. His last words were, *"Thomas Jefferson survives..."* (Thomas Jefferson is alive...), not knowing that a few hours before, Jefferson had also died. Adams is buried in the crypt of the United First Parish Church in Quincy, alongside his wife Abigail, his son John Quincy Adams and his wife Louisa.

3. Thomas Jefferson (1801-1809)

Democratic-Republican party | Vice presidents: Aaron Burr and George Clinton

"If you want something you've never had you must be willing to do something you've never done."

Thomas Jefferson (Shadwell (Virginia), April 13, 1743 - Monticello near Charlottesville (Virginia), July 4, 1826) was an American statesman, philosopher, architect, slave owner, artist, and the third president of the United States. The draft of the Declaration of Independence of 1776 (adopted on the 4th of July that year) was largely to his credit. He also authored the Virginia Statute for Religious Freedom, adopted in 1786, which established religious freedom.

Life

Thomas Jefferson was born in Albemarle County, Virginia, into a wealthy family of large landowners. His father, Peter Jefferson (1708-1757), was a self-taught surveyor who had acquired a modest estate of 60 slaves. His son would later become a gentleman farmer and slaveholder himself. His mother, Jane Randolph Jefferson (1720-1776), was among Virginia's leading families. Of her two sons, Thomas was the oldest. She also had six daughters. About his mother, Thomas had almost nothing to say in his memoirs. When his father died in 1757, he did everything he could to escape her scrutiny. He moved in with a local school teacher and learned Latin and Greek there until he entered college (College of William and Mary in Williamsburg) in 1760.

Thomas Jefferson was a multifaceted man. In addition to being a politician and philosopher, he was a scientist, lawyer, inventor, writer, and founder of Jeffersonian architecture. In 1767, he joined the Virginia Court as a jurist. During his time as ambassador to France (see below), he immersed himself in the wines of that country. From the evaluations of the wines that have survived, it can be seen that he was a great connoisseur. Jefferson collected thousands of books during his lifetime in his personal library at Monticello. After the death of his father, Peter Jefferson, the future president inherited his library, among others. He also inherited many books from George Wythe. After the British burned the Library of Congress in 1814, Jefferson turned over his collection of more than 6,000 books to Congress for four dollars a book.

In 1772 he married Martha Wayles Skelton, who thus became Mrs. Martha Jefferson. Together they had six children. However, she never lived to see her husband become president of the United States, as she died as early as 1782 at the age of 33. Their oldest daughter Martha Jefferson Randolph was considered *first lady* during Jefferson's later presidency. Jefferson never remarried, but it is generally assumed that he had a (sexual) relationship with his slave wife Sally Hemings, and that he was the father of her six half-breed children.

To his election to *the House of Burgesses* he seems to have lent a hand himself by handing out free rum punch. As a politician he wrote pamphlets. These caught the eye of the later President John Adams, who put him forward as the right person to write the Declaration of Independence. In addition to this *American Declaration of Independence,* he wrote the *Statute of Virginia for Religious Freedom.*

Declaration of Independence

Jefferson is considered the spiritual father of the United States. He designed the foundations of the nation: 'all men are created equal', popular sovereignty, the right to resist the government when it would not obey the law itself, and the 'natural' right to individual freedom, life and *the pursuit of happiness*. These basic values he had gained in part from writings of the English liberal Enlightenment philosopher John Locke, from whom he found the principle of 'natural law'. He may also have been inspired by various writings and statements from the Low Countries at the time of or after the onf independence struggle against the Spanish ruler in the 16th century, such as Spinoza who went further than Locke in his political thinking about (the role of) religion. Among Enlightenment thoughts and ideas, one can think of values such as individual freedom, freedom of religion, conscience, commerce, and the right to resist unlawful behavior by the government.

In the Declaration of Independence, Jefferson fiercely outlined the exploitation and oppression that he and many others experienced of Americans; he referred to the English king as a tyrant. The fact that Americans were not allowed to process their own agricultural products, for example, but had to ship them to England, only to have to buy them expensively after processing, was indigestible to most Americans.

However, Jefferson's role in American history is not undisputed. Many people see him as the embodiment of the struggle around racism and freedom in the US. The U.S. advocates great individual freedom; after all, everyone is equal. This is therefore diametrically opposed to racism, which has always played a major role in American politics. Jefferson is a good example of this. Although he wrote the words "all men are created equal" in the Declaration of Independence, he still owned hundreds of slaves. This was also blamed on him by abolitionists at the time. Many historians, however, comment on this alleged hypocrisy. After all, the ownership of slaves must be viewed in the context of his time. Of the so-called *Founding fathers,* John Adams was the only one who did not own slaves. Jefferson also wrote a book defending slave ownership through racial theory.

Role in Indian Removal Act

Although often only Andrew Jackson is mentioned in connection with the Indian Removal Act, it was probably Jefferson who first proposed the idea. Jackson merely provided the implementation and execution of the plan Jefferson had devised. Jefferson explained his plan in a series of private letters to William Henry Harrison. His first actions to promote the Indian Removal Act occurred between 1776 and 1779, when he recommended that the Cherokee and Shawnee be driven from their territories to the area west of the Mississippi River. When he was already president, he wrote a letter to the governor of Indiana Territory on February 27, 1803, making clear his plans for the Indians.

Republican

Jefferson also played a major role in the political divide between federalists (then led by Alexander Hamilton) and republicans. Jefferson chose the latter party. He favored small government, a leading role for agriculture with many small farmers, and decentralized policies. One of his supporters was James Madison, whom he would later appoint as his Secretary of State. The Federalist Hamilton, however, advocated a strong federal government, a solid financial system, and a government of the rich, wealthy, and highborn, in short, the elite.

From 1779 to 1781 he was governor of Virginia.

From 1785 to 1789, Thomas Jefferson was ambassador to France, which allowed him to study the French Revolution closely. Then from 1790 to 1793, under President George Washington, he was *secretary of state*. Having already been a presidential candidate in 1792, he became vice president under John Adams in 1797 after the US presidential election of 1796. After the election of 1800, he became president in 1801. He remained so for two terms, having also won the 1804 election, until 1809.

As Secretary of State and as Vice President, Jefferson rebelled against what he saw as the government's overly centralized power, bringing him into conflict with both Hamilton and John Adams. As president, however, Jefferson himself was quite domineering. He preferred to consult with his ministers by one-two punch, rather than in full ministerial session. He was accused of "monarchist" behavior, which violated his own ideas about governing.

Jefferson and Adams were both Founding Fathers, and also friends for a long time. However, this changed drastically during the 1800 election when it became apparent how far apart the two men were politically. Jefferson disagreed with the policies Adams had pursued during his presidency and planned to take a drastically different approach. To win the election, both men went about their business in a devious manner, spreading lies about each other. Jefferson, for example, spread the word that Adams would like to start a war with France. Partly because of these mutual lies, the situation quickly escalated and the two men could no longer stand each other. Years after Jefferson's presidency, Adams writes a letter to Jefferson, taking the first step toward renewed friendship. The two men write regularly; 158 letters have been recovered. Thus their intense rivalry comes to an end. Both men eventually die on the same day, July 4, 1826.

President

Perhaps his greatest success as president was the purchase in 1803 of the vast territory of the French, the *Louisiana Territory*. In doing so, he doubled the territory of the Union in one fell swoop. It included in whole or in part the following states: Louisiana, Arkansas, Missouri, Iowa, Minnesota, North Dakota, South Dakota, Nebraska, Kansas, Oklahoma, Texas, New Mexico, Colorado, Wyoming, and Montana. This purchase is very appropriately known as the Louisiana Purchase.

Napoleon also transferred Florida, New Orleans, and the navigation rights of the Mississippi River to the Union without objection. In addition, as part of the Lewis and Clark expedition (designed to investigate the possibility of a shipping route from the Mississippi River to the Pacific Ocean), the Americans extended their power over large areas of the western part of the country. These territorial expansions, incidentally, would later cost the lives of large numbers of Native Americans.

Other things Jefferson was able to take credit for during his first term in office were the elimination of the whiskey tax, the reduction of government, and the elimination of the national debt. This was possible because of the peace in Europe, which allowed trade to flourish. It was also a success for his finance minister, Albert Gallatin.

His second term as president was considerably more difficult. France and England had conflicts again. Maritime trade became unsafe and stagnant, even as Jefferson had decimated the Navy. Jefferson responded by prohibiting trade with Europe, but the only result was that the American economy took a huge hit. Domestically, he faced opposition. Jefferson did not want to run for office again and withdrew.

After the presidency

After his two terms as president, Jefferson went to live in Monticello. There he founded the University of Virginia, for which he designed himself. The University of Virginia is an ode to Roman art; it is literally a copy of the Roman Pantheon. One can clearly see this in the podium on which the structure is placed and the dome. (*See also: Jeffersonian architecture.*) Furthermore, he built his own house, called Monticello. Here he kept a huge supply of imported French wine. During his time as ambassador to France, he developed a love of French cuisine and dress.

Jefferson died at the age of 83 on July 4, 1826, fifty years to the day after the U.S. Congress adopted the Declaration of Independence. On the evening of July 3, he spoke his last words. He is said to have asked, *"Is it the fourth?"* He was answered that it would soon be the fourth, upon which he fell asleep. He died on the afternoon of the next day (the 4th). On the same day, pastor and former political rival John Adams died at the age of 90. Adam's last words would have been: "Thomas Jefferson survives." He did not know, however, that Jefferson had died a few hours earlier.

Jefferson was buried at his Monticello estate.

Monuments and Legacy

Several buildings were named after Jefferson after his death. Also, his face was printed on stamps and money. In the early twentieth century, Jefferson was chosen along with George Washington, Theodore Roosevelt and Abraham Lincoln for the Mount Rushmore Memorial. Jefferson is also depicted on the Jefferson Memorial, in Washington D.C. This monument was erected in 1943, in honor of Jefferson's bicentennial. Inside the building is a six-foot tall statue of Jefferson, with inscriptions of some of his written passages.

4. James Madison (1809-1817)

Democratic-Republican party | Vice presidents: George Clinton and Elbridge Gerry

"Equal laws protecting equal rights...the best guarantee of loyalty and love of country."

James Madison (Port Conway (Virginia), March 16, 1751 - Montpelier (Virginia), June 28, 1836) was an American statesman, political philosopher, and slaveholder. Between 1809 and 1817 he served as the fourth president of the United States. During his presidency, the country again went to war with the United Kingdom.

James Madison played an important role in the creation of the United States of America. He was one of the main authors of the Constitution of the United States and the subsequent *Bill of Rights*. With his articles in the *Federalist Papers* defending the new Constitution, he influenced public opinion. Thanks in part to Madison, the United States was given a federal form of government. He served as a delegate to the House of Representatives and was Secretary of State in President Thomas

Jefferson's cabinet. James Madison is one of the *Founding Fathers* of the US and is known as the *Father of the Constitution.*

On September 14, 1794, Madison married Dolley Payne Todd, later first lady, with whom he would have no children. The couple differed considerably in age and temperament: the fourteen years younger Dolley was a cordial and cheerful woman and a hostess who furthered her husband's political career. Madison was gruff and reserved.

Youth

James Madison was born in Port Conway the oldest of twelve children of Colonel James Madison Sr. (1723-1801) and Eleanor *Nellie* Conway (1731-1829). His slaveholding parents owned a tobacco plantation in Orange County, Virginia, an estate called Montpelier. He received his earliest education at home and in 1769 left for Princeton University in New Jersey, where he studied history, public administration, and law. He became involved with a circle of students and faculty members who had revolutionary ideas and became a member of the *American Whig Society*. He received his academic degree as early as 1771, after which he continued his studies with the rector magnificus of Princeton for several months before returning to Virginia.

From 1772 to 1775 Madison resided at his father's *Montpelier* estate, where he became increasingly interested in politics and government. During this period he also became convinced of the need for the British colonies to become independent of the mother country. Beginning in 1776, Madison was a member of the Virginia Constitutional Convention, where he helped draft the *Virginia Declaration of Rights* and worked closely with Thomas Jefferson. After Virginia adopted a new constitution in June 1776, Madison became a member of the Legislative Assembly of the future state of Virginia.

Father of the Constitution

Still young and timid, Madison joined Virginia's delegation to the Continental Congress in 1779, where he assumed a more leading role at the end of the American War of Independence. Madison favored a strong central federal authority and felt that the *Articles of Confederation* provided too weak a framework for the government of the newly independent United States. In 1784, Madison was again elected to the Virginia Legislative Assembly, the *General Assembly*. In the *Assembly,* he was one of the leading advocates of a stronger central government, a not too popular position in Virginia. Madison also advocated religious freedom and the separation of church and state.

In September 1786, at Madison's suggestion, a convention was held in Annapolis, Maryland where, Madison hoped, the states could agree on a more uniform trade policy. Only four states sent a delegation, and little more was accomplished than to convene another convention. At this second convention, held in Philadelphia, all the states were present. The intended purpose of this convention was to reform the Articles of Confederation. In May 1787, Madison was elected as one of Virginia's delegates.

Constitutional Convention

Three weeks before the Convention was to start, James Madison arrived in Philadelphia. He presented his plan for a new constitution to the other Virginia delegates. The proposal was based on his *Study of Ancient and Modern Confederacies* and *Vices of the Political System of the United States*. In Madison's vision, the three pillars of statehood were to be: an elected executive, a legislature consisting of two chambers in which the states would be represented according to their population size, as well as a strong national judiciary. This system would become the foundation for the entire political framework of the United States. It rested on Montesquieu's trias politica: there are three powers of government that control each other through *checks and balances* so that none can dominate.

At the Convention, the *Virginia Plan* was nominated by Governor Edmund Randolph of Virginia. Opposed to this was the *New Jersey Plan*, which differed from Madison's ideas primarily in that it advocated a parity in the distribution of representatives in the future U.S. Congress. Ultimately, the compromise was reached that the House of Representatives would be composed based on population size, while in the Senate each state, regardless of size, would have two senators.

During the Constitutional Convention, Madison attended almost all meetings so as, he said, "not to miss any important speech." His goal was to create a constitution, *"on which would be staked the happiness of a people great even in its infancy, and possibly the cause of liberty throughout the world"* ("which has the purpose of securing the happiness of a people, great even in this early stage, and perhaps liberty throughout the world").

After the Constitutional Convention, Madison worked for the adoption of the Constitution which he co-signed. At the Virginia State Convention where the ratification of the new Constitution was being discussed, the "Father of the Constitution" had several debates with Patrick Henry, who opposed the constitutional proposal. Madison was one of three authors of a series of 85 influential articles that appeared in mostly New York newspapers and were later published as the *Federalist Papers*. Madison, Alexander Hamilton, and John Jay published these articles as a counterweight to the negative coverage of the Constitution in various newspapers. They hoped to convince the American public of the need to adopt the Constitution. It is generally believed that Madison wrote 26 of the 85 *Federalist Papers*.

The Virginia State Convention voted to ratify the Constitution in 1788 by 89 to 79 votes. Madison failed to be elected to the Senate in 1789, but was elected to the House of Delegates in his home district.

Bill of Rights

One of the arguments that opponents of the Constitution made against it was the absence of a *Bill of Rights*, which was supposed to guarantee the rights of citizens. Although Madison initially opposed this *Bill of Rights*, he gradually became one of its biggest supporters. In all, Madison proposed twelve amendments as part of this *Bill of Rights* and in December 1791, ten of them were ratified by the states and thus became part of the Constitution. More than 150 years after his death, in 1992, another of Madison's amendments was ratified, as the 27th Amendment to the Constitution.

During the eight years that Madison served in the House of Representatives, the two-party system that still exists in the U.S. today began to emerge. Madison initially aligned himself with Alexander Hamilton's faction, which advocated a close relationship with old motherland Britain and wanted to give more power to the central government. Thomas Jefferson and his followers opposed this. Gradually, Madison began to identify more and more with Jefferson's views, and by the end of his four terms as Congressman, Madison was one of the leaders of the Democratic-Republican Party in the House. Hamilton's Federalist Party and Jefferson's Democratic-Republican Party differed on measures Hamilton wanted to implement, such as the creation of a national bank, the assumption of debts incurred by the individual states by the federal government, and the introduction of trade tariffs, although Madison had proposed many of these measures himself in the *Continental Congress*. Madison feared that the Federalists would give the northern states too much influence, and his original nationalism gradually changed to regional loyalty.

This split in American politics caused a chilling of the relationship between Madison and George Washington, who, like Hamilton, was a Federalist, although party-less for form's sake. Previously, Washington maintained close contacts with Madison and, as president, sought Madison's advice on various policy issues.

Madison and foreign policy

In foreign policy, the anti-Federalists were more pro-French shortly after the introduction of the Constitution, while the Federalists held pro-British sentiments. In the wars between France and Britain that followed the French Revolution, President Washington sought to maintain American neutrality, which the anti-Federalists saw as pro-British action. In 1794, the United States entered into the Treaty of Jay with Great Britain that resolved various differences between the two countries, often still dating from the American War of Independence, and established American trade rights. Madison had fought unsuccessfully against the ratification of this treaty: he felt that America was better able to withstand any trade war than Britain. Madison and other anti-Federalists gradually lost influence during this period, while the Federalists gained the upper hand in Congress.

Madison did not run for re-election to Congress in 1797 and retired with his wife Dolley to *Montpelier*, his father's estate, which he had since inherited. Two years later, however, he was again elected to the Virginia *Assembly*. After Thomas Jefferson was elected president in 1801, he appointed his old political friend and kindred spirit Madison to the highest post in the cabinet, that of *Secretary of State*. In this position, it was up to Madison to manage relations with the two great rivals Britain and France. Both European powers were at war with each other almost constantly during this period and had declared a blockade of each other's ports. Because American merchant ships carried much of both countries' trade with their West Indian colonies, they regularly suffered from French and British warships confiscating their cargoes. The British forcibly forced British nationals serving on the neutral American ships to serve in the British navy (*impressment*).

Madison initially tried unsuccessfully to put an end to these practices through diplomatic means. As a last-ditch effort to prevent war with one or both of the European powers, Jefferson and Madison introduced the *Embargo Act* passed by Congress in 1807. This act prohibited all trade of American ships with foreign countries. This *Embargo Act* was difficult to implement and led to an economic downturn especially in the southern states. The law was soon repealed again, although the underlying problems were not solved.

Presidency

In the run-up to the 1808 U.S. presidential election, the Democratic-Republican Party nominated Madison as its candidate for the White House. The Federalists nominated the diplomat Charles Cotesworth Pinckney. Madison won the election easily, capturing 122 of the 175 Electoral College votes. George Clinton retained the position of vice president, which he also held under Jefferson. On March 4, 1809, Madison was sworn in as the fourth president of the United States by the chief justice of the *Supreme Court*, John Marshall.

Madison's presidency was largely dominated by deteriorating relations with Britain and France. While the *Embargo Acts* were repealed, the subsequent *Non-Intercourse Act* that allowed trade with all countries except Britain and France was also quickly dismissed as ineffective and abolished.

War of 1812

From November 1810, trade with Great Britain, which had been allowed again after the abolition of the *Non-Intercourse Act*, was again prohibited. Together with the continuation of the British policy of conscription (*impressment*), this made for very tense relations with the former mother country. Madison's foreign minister, James Monroe, conducted negotiations with Britain, but little to no progress was made and war seemed inevitable. In addition, there were members of Congress who called for war because they wanted to use the opportunity to expand the territory of the United States. Prominent members of this group were Henry Clay and John C. Calhoun.

In the spring of 1812, Madison asked Congress to declare an embargo on Britain and, if American demands were not met, to take harsher measures, if necessary a declaration of war. An ultimatum to Britain expired on June 1, 1812, and Madison made a speech to Congress. He argued that British policy was in fact hostile. Measures against American merchant ships and British support for Indian uprisings in the western territories of the United States had led to *"on the side of Great Britain a state of war against the United States, and on the side of the United States a state of peace toward Great Britain"* ("on the side of Great Britain a state of war toward the U.S. and on the side of the U.S. a state of peace toward Great Britain"). The President asked Congress whether it wanted to stand idly by in this situation, or stand up for the rights of the United States. On June 17, Congress responded with a declaration of war, which Madison signed a day later. Ironically, two days earlier Britain had still partially met American demands, but news of these British decisions had not yet reached the United States. The War of 1812 was a reality.

The United States was ill prepared for war. Madison personally sought to assume leadership of the armed forces. In addition, there was little appetite for war in some regions. In New England in particular, there was fierce resistance, led by the Federalists, and a convention was even held in Hartford where a separate peace with Great Britain was considered.

The presidential election of 1812 was held during this difficult time. New England's opposition to the war and the poor military record in the early stages of the war dominated the election campaign, in which Madison ran against his party colleague DeWitt Clinton. In the end, Madison won in the Electoral College by 128 votes to 89, re-electing him to a second term. His *running mate* and new vice president was Elbridge Gerry.

Militarily, the war was far from successful for the first two years, although the U.S. Navy had some successes against the superior British *Royal Navy*. During 1814, the tide began to turn in favor of the Americans, although Madison was forced to flee the capital of Washington in August 1814. British troops took the seat of American government and set fire to the White House and other government buildings. Madison had joined fleeing army units and rode around on horseback for several days before returning to the partially destroyed capital.

In the summer of 1814, Madison sent envoys to Ghent to negotiate peace with the British government. On December 24, the Peace of Ghent was signed, effectively restoring the *status quo* before the war. The American goals had not been achieved, but the war that had been endured had resulted in the United States gaining a new self-confidence. Madison was praised by his countrymen for leading the country through the war in one piece.

Postwar policies

The last two years of Madison's presidency were marked by growing prosperity and increasing nationalism in the United States. The president signed some laws that decided on the creation of a new national bank and the introduction of trade tariffs, which he had fiercely opposed years earlier. This brought him a little closer again to the position of his old friend and later political rival Alexander Hamilton.

Where "domestic improvements" were concerned, Madison vetoed some laws passed by the federal Congress that particularly affected the country's infrastructure. Madison argued that the Constitution reserved it to the states to build and maintain roads, bridges and the like.

The War of 1812 proved very important to the growth of American self-consciousness. As a result, the link with Europe was permanently severed and people now focused entirely on their own expansion into the West. With this isolationism towards Europe, the first step was taken under Madison in an evolution that would eventually lead to the Monroe Doctrine of 1823, which would deny the European powers the right to interfere in internal American affairs.

After the presidency

In 1817, Madison ceded the presidency to James Monroe and retired to his Montpelier estate. In 1829, Madison returned to public life for a short time when he attended the *Virginia Constitutional Convention* as a member of the delegation, where a new Constitution for Virginia was negotiated. Madison became president of the *University of Virginia,* founded by his political friend, in 1826, after Jefferson's death.

During the last years of his life, Madison was in poor health. Despite this, he continued to follow politics intensively. On June 28, 1836, the statesman died at Montpelier at the age of 85. Madison was the last living signer of the U.S. Constitution.

5. James Monroe (1817-1825)

Democratic-Republican party | Vice President: Daniel D. Tompkins

"We must support our rights or lose our character, and with it, perhaps, our liberties."

James Monroe (Westmoreland County (Virginia), April 28, 1758 - Albany (New York), July 4, 1831) was an American politician and slaveholder. He was the 5th president of the United States from 1817 to 1825.

After serving in the army in the American War of Independence, Monroe joined the anti-federalists. He subsequently served as a member of the Senate, Governor of Virginia, Secretary of War, and Secretary of State.

Lifetime

Youth and involvement American War of Independence

His father was a planter. When he died in 1774, James Monroe
inherited a small plantation, including a number of slaves. He entered
the College of William and Mary that same year and, like most of his
fellow students, was enthusiastic about the American rebellion against
King George III. When the rebellion turned into a full-scale war, Monroe
enlisted in the Continental Army in early 1776. He did not return to
school. His good background earned him a position as an officer. He
was involved in the raid on the Governor's palace in Williamsburg,
where two hundred muskets and three hundred swords were captured
to arm the Williamsburg militia. With the rest of General Washington's
army, Monroe was driven off Long Island by the British.

On Christmas Eve 1776, Washington attacked the Hessians at Trenton
and won a victory that did much to boost the morale of the colonial
troops. During an artillery attack, Monroe was hit by a bullet in his left
shoulder and had to be carried off the battlefield. The bullet was not
removed and remained lodged in his shoulder for the rest of his life.
After his recovery, he enlisted as a lieutenant colonel in the Virginia
militia. In September 1779 he left there and went to study law, first with
George Wythe and later with Thomas Jefferson. When the British
attacked Richmond Jefferson, at that time governor if Virginia
appointed him as liaison to the Continental Army in North Carolina. In
1783 he was admitted to the Bar and started his own law practice in
Fredericksburg, Virginia.

Entrance into politics

Monroe made his entrance into American politics in 1782 with his
election to the Virginia House of Delegates. From 1783 to 1786 he was
a member of the Continental Congress. Monroe played an important
role in Virginia's ratification of the Constitution. On one side were the
supporters, led by George Washington and James Madison. Patrick
Henry and George Mason led the way in opposition. This left the
deciding vote with the moderate figures like Monroe and Edmund
Pendleton. They were concerned about the absence of a Bill of Rights
and the ability of the federal government to tax. They wanted only the
individual states to have that option. Finally, they decided to agree that
once the Constitution was adopted, they would try to make the changes
they wanted. With a narrow majority, Virginia then ratified the
Constitution. Monroe ran for the first House of Delegates, but was
defeated by Madison. In 1790, the Virginia Legislative Assembly did
elect him to the Senate. There he soon joined the Democratic-
Republican Party of Jefferson and Madison and after a short time was
leader of the Senate.

Ambassador to France

The government appointed Monroe as ambassador to France in 1794. There he campaigned for the release of Thomas Paine, who had been arrested for his objection to the execution of King Louis XVI. The French government insisted that Paine leave immediately for the United States. Furthermore, he reached an agreement for the release of all American prisoners, including Adrienne de La Fayette and her family, all of whom had been granted American citizenship through their efforts during the Revolution.

The American ambassador tried to convince the French government that President Washington's policy of neutrality did not work in favor of Great Britain, with whom France was at war at the time. This could no longer be maintained after the United States and Britain signed the Treaty of Jay ("treaty of Jay"), much to Monroe's own dismay. President Washington felt that Monroe was not serving his country's interests well and called him back.

Governor of Virginia

The fired ambassador returned to his law practice until he was elected governor in 1799. He had to deal with a slave revolt led by Gabriel Prosser in 1800. Monroe sent in the state militia, who put down the uprising. Prosser and 26 other slaves were hanged. Monroe also considered using the state militia to help Jefferson gain power as president in 1800.

Ambassador to Britain

President Jefferson sent Monroe to France in 1803 to assist Robert Livingston in negotiating the Louisiana Purchase. Then the president appointed him ambassador to Britain. He negotiated a new treaty with Britain to replace the Jay Treaty, as it was expiring after ten years. At the time, Jefferson had been dismissive of that treaty, even though the treaty had provided ten years of peace during which a lot of money came into the country through trade. Monroe concluded the Monroe-Pinkney Agreement in December 1806, which would have given America a new period of peace, but the treaty did not end the forced admission of American sailors into the British Navy. Britain desperately needed these men to man all the warships in the fight against Napoleon Bonaparte. Jefferson did not even submit the treaty to the Senate for ratification, nor did he make any attempt to negotiate a new agreement. As a result, the two countries grew further apart, eventually culminating in the War of 1812. Monroe himself was angered by the rejection of the agreement and became embroiled with Secretary of State James Madison over it.

Leading up to the 1808 presidential election, the Democratic-Republican Party was quite divided. Part of the party wanted little of Jefferson's policies and asked Monroe to run for president. The plan was to elect him president in cooperation with the Federalist Party. Monroe's supporters did not prevail and at the party convention Madison was chosen and subsequently elected as president.

Minister of War and Foreign Affairs

Monroe returned to the Virginia House of Delegates and was re-elected governor in 1811. He held that position for only four months because Madison asked him to be his Secretary of State. In this way the president hoped to win support from opponents within his own party. Monroe did not have a major stake in the War of 1812, because he was outflanked by President Madison and the war hawks in Congress. The war went disastrously for America. In August 1814, the British captured Washington D.C. and burned down the Capitol and the White House. Madison replaced John Armstrong as Secretary of War and asked Monroe for that post. The latter stepped down as Secretary of State, but Madison did not appoint a replacement, so Monroe effectively occupied two ministerial posts. He launched another plan to invade Canada, but a peace treaty ended the war in March 1815.

President of the United States

Madison no longer stood for election in 1816 and Monroe was his intended successor. The Federalist Party had lost much support because it had not supported the War of 1812. They did not even nominate an official candidate. Most Federalists supported Rufus King, twice previous candidate for vice president. Monroe therefore won the election easily. The dissolution of the Federalist Party continued and four years later he did not even have a single opposing candidate, something that had previously only occurred in the election of George Washington. After 1820, this never happened again.

Monroe faced a major economic crisis in 1819 as an aftermath of the Napoleonic Wars. Britain had increased its industrial capacity to meet all the war effort. Europe was in ruins and as a result much of Britain's excess production was dumped on the American market at low prices. Many American companies could not compete with this and went bankrupt. In addition, there was a lack of proper supervision of the rapidly growing banking sector. As a result, there was a lot of money in circulation and massive speculation on land took place. Due to food shortages, this was seen as an interesting investment, especially since the government sold a lot of land under favorable conditions. Investors lost a lot of money when land prices plummeted. Despite the crisis, which lasted until 1821, Monroe remained popular.

The biggest challenge in his presidency was Missouri's entry into the Union. In the Senate, the number of states where slavery was and was not allowed was balanced, but that would change with Missouri's accession. Supporters and opponents concluded the so-called Missouri Compromise in which it was agreed, among other things, that Maine would be split off from Massachusetts and join the Union as a separate state, where slavery was prohibited, thus restoring the balance.

Congress required many grants for national infrastructure improvements. Monroe vetoed a law that would have made the federal government pay for the maintenance costs of the Cumberland Road, a road built from Cumberland, Maryland to Vandalia, Illinois. He felt that the states were responsible for this themselves.

Monroe caused a major controversy when it was revealed that he had sent General Andrew Jackson to Spanish Florida in 1817. Jackson launched a military campaign there against the Seminole Indians and the Spanish who were protecting them. Many believed he had the president's permission to do so, but Monroe denied it. The president had the advantage that most members of Congress were in favor of further expansion, and all resolutions against Monroe and Jackson were voted down. Secretary of State John Quincy Adams entered into a treaty with the Spanish a year later buying Florida for five million dollars.

Monroe's name lives on for posterity primarily through the Monroe doctrine he established. This was a principle in the foreign policy of the United States. The term itself is derived from a speech Monroe made to Congress in 1823. Monroe declared any form of European interference in the Western Hemisphere taboo, by which he meant political intervention in the only recently independent nations of South America and new attempts to colonize the Americas. Monroe did, however, promise to respect the existing colonies held by European powers. The Monroe doctrine would be standing American policy for a long time. Many historians believe that the doctrine was taken out of context after his presidency, however, and used to justify foreign policy. Monroe intended his doctrine to be defensive, to curb expansion of power from

Europe into the West. However, this doctrine was later used as an excuse for US expansion.

During his presidency, Monroe supported the settlement of freed slaves in what would later become known as Liberia. The white elite preferred to get rid of the freed slaves because they feared they might rebel against their former masters. The federal government purchased some hundred thousand dollars worth of land in Liberia. In gratitude, Liberians named their capital city Monrovia after the U.S. president.

A third term passed Monroe by. He was succeeded by his Secretary of State, John Quincy Adams.

Last years of life

He returned to Virginia and after the death of his wife lived in New York. He died on July 4, 1831, becoming the third president to die on American Independence Day; five years earlier, both John Adams and Thomas Jefferson had also died on this date.

6. John Quincy Adams (1825-1892)

Democratic-Republican party and National Republican party | Vice President: John C. Calhoun

"Try and fail, but don't fail to try."

John Quincy Adams (Braintree (Massachusetts), July 11, 1767 - Washington D.C., February 23, 1848) was the 6th president of the United States from 1825 to 1829.

He was the son of John Adams, the second president of the United States. He studied at Leiden University during his father's envoy to the Netherlands. He also held a number of envoys (including the Netherlands 1794-1797). As an envoy, he played a key role in the negotiation of important treaties, particularly the Treaty of Ghent (1814), which ended the War of 1812. He served as Secretary of State from 1817 to 1825. Adams is also considered the creator of the Monroe

Doctrine, which would be a key political principle for 19th-century America.

Adams became president after the hard-fought election of 1824, in which he defeated Andrew Jackson. His presidency followed 24 years after his father's. It was the first time in the United States that a son of a president became president himself (later this happened again with George H.W. Bush and George W. Bush). John Quincy Adams' presidency, like his father's, lasted only one term. It was not a great success because he was ahead of his time with his vision of a strong central authority.

Adams is to date the only president to return to Congress after the end of his term. He was elected to the House of Representatives in 1831 and would hold that position until his death in 1848. Late in life he emerged as an ardent opponent of slavery.

He was also the first president (by tenure) of whom a photograph is known.

Lifetime

Youth and education

John Quincy Adams was the son of John Adams and Abigail Adams (birth name Smith). He was named after Colonel John Quincy, his mother's grandfather. His father was the American ambassador to France from 1778 to 1779 and to the Netherlands from 1780 to 1782. His son accompanied him on these trips and thus spent much of his childhood abroad.The young Adams studied at Leiden University. At the age of fourteen he accompanied Francis Dana on a mission to St. Petersburg, Russia. He stayed in Finland, Sweden and Denmark. The many travels in his youth allowed him to develop his language skills well, so he spoke fluent Dutch and French. During his youth he was prepared for a life in politics. His father pointed out his privileged position and believed that John Quincy should use his privileges in the service of his country.

Back in the United States, he enrolled at Harvard and earned a Bachelor of Arts in 1787. He then apprenticed with a lawyer for two years. Back at Harvard, Adams also earned a Master of Arts. In 1791, he was admitted to the legal profession.

Ambassador to the Netherlands, Portugal and Prussia

Adams first made himself heard on the national stage through a series of articles praising the decision of the first U.S. President George Washington not to interfere in the French Revolution. The president appointed Adams as ambassador to the Netherlands in 1793. Adams was not happy about the appointment. He was content with his quiet life in Massachusetts and only accepted the appointment at his father's urging. On his way to Holland, Adams delivered a number of documents to John Jay, who at the time was engaged in negotiations with Britain to avert a possible trade war. After Holland, ambassadorships in Portugal (1796) and Prussia (1797) followed. Four years later he returned to the US.

Senator

Back in America, Adams initially returned to work in the legal profession. In 1802 he was elected to the Massachusetts State Senate. That same year he ran for the House of Representatives on behalf of the Federalist Party, but lost the election. A year later, however, he was elected to the Senate. During this same period, Adams also went to work at Harvard as a professor of rhetoric. In the Senate, he supported President Thomas Jefferson's Louisiana Purchase and Embargo Act, losing the support of the Federalists in his home state. At that time, members of Congress were not yet elected directly by the people, but by the popular vote of the respective state. The Federalists in Massachusetts were in the majority in the legislative chambers in their home state and replaced Adams for someone else in June 1808. Adams then broke with his own party and switched to the Democratic-Republican Party.

Ambassador to Russia and Britain

President James Madison appointed Adams as the first American ambassador to Russia in 1809. Almost immediately upon arrival, he asked Russia's Tsar Alexander I to pressure Denmark into releasing several American sailors and ships. Denmark was at that time engaged in a war with Britain. However, Denmark had not only attacked British ships, but also American ships. Denmark cooperated with the request, and the American ships and sailors returned to the U.S.

Adams was nominated as a judge of the Supreme Court in 1811, but declined the nomination. In 1812 he reported on Napoleon's invasion of and retreat from Russia. In 1812, meanwhile, the Americans had gone to war with Britain, but on the losing side. The US accepted an offer from the Tsar to mediate between the two sides. The British, however, did not go along with this. Adams was called back from Russia in 1814 to lead the team that negotiated with Britain to end the war. This eventually culminated in the Peace of Ghent.

Adams then served as ambassador to Britain for two more years, a post previously held by his father.

Minister of Foreign Affairs

President James Monroe asked Adams to be his Secretary of State in 1817. In that capacity, he entered into the Adams-Onís Treaty with Spain in 1818. In it, Spain pledged to cede Florida to the United States. To the west, the United States gave up its claims to Texas and other territories under Spanish rule, and a mutually accepted boundary was established: along the Red River, the Arkansas, and the forty-second parallel.

With Great Britain, Adams concluded the Treaty of 1818. This resolved a number of border disputes and laid the groundwork for a better relationship with neighboring Canada.

At the time Monroe came to power, several European countries, especially Spain, were trying to regain her control over South America. In 1821 on Independence Day, Adams gave a speech in which he announced that the United States supported the independence movements in the various countries morally, but never through armed intervention. In doing so, he was a key architect of what came to be known as the Monroe Doctrine. Adams is known as one of the most important foreign ministers in American history.

President

The people of New England admired Adam's patriotism and his political skill. It was largely because of their support that Adams ran for president in 1824. With the demise of the Federalist Party, he faced opposition only from within his own party, the Democratic-Republican Party. His opponents were John C. Calhoun, William Crawford, Henry Clay, and Andrew Jackson. During the campaign, Calhoun withdrew and Crawford fell ill, leaving three serious candidates. Jackson obtained the most electoral votes, but not an absolute majority. Therefore, a vote in the House of Representatives had to be the deciding factor. Clay was president of the House of Representatives and did not want anything to do with Jackson. He supported Adams who was thus elected president. John Quincy Adams was the first and until now (2021) only president who did not take an oath on the Bible, but on the Constitution because he was a fervent supporter of separation of church and state.

Adams launched an extensive program on improving the domestic infrastructure. This included beginning construction of the Chesapeake and Ohio Canal and establishing a connection between the Ohio and Great Lakes. He proposed the establishment of a national university and federal support for science and the arts. As president, he favored high tax rates to pay for building industry. He also wanted to allow only limited land sales to prevent settlers from moving too quickly westward. However, Adams had to deal with a hostile Congress beginning in 1827 that caused many of his proposals to be shot down. He did manage to reduce the national debt from $16 million to $5 million.

In Europe, the Greek War of Independence broke out in 1821. American public opinion was behind the Greeks trying to throw off the Ottoman yoke. Henry Clay, his Secretary of State, wanted the U.S. to support Greece militarily, but Monroe opposed it.

Jackson's defeat in 1824 had embittered him and he was keen to win the 1828 presidential election. In the campaign, Jackson faced personal attacks from Adams' camp; the circumstance that Jackson's wife Rachel had not yet been divorced from a first husband during their marriage played a major role. The Democrats on the other side portrayed Adams as "elitist," while Jackson was the "man of the people." The election ended in defeat for Adams.

Adams' presidency is known to have been unfruitful, thanks in part to his unwavering ideology. As president, he was unwavering in his principles and in no way open to compromise with political opponents. His political ideas were prescient for his time, and his inability to compromise meant that he got very little done in his four years as president.

Delegate

After his time as president, Adams worked on a biography of his father, but did not enjoy it. In his diary he wrote of missing a goal. After his brief period of political absence, he was elected to the House of Representatives. There he served from 1831 until his death in 1848. In 1833 he ran for the governorship of Massachusetts on behalf of the Anti-Masonic Party. None of the candidates obtained an absolute majority. The Legislative Assembly of that state then had to tie the knot. Adams then withdrew in favor of John Davis.

In 1829, James Smithson died. He left his money to the U.S. government to build an institute of learning. Many politicians wanted to use the money for other purposes, but Adams made sure that the money was eventually used to build the Smithsonian Institution.

Adams, who had been an opponent of slavery all his life, used his new position to further criticize it. In Congress, a rule ("gag rule") had been introduced to prevent the subject from being discussed. The former president, however, did not care about that and came up with proposals anyway. His political opponents then wanted to limit his right to speak. Adams used the debate about this to fiercely criticize the slave owners. He argued that if he were limited in his right to speak he would resign as a Delegate, run for President and be elected with great ease. When his opponents realized that they were playing into Adams' hands in this way, they tried to let the debate about restricting his right to speak bleed to death. Adams would not allow that to happen, and the debate dragged on. A vote two weeks later fell in his favor.

Along with Henry Clay, he was one of the political leaders of the abolitionist movement. They both opposed the annexation of Texas and the American-Mexican War because it would eventually lead to civil war. They saw it as an attempt by the southern states to increase the area where slavery was allowed.

In 1841, Adams defended the Amistad prisoners before the Supreme Court. This was a group of prisoners who had been illegally kidnapped in Africa and were to be sold as slaves. However, they rebelled. The Africans were later arrested on the vessel near Long Island in upstate New York by the United States Navy. The resulting lawsuits gave the abolitionist movement a boost.

In 1840, a federal court case concluded that the initial transport of Africans across the Atlantic (which had nothing to do with the *Amistad*) was illegal, given that the international slave trade was banned. Consequently, the captives were not lawful slaves, but free individuals. Further, given their illegal confinement, the Africans had the right to take any lawful action to preserve their freedom, including with the use of force. The U.S. Supreme Court upheld these findings on March 9, 1841.

Death

On November 20, 1846, Adams suffered a stroke from which he would never fully recover. He died on February 23, 1848 in the Capitol building of a cerebral hemorrhage at the age of 80. Adams is buried in the crypt of the United First Parish Church in Quincy, alongside his parents and his wife.

Family

John Quincy Adams married Louisa Catherine Johnson, whom he had met in London, in 1797. The marriage took place there at All Hallows-by-the-Tower. They had three sons and a daughter. Their daughter Louisa was born in 1811 but died in 1812 when the family was in Russia. They named their first son George Washington Adams (1801-1829) after the first president of the US. George and their second son, John (1803-1834), had turbulent lives and died young (George committed suicide, while John was expelled from Harvard and died an alcoholic).

Adams' youngest son, Charles Francis Adams (who named his own son after his father, John Quincy), also built a career in diplomacy and politics. In 1870, to honor his father, Charles built the first "memorial presidential library. The "Stone Library" contains more than 14,000 books written in twelve languages. The library is located in "the Old House" (also called Peacefield) at Adams National Historical Park in Quincy, Massachusetts.

Personality and legacy

Adams' personality and political beliefs were similar to those of his father, John Adams. He was not very social and preferred a book to company. During his presidency he struggled with a persistent depression. He himself blamed the high expectations of his father and mother for his poor mental state. Adams had deep respect for his father, but a difficult relationship with his mother. His mother regularly expressed her high expectations of her children, afraid as she was that her children would become alcoholics like her brother.

Adams is known as one of the most effective diplomats and foreign ministers in American history. However, his presidency is usually seen as mediocre. Adams was one of the first major political leaders to question whether the United States could continue to exist united as long as slavery existed. He wrote about this in his diary, *"It establishes false notions of virtue and vice: for what can be more false and*

7. Andrew Jackson (1829-1837)

Democratic party | Vice presidents: John C. Calhoun and Martin Van Buren

"Never take counsel of your fears."

Andrew Jackson (Lancaster County (South Carolina), March 15, 1767 - Nashville (Tennessee), June 8, 1845) was the 7th president of the United States from 1829 to 1837 and a slaveholder. Jackson was a founding member of the Democratic Party and was the first Democratic president. Jackson was known as *Old Hickory* (literally: old nut tree, but in the United States an expression used to indicate strong, tough people).

Early life

Andrew Jackson was born on March 15, 1767. His parents, Andrew and Elizabeth Hutchinson Jackson, were Scots-Irish settlers who had emigrated two years earlier from what is now Northern Ireland. After arriving in British America, they traveled overland through the Appalachians to a Scotch-Irish community in the Waxhaws, an area on the border between the present-day states of North Carolina and South Carolina. They brought with them their two children, Hugh (born 1763) and Robert (born 1764). In February 1767, three weeks before their third son Andrew was to be born, father Jackson died at the age of 29 in an accident while working as a farmer. In response, Elizabeth and her children moved in with relatives.

The exact birthplace of Andrew Jackson is unclear. In 1824 he wrote in a letter that he was born on his uncle James Crawford's plantation in South Carolina, but this statement may have had political motives. In the 1950s, indications emerged that Jackson could also have been born in the home of another uncle, in North Carolina.

Beginning in 1780, during the American War of Independence, 13-year-old Jackson (like his two older brothers) was employed as a courier. That same year, he and his older brother Robert were captured by the English. During his captivity, young Andrew once refused to polish the shoes of an English officer. This officer lashed out at him with his saber, leaving him with scars on his head and left hand. Also, both he and his brother Robert contracted smallpox during their captivity. Jackson survived the disease, but his older brother died a few days after their release. These experiences with the English, as well as the fact that the war took the lives of his immediate family, caused Jackson to develop an enormous dislike for the English. He was the last president of the United States to have fought against the English, and the second president to have been a prisoner of war (George Washington was held by the French during the Seven Years' War).

War of 1812

In the War of 1812, Jackson fought primarily against local *Native Americans* from western Florida, including the Creek. These tribes resisted the American push westward and submission to the United States. Jackson managed to defeat them, however, and through the Treaty of Fort Jackson, the Creek Indians were deprived of an area of about 90,000 square miles.

Furthermore, Jackson was also the American commander in the battle of New Orleans (January 8, 1815). Here he managed to inflict a crushing defeat on the British, but the battle was fought when an agreement had already been reached between the British and American governments in Ghent. Due to slow communication, this was passed on too late to the troops near New Orleans, so the armies fought each other anyway. By defeating the British, there was nationwide recognition for Jackson. Suddenly he was one of the country's best-known characters and considered a war hero. A status that benefited him later, during his bid to become president.

First Seminole War and annexation of Florida

In 1818 he was given command in the war against the Seminole in Florida, because of his previous experience fighting *Native Americans*. He won the battle against both the Seminole and the Spanish (to whom Florida belonged) and occupied the area. His brusque invasion of Florida became even more controversial when he executed two captured British secret agents, causing a diplomatic row. In 1819, however, Spain officially ceded Florida to the US. It became a territory within the United States in 1821 after ratification by the US Congress. Andrew Jackson became the first governor.

Political career

Jackson became a member of the Tennessee Congress in 1796, and a senator for that state in 1797. Between 1798 and 1804 he was a member of the Tennessee Supreme Court. He became military governor of Florida (1821) and was again senator for Tennessee from 1823 to 1825.

In the 1824 presidential election, Jackson was one of four candidates on behalf of the Democratic-Republican Party. The others were John Quincy Adams, William Crawford, and Henry Clay. None of them obtained a majority; Jackson still had the most success with 99 electoral votes, but the House of Representatives ultimately elected Adams as president. Jackson was very bitter about this and continued to actively oppose Adams in the period that followed. He withdrew from the Democratic-Republican Party and eventually founded the Democratic Party with Martin van Buren and others in 1828.

Four years later, in the presidential election of 1828, Jackson was still elected president. This time he defeated Adams by a large margin and was sworn in as the seventh president of the United States on March 4, 1829. In 1832 he was re-elected to a second term. After an eight-year presidency, Jackson was succeeded by his vice president, Martin Van Buren, on March 4, 1837.

Many of his supporters compared Jackson to George Washington, the first president of the United States. Many people felt the same sentiment with both men; both had fought the British and won.

Indian Removal Act and controversy

As president, Jackson was responsible for the *Indian Removal Act* of 1830, a law that required all *Native Americans* in the east to be relocated to the area west of the Mississippi River. This was a major factor in the subjugation of *Native Americans*, their absorption into the U.S. capitalist economy, and thus the destruction of their traditional hunting culture. Most *Native Americans* settled in what is now Oklahoma. About ten thousand of them died during this journey, which is why it came to be known as *The trail of tears*.

Andrew Jackson has always been a controversial figure because of his hard-line approach, but especially his treatment of the original inhabitants of the U.S. caused him to be viewed today as one of the most controversial presidents in U.S. history. At the time, political relations were different and the vast majority of the people supported Jackson. Thus, Jackson cannot be held solely responsible for the atrocities committed; after all, he represented the country.

Jacksonian democracy

Nevertheless, Jackson was very popular in his day because of his ideology, and supporters of it can still be found today. This so-called Jacksonian democracy, which has its roots in rural America of the early 19th century, has a number of prescribed points:

- Universal suffrage for all white men.

- Manifest Destiny.

- Patronage: the Spoils System was introduced whereby followers and relatives were given political positions in the new government. This contrasted with the meritocratic system where competence was taken into account rather than adherence or kinship.

- Curbing the power of the federal government over individual states. Over time, however, Jackson will amass as much presidential power as possible.

- Strict interpretation of the United States Constitution.

- Opposition to banks: Jackson was a fierce opponent of the banking industry and the monopolies that some banks acquired, especially the National Bank (*Second Bank of the United States*).

Attack

In 1835, Jackson attended the funeral of a Congressman. Afterwards, the unemployed Richard Lawrence, dissatisfied with his situation, drew a pistol. This weapon refused and even when the assailant drew a second pistol the weapon refused to fire. According to lore, Jackson then began beating on the man with his cane until he was calmed down. Lawrence, meanwhile, was also overpowered.

Lawrence was acquitted on grounds of insanity and spent the rest of his life in a mental institution. Jackson was convinced that the attack was planned by his political opponents in his fight against the National Bank (*Second Bank of the United States*).

Personal life

Marriage and family

After Jackson left for Nashville in 1788, he met Rachel Donelson there. She had been unhappily married to Captain Lewis Robards, from whom she divorced in 1790. She then entered into marriage with Jackson. However, it was later discovered that the divorce between Donelson and Robards had not been officially finalized, so the marriage to Jackson was declared invalid. After finalizing her divorce, Jackson and Donelson remarried in 1794. They had no biological children, but did have three adopted sons:

- Andrew Jackson Jr. the son of Rachel's brother Severn Donelson (adopted in 1809).

- Lyncoya, an orphan boy belonging to the Creek Indians (adopted in 1813 after the Battle of Tallushatchee, in which he had been found on the battlefield with his dead mother). Lyncoya died of tuberculosis in 1828, at the age of sixteen.

- Andrew Jackson Hutchings, the grandson of Rachel's sister Catherine and the son of a former Jackson business partner (adopted in 1817).

The Jacksons also acted as guardians for several children here, although not all of them lived with them full time:

- John Samuel Donelson, Daniel Smith Donelson, and Andrew Jackson Donelson, the three sons of Rachel's brother Samuel Donelson, who had died in 1804. Andrew Jackson Donelson later served as Jackson's personal secretary during his presidency.

- Caroline Butler, Eliza Butler, Edward Butler and Anthony Butler, the four children of General Edward Butler, a family friend. They were taken in by the Jacksons after the death of their father.

Andrew Jackson became a widower when Rachel died on December 22, 1828. He had just won the presidential election at that time and was preparing to run for president. She was buried on Christmas Eve, wearing the dress she would wear to the inauguration. Rachel thus never served as first lady of the United States. This role was filled at Jackson's request by Emily Donelson, the daughter of Rachel's brother John Donelson and wife of her own cousin Andrew Jackson Donelson, who acted as personal secretary to the president. After Andrew Jackson Jr. also came to the White House in 1834, his wife Sarah Yorke Jackson was also designated as hostess. It was the only time in history that two women simultaneously served as (unofficial) First Lady. After Emily died of tuberculosis in 1836, Sarah assumed all duties.

The Hermitage

With the exception of the years in Washington D.C., Jackson and his family lived primarily on his estate, The Hermitage, near Nashville, which he had purchased in 1804. It was a 1,000-acre plantation on which mainly cotton was grown. The heavy labor was performed by African-American slaves, including women and children. The more profit he made, the richer Jackson became and could thus increase the number of slaves. When he bought the plantation, Jackson owned nine slaves; 25 years later there were 100. At the time of his death in 1845, Jackson had about 150 slaves living and working on the grounds of The Hermitage.

Temperament

Jackson's short fuse was notorious. His difficult childhood is often given as the main reason for this. Even at a young age, Jackson developed a defense technique in this way that he would continue to use for the rest of his life. On the last day of his presidency, he said he regretted two things: that he was unable to shoot Henry Clay, and that he had not hanged John C. Calhoun. During his time in the army, he also had some of his men killed for treason. During his election campaign, this was frequently used against him and he was portrayed as a murderer.

The controversy surrounding his marriage to Rachel bothered him. When Charles Dickinson attacked Jackson in an article in the local newspaper, Jackson challenged him to a duel. Dueling was illegal in Tennessee, so the two men met in Kentucky. Jackson's strategy was to get Dickinson to shoot first. This happened, Jackson was hit in the chest. Then Jackson took his time and did fatally hit Dickinson in the chest. Jackson survived the duel, Dickinson bled to death. The bullet could not be removed because it was too close to the heart. He continued to walk around with it for the rest of his life. In Tennessee, people were seething; his local reputation had been destroyed.

Death

Andrew Jackson died on June 8, 1845, at the age of 78, from a combination of chronic tuberculosis, heart failure and pulmonary edema. He was buried on the grounds of his plantation The Hermitage, next to his wife Rachel.

Honors

Many places in the United States are named after Andrew Jackson, including major cities such as Jacksonville (Florida) and Jackson (the capital of the state of Mississippi). Several counties also bear his name.

Since 1869, Jackson's portrait has appeared on U.S. banknotes. Since 1928, he has been featured on the $20 bill.

8. Martin Van Buren (1837-1841)

Democratic party | Vice president: Richard Mentor Johnson

"It is easier to do a job right than to explain why you didn't."

Martin Van Buren, christened **Maarten Van Buren** (Kinderhook (New York), December 5, 1782 - there, July 24, 1862), was the eighth president of the United States (1837-1841). Prior to his presidency, he was the eighth vice president (1833-1837) and the tenth secretary of state under Andrew Jackson (1829-1831).

He was a key organizer of the Democratic Party, a dominant figure in the two-party system.

Van Buren's predecessors had been born in the territory of the later United States, but were British subjects before the American

Revolution. Van Buren was the first president to be born an American citizen and, moreover, the first president who was not of British descent-his family was Dutch and his native language was Dutch.

As Secretary of State under Andrew Jackson and then as Vice President, he was an important figure in building an organizational structure for the Jacksonian democracy, especially in New York State. As president, he did not want the United States to annex Texas, an act that would reach his successor, John Tyler, eight years after Van Buren's initial rejection. Between the nonviolent Aroostook War and the Caroline Affair, relations with Britain and its colonies were strained.

His government was largely marked by the economic problems of his time, the Panic of 1837. He was scapegoated for the Depression and called "Martin Van Ruin" by his political opponents. Van Buren was voted out after four years and lost to Whig candidate William Henry Harrison.

In 1848 he ran for the presidency for a third party, the Free Soil Party.

Biography

Van Buren was born in Kinderhook in upstate New York. His great-great grandfather Cornelis Maessen emigrated from Buurmalsen in the Netherlands in 1631. His father Abraham Van Buren (17 February 1737 - 8 April 1817) was a farmer and café owner. His mother, Maria Goes van Alen (27 February 1747 - 16 February 1817) also had children from an earlier marriage.

Van Buren attended public school at Kinderhook Academy, and in 1796 he entered law school in New York City. One of his teachers was William Peter van Ness, a prominent lawyer and later Aaron Burr's second-in-command in the duel against Alexander Hamilton for the presidency. After graduation, Van Buren was a practicing lawyer for 25 years.

Van Buren married Hannah van Buren, his niece in the third degree, at Catskill in Greene County on February 21, 1807. They grew up together in Kinderhook.

Beginning of political career

Van Buren's practice made him financially independent, and it led him down the political path. The political situation in New York after 1800, the year Jefferson was elected and the Federalists lost power, was particularly bitter and personal. The Democratic-Republican Party was split into three pieces, followers of George Clinton (and later his nephew De Witt Clinton), Robert Livingston and Aaron Burr, respectively.

Federalist power after 1799 depended on coalition with one of these groups. Van Buren, who had joined the Clintons early on, entered the state Senate in 1812 and also became a member of the *Court for the Correction of Errors*, the highest court in New York until 1847.

National Politics

In 1821, Van Buren was elected as a senator. In the Senate he was very active. In the disputed presidential election of 1824, eventually won by John Quincy Adams, he sided with Secretary of the Treasury William Crawford. After the election, he sided with Andrew Jackson and played an important role in the formation of the Democratic Party. In 1828 he was elected governor of New York He stepped down from the Senate and returned to New York. After a few months he also resigned as governor to become Secretary of State under the new President Andrew Jackson. For the next four years he was a loyal supporter of Jackson. First as minister (until 1831) and then as ambassador to the United Kingdom. In 1832 he was elected vice president. Four years later he was elected president.

President

The presidency of Martin Van Buren was not a success. The fact that he succeeded Andrew Jackson did not help, but the economic crisis was a bigger problem. For four years he tried to solve the crisis, but he ultimately failed. Finally, in 1840, he lost the election to William Henry Harrison.

Under his reign, the so-called Trail of Tears took place. The relocation of the Cherokee Indians, or Native Americans, from their land to present-day Oklahoma. This movement of people had begun under Jackson's reign and was made possible in part by Van Buren. Van Buren expressed his pride in this victory for the Americans in several letters. One-fourth of the Indians who had to change territories eventually died from disease, overheating, and other conditions.

During his presidency, Van Buren's views on slavery were in line with those of his party. The Democrats enjoyed a great deal of support in the southern United States and so they were also in favor of the use of slavery. After his presidency, however, Van Buren changed his mind and in the later years of his life he began to support laws that sought to eliminate slavery. At the start of the American Civil War, he was on the side of the Union, or North.

Campaign and party split

Van Buren is known today as the founder of modern campaigning. In the 1824 election, there were four candidates on behalf of the Democratic-Republican party. Although the candidates had largely the same ideas, they were pitted against each other. As a result, Andrew Jackson, who was supported by Van Buren, lost. Instead of substance, local sentiment became more important in this political system. Van Buren saw the ineffectiveness of this setup and pushed for reforms. Due to previously visible fractions in the Democratic-Republican party, and Van Buren's intended reforms, the party eventually split. Van Buren is thus recognized as one of the founding fathers of the Democratic party.

Later years and inheritance

For the 1844 election, Van Buren hoped to regain his party's nomination for the presidency. He lost to James K. Polk who eventually became president. In 1848 he did run for president, on behalf of the Free Soil Party. He lost, but still got a fair number of votes. After this election, he retired.

Van Buren was known as a great political leader who thrived behind the scenes. Within the Democratic party, he had considerable power and knew how to compromise and get things done. As president, however, he proved unable to get these things done. He was not very social and lacked a certain charisma necessary for an effective presidency.

He died on July 24, 1862, at his Lindenwald estate, of asthma and heart problems.

9. William Henry Harrison (1841-1841)

Whig party | Vice President: John Tyler

"There is nothing more corrupting, nothing more destructive of the noblest and finest feelings of our nature, than the exercise of unlimited power."

William Henry Harrison (Charles City County (Virginia), February 9, 1773 - Washington D.C., April 4, 1841) was a military officer and politician of the Whig Party. He was the 9th president of the United States from March 4 to April 4, 1841. Harrison died on the 32nd day of his presidency at the age of 68.

His father owned a plantation in Virginia and had signed the Declaration of Independence. His brother was a member of the House of Representatives. Harrison joined the army when he was 18 years old, and quickly promoted to governor of Indiana. It was in this position that he crushed a rebellion of Indians led by Tecumseh at the Battle of Tippecanoe in 1811. This earned him a promotion to general and he fought with distinction in the War of 1812.

After the war, he was elected to various political roles, including as a member of the House of Representatives and the Senate. He was a presidential candidate for the Whig party in 1836, but lost to Martin Van Buren. He won the election in 1840, mainly because the economy was doing poorly. His vice president was John Tyler. The slogans for their campaign "Log Cabins and Hard Cider" and "Tippecanoe and Tyler too" are among the most famous in American politics. This first slogan was a response to propoganda from the Van Buren camp, who said that with some money and some Hard Cider he could live out the rest of his life. Harrison's campaign put a spin on this by portraying Harrison as a commoner, when in reality he belonged to the elite. The second slogan originally came in the form of a song. Tippecanoe refers to the victory in the battle against Tecumseh's army at Tippecanoe and Tyler logically refers to John Tyler, who would become Harrison's vice president.

It was a very cold day on March 4, 1841 when Harrison gave his first speech as president. He gave the longest inaugural address in American history, almost two hours. On March 26, he caught a cold, according to the views of the time because of the bad weather during his speech. The cold became pneumonia, and despite several treatments, he died a month after his speech-the first president to die while in office.

It was not until the 21st century that a thorough investigation was conducted into the president's cause of death, which at the time could not be determined by doctors. Since Harrison became ill only three weeks after his speech, it is very unlikely that pneumonia was his cause of death. The relevant study attributed his death to Washington's poor sanitation system. The two investigators involved, named Jane McHugh and Philip A. Mackowiak, discovered that the water used by the White House was downstream from where people went to relieve themselves. Most likely, Harrison contracted an illness as a result. His last words he spoke to his doctor, although many people think they were addressed to the vice president, John Tyler: "Sir, I wish you to understand the true principles of the government. I wish them carried out. I ask nothing more."

Benjamin Harrison, Harrison's grandson, also later became president. They are the only grandfather/grandchild combination of presidents to date.

10. John Tyler (1841-1845)

Whig party and Unaffiliated party | Vice president: None (vacant)

"Everything dependent on human action is liable to abuse."

John Tyler Jr. (Charles City County (Virginia), March 29, 1790 - Richmond (Virginia), January 18, 1862) was an American politician and slaveholder. He was the 10th president of the United States. Previously, he was the 10th Vice President of the United States under President William Henry Harrison, but after his untimely death, Tyler was sworn in as President after only one month. Prior to that, he was governor of Virginia, a senator and a member of the House of Representatives.

Lifetime

Youth and early career

Tyler came from an aristocratic family. His father was a friend of Thomas Jefferson, served in the Virginia State House of Delegates and later was governor of the same state. He studied law and was admitted to the Bar at the age of 19. Two years later he made his entrance into politics with his election to the Virginia House of Delegates. Of that, he was a member for five years. Tyler had little to do with the British, as did most of his contemporaries. During the War of 1812, when Hampton was occupied and an attack was threatened on Richmond, the capital of his home state, Tyler organized a small militia, but an attack did not occur. During the same period, Tyler's father died and he inherited his plantation, including thirteen slaves.

Member of the House of Representatives

A seat in the House of Representatives became vacant in the interim in late 1816. Tyler stood for election and won the election on behalf of the Democratic-Republican Party. This party wanted the federal government to provide more (financial) support for domestic infrastructure improvements, such as the construction of (rail) roads and the ports. However, Tyler maintained his own views that the individual states were responsible for such improvement and should bear the costs themselves. He had a similar position when it came to slavery. He saw slavery as evil and made no attempt to justify himself, but also never granted freedom to any of his own slaves, although he took good care of them and did not use force against them. He believed that the federal government should stay away from the subject and that it was a choice of the individual states whether or not to allow slavery.

Tyler therefore also voted against the Missouri Compromise in 1820. This compromise revolved around Missouri's entry into the Union. In Missouri, slavery was allowed. In the Senate, the number of states where slavery was and was not allowed was balanced, but that would change with Missouri's accession. The compromise would see Maine split off from Massachusetts and join the Union as a separate state, where slavery was prohibited, thus restoring the balance. Despite Tyler's dissenting vote, the compromise was adopted. In 1821, he decided not to run again and returned to his law practice.

Governor of Virginia

After two years, law school began to bore him again, and Tyler again - successfully - ran for the House of Delegates as a Virginia delegate. His reputation grew and in December 1825 the Virginia Legislative

Assembly elected him as its new governor. Under Virginia's old constitution, he had little power; he could not even veto laws. His most notable performance was the funeral speech after the death of former President Thomas Jefferson.

The Virginia Legislative Assembly had to decide in January 1827 whether to grant the incumbent Senator John Randolph another term. This one did not differ much from Tyler in terms of views, but had also made political enemies because of his unstable character and fierce opposition to President John Quincy Adams and Senator Henry Clay. Their political allies sought an acceptable alternative to Randolph and came to Tyler. The latter at first refused to run, but political pressure grew, he gave in and won the election by a few more votes at Randolph's expense.

Senator

Simultaneously with Tyler's election to the Senate, the presidential campaign was also underway. Incumbent President John Quincy Adams was being challenged by Andrew Jackson. The Democratic-Republican Party fell apart into the National Republicans who supported Adams and the Democrats who supported Jackson. Tyler did not have much confidence in Adams because he believed in a strong federal government. He was afraid that Jackson would do the same, but had more confidence in him and therefore the latter could count on his support.

Jackson was elected president and Tyler clashed with him in the Senate fairly quickly. He disagreed that the new president was nominating many friends and political allies for important government positions and voted against many of his nominations. He had particular difficulty with the appointment during a recess of three commissioners to negotiate a trade treaty with the Ottoman Empire. Despite his objections to his policies, Tyler remained on relatively good terms with the president. He supported Jackson when he successfully ran for re-election in 1832.

At the beginning of Jackson's second term, the federal government became embroiled in a conflict with the state of South Carolina. In response to tariffs levied on some commodities, South Carolina invoked *Nullification*, the right of a state not to enforce laws if they did not serve the state's interest. South Carolina declared the Tariff Acts of 1828 and 1832 null and void within their own borders. Jackson sent armed units to enforce federal laws while South Carolina threatened to secede from the Union. Tyler disagreed with that armed intervention and made that clear, and in the period that followed he further alienated himself from the president. He joined the new Whig Party formed by Henry Clay. By his party colleagues, Tyler was elected President pro tempore of the Senate in 1833.

Shortly thereafter, the Democrats seized power in the Virginia House of Delegates. In the Senate, a motion of censure against President Jackson was in the works at the time. The Virginia House of Delegates could instruct Tyler to vote for it, something he was not at all comfortable with. Earlier, as a state politician, Tyler had agreed to a motion of censure against two politicians who had disregarded an instruction. He found himself in an awkward position, so in February 1836 he submitted his resignation and left the Senate.

Vice President

Tyler's name was mentioned early in 1835 as a candidate for the vice presidency. The Whig party was not yet organized enough to hold one national convention. Instead, they nominated three candidates, each of whom enjoyed great popularity in their respective regions. In a few states, Tyler was chosen as the running mate. By doing so, they hoped to deny the Democratic nominee and incumbent Vice President Martin van Buren a majority in the Electoral College, after which the House of Representatives would have to decide. Tyler hoped that he would end up as one of the two vice presidential candidates with the most votes and that, if the Electoral College could not reach a decision, the Senate would then have to decide, would choose him. Van Buren, however, immediately won a majority of votes. His running mate Richard Mentor Johnson just failed to get enough votes in the Electoral College to become vice president, but in the House of Representatives he subsequently did.

Again Tyler withdrew from politics, but he returned in 1838 already with in the Virginia House of Delegates. In March 1839, a Senate seat became vacant, for which Tyler was one of the candidates. Some party members continued to support the incumbent Senator William Cabell Rives and so an impasse developed, leaving the Senate seat vacant for two years.

Leading up to the 1840 presidential election, America had been in an economic crisis for three years, caused by the Panic of 1837. President Van Buren had not been able to end that crisis and it was costing him a lot of political support. The Democratic Party was split into several factions, leaving the way open for the Whigs to the presidency. Their candidate would likely become the new president. At their 1839

National Convention in Harrisburg, Pennsylvania, the party chose William Henry Harrison, but he was suspected of having abolitionist sympathies. To counterbalance this, the slave owner Tyler was chosen as his running mate, who was also from a large Southern state. Painfully, the delegates from his own state abstained because of the conflict surrounding the vacant Senate seat. The subsequent election was indeed won by the Whigs duo.

Leading up to the formation of a new cabinet, Tyler largely kept his distance. Harrison's advanced age and ailing health had already been a theme during the election campaign, and in the first weeks of his presidency, his health deteriorated rapidly. Barely a month later, on April 4, 1837, Harrison died. Tyler received the news a day later. The U.S. Constitution was unclear about what exactly the status of the vice president was when the president died. The section on it read, *"When the President shall be removed from office, or when he shall die, resign, or be unable to discharge the powers and duties of his office, such office shall pass to the Vice President."* The cabinet decided that Tyler would be referred to as the "vice president acting president," but Tyler immediately made short work of that and chose the designation president, indicating that he had the same role and status as his predecessors. During his term, some of the opposition took issue with this and continued to refer to him as the "acting president." Letters addressing him as anything other than "president" were returned unopened.

Tyler's transition from vice president to president was controversial at the time. However, it later set a precedent for later vice presidents, called the Tyler precedent. Each of the seven presidents who died during their presidency after Harrison was succeeded by the vice president. It was not until the twentieth century that the Tyler precedent was also immortalized in law, this became the 25th Amendment. This law states that when a president dies, he will be succeeded by the vice president. When a president becomes ill, or due to other circumstances is unable to effectively lead the country, it will be replaced by the vice president, who in this case will only act as "acting president." Tyler, by his example in the 19th century, thus drastically changed the vice-presidency for the rest of American history. The vice-presidency, first seen as a dishonorable job, now became an important part of American politics.

President

When Tyler succeeded Harrison, he initially agreed with proposed laws of his Congressional party colleagues. However, he clashed with the

Whigs when he twice vetoed a law to extend the existence of the Second National Bank. That Second National Bank had been established by law in 1816, and its continued existence had to be extended by law. Tyler, however, was vehemently opposed to the bank, which he believed would give the elites and larger corporations too much advantage over the "common people." In September 1841, all ministers resigned in protest of the veto, with the exception of Secretary of State Daniel Webster. They did so at the urging of Henry Clay who hoped that this would force Tyler to resign so that he could be replaced by Samuel L. Southard, the President pro tempore of the Senate. When Tyler did not resign, he was expelled from the party. His former party colleagues in the former Congress were so angry that they denied him the funds for needed repairs to the White House. In the following year, the president clashed with Congress again when he twice vetoed new tariff laws. His former party colleagues investigated whether they could depose him through impeachment proceedings, but sufficient support for this was lacking.

Tyler had to form a new cabinet because most of his ministers had resigned. Out of remorse, the Whigs did not support most of the nominated candidates. Because of the death of two members of the Supreme Court, Smith Thompson in 1843 and Henry Baldwin in 1844, Tyler was allowed to nominate two new candidates, but his nominations were rejected four times, more often than any other president in the history of the United States. Clay's allies wanted to wait until he himself had been elected president in 1844 so that he could nominate his own candidates (Instead of Clay, James Polk won that election). In February 1845, Congress still agreed to one nomination, that of Samuel Nelson.

The difficulties Tyler faced in domestic politics contrasted sharply with his successes in the foreign field. He had long advocated free trade and expansion into the West. He concluded a trade agreement with China and the Zollverein, an association of several free German states. He informed Britain in 1842 that they should stay away from Hawaii. This started a process that would eventually lead to the American annexation of the archipelago. Secretary of State Webster entered into the Webster-Ashburton Agreement with Britain in 1842, which established the precise course of the Maine-Canada border. This ended a conflict between the United States and Great Britain that had almost caused war on several occasions. Further, in 1842 the president ended the Second Seminole War, a conflict that had been dragging on since 1835 with various Native American tribes in Florida. Tyler favored forced cultural assimilation of the Indians.

Almost immediately upon taking office, Tyler saw the annexation of the Republic of Texas as a major issue he wanted to bring in. Texas had declared its independence from Mexico in 1836, although Mexicans still did not recognize it as a sovereign state. The people of Texas wanted to join the United States, but Tyler's predecessors Jackson and Van Buren had been reluctant to do so, fearing that the accession of a new Southern state would further increase tensions around the issue of slavery. Secretary of State Webster advised Tyler to go easy on the issue, but from 1843 onward he made it the spearhead of his policy. He also saw it as his only chance to be re-elected as an independent candidate in 1844, now that he was without a party. The President knew that he would need a Secretary of State who supported him on this issue and so replaced Webster for Hugh Legaré. With the help of his Treasury Secretary John Spencer, he replaced many public servants who opposed annexation with supporters. In the spring of 1843, he made a political tour of the country to do something about his waning popularity, but during the tour he received news of Legaré's sudden death. As his successor, Tyler appointed Abel Upshur.

Tyler and Upshur entered into negotiations with the government of Texas and promised military protection against Mexico. Under the Constitution, they needed the consent of Congress to do so. The Northern states were reluctant to allow a new slave state. To put pressure on the Northern Congressmen, Upshur spread rumors that Britain was also seeking rapprochement with Texas.

The ship the USS Princeton was commissioned in February 1844. A cannon was defective and exploded when a gun salute was to take place. President Tyler was unharmed because he was below deck, but among the dead were Secretary of State Upshur, Secretary of the Navy Thomas Gilmer, Tyler's personal slave Armistead, and David Gardiner, father of Tyler's then fiancée and later second wife Julia Gardiner.

The president appointed former Vice President John C. Calhoun as Secretary of State in March 1844, something that was later seen as a political blunder. Calhoun was an outspoken supporter of slavery, which made it much harder to gain support from Northern Congressmen for the annexation of Texas. Clay (Whig) and former President Van Buren (Democrat) were both the most likely presidential candidates for their party at the time and, after joint deliberations, both decided against annexation. Tyler sent the annexation treaty to the Senate for ratification in April 1844, although he anticipated that it would not be approved. Van Buren's action, however, had antagonized the Southern Democrats, making him unacceptable as a presidential candidate to part of the party. The Democrats eventually designated the relatively unknown James Polk, a supporter of annexation, as their candidate. Former President Jackson persuaded Polk to allow Tyler to join the Democratic Party. Polk agreed, and Tyler subsequently withdrew as a presidential candidate. In the November election, Polk defeated Clay by a narrow margin. In late February 1845, the House of Representatives, by a large majority, and the Senate, by 27 votes to 25, agreed to the annexation of Texas. Three days before his resignation, Tyler signed the annexation bill.

Later years

After his presidency, Tyler left the political arena and spent much time on his plantation in Virginia. In February 1861, he made one more appearance during his participation in a peace conference in Washington D.C. on the eve of the American Civil War. He hoped that compromise could be reached, but when the conference's proposals were rejected by Congress, Tyler saw secession of all Southern states as the only option. When war broke out, Tyler went along with the decision of his state of Virginia joining the Confederate States of America. He was elected to the Confederate House of Representatives and left for the new capital city of Richmond in early January 1862 to attend the inaugural session. That came to nothing, as he died shortly after arriving in Richmond. Tyler died on January 18, 1862 from the effects of bronchitis at the age of 71. He spoke to his doctor, "Doctor, I am going. Perhaps that is for the best".

Tyler had wanted a simple funeral, but the President of the Confederacy Jefferson Davis organized a large state funeral that portrayed Tyler as a hero of the new nation. He was the only American president to be buried under a non-American flag.

11. James K. Polk (1845-1849)

Democratic party | Vice president: George M. Dallas

"No president who performs his duties faithfully and conscientiously can have any leisure."

James Knox Polk (Pineville (North Carolina), November 2, 1795 - Nashville (Tennessee), June 15, 1849) was the 11th president of the United States from 1845 to 1849 and a slaveholder.

Polk was born in Pineville, North Carolina. He was a member of the House of Representatives from 1825 to 1839 and governor of Tennessee from 1839 to 1841. In the election of 1844, he was elected the eleventh president of the United States. He was helped during his campaign by Jefferson Davis, later President of the Confederate States of America. He emerged as a very powerful and energetic executive. He lowered tariffs (1846), restored the independent treasury system (1846), and settled border disputes with England over Canada (1846).

Oregon Treaty

Those disputes with Canada eventually led to the Treaty of Oregon. This treaty established the borders between the U.S. and Canada at the 49th parallel, which meant that the U.S. gained a great deal of territory. This territory would, broadly speaking, eventually lead to three new states: Washington, Oregon and Idaho.

Mexican-American War

But he also bore heavy responsibility for the outbreak of the Mexican-American War, in which the U.S. annexed some states of Mexico. Shortly before he was sworn in, the Republic of Texas had seceded from Mexico. War soon broke out, as strife ensued over the exact demarcation of the Texas/U.S. border with Mexico. After the war, it was determined that the border would be the Rio Grande. The entire area north of the Rio Grande with the states of Alta California, Nuevo Mexico, and Texas was ceded to the U.S., thus fulfilling Manifest Destiny: the United States now effectively encompassed an area from "sea to shining sea."

The Mexican-American War was always Polk's goal. Before declaring war on Mexico, he repeatedly expressed his desire to own California. Polk provoked a war by bringing American soldiers to the Mexican border. A group of Mexicans then crossed the agreed upon border and killed a number of American soldiers. This was the moment for Polk to start a war. He stated that it was unacceptable that American blood had been shed on American soil. Among others, he sent the later president, Zachary Taylor, to Mexico where the war was then fought. The U.S. won by a large margin, but there was much discontent, especially in the north, about the way things were going. The later president, Ulysess S. Grant, fought on the American side in the war, but opposed Polk's policies. He praised the Mexican soldiers, who he said were very brave, and complained in letters about the futility, and injustice of this war.

Eventually, the newly gained territories would be incorporated as states of the U.S., after achieving certain conditions, such as attaining a certain population. States that would eventually emerge from the won territories of the Mexican-American War include: Arizona, California, Colorado, Nevada, New Mexico and Utah.

Personality and legacy

Polk was not known for his charisma. He possessed no humor, or other social skills. During his campaign, he tirelessly went around the country trying to convince people of his political position. To do this, he was carefully trained by members of the Democratic party. He memorized jokes and adopted a more folksy way of speaking. In his campaign, he was portrayed as a man of the people.

His presidency was rarely effective. Many historians attribute this to his willingness to deceive his own party members. He promised everyone all sorts of things to get his way, only to not go back on these promises. Through his effective policies, he was able to make a few important changes, but these were mostly overturned by his successors, so his policies do not enjoy special recognition. He is mostly remembered for the Mexican-American War, which to this day many people consider unjust.

Weak health and death

Polk's time in the White House took its toll on his health. When he became president he entered the White House with enthusiasm and vigor. On March 4, 1849, he left the White House exhausted. He had lost weight and had dark lines in his face and dark circles under his eyes. It is believed that he had contracted cholera in New Orleans while traveling through the South.

Polk died on June 15, 1849 at the age of 53, 103 days after leaving the White House and was buried in the grounds of his home. He died as the youngest president not to die by assassination. His wife, Sarah Childress Polk, lived in the house for another 42 years after his death until she died on August 14, 1891. She spent the last thirty years of her life trying to improve her husband's image, without success. She was known as a hard-working woman who asserted herself as an unofficial advisor to the president. Presidents before Polk often had no wife, or were widowed. So a strong woman in the White House was rare at the time. Also, she was strongly religious. She disapproved of horse races and other forms of entertainment. Alcohol was officially prohibited in the White House during her husband's reign, but wine was served in abundance at parties.

12. Zachary Taylor (1849-1850)

Whig party | Vice president: Millard Fillmore

"I have always done my duty. I am ready to die. My only regret is for the friends I leave behind me."

Zachary Taylor (Barboursville, Virginia, November 24, 1784 - Washington D.C., July 9, 1850) was the 12th president of the United States (1849-1850), a slave owner and a U.S. military leader.

Initially uninterested in politics, he nevertheless entered the 1848 U.S. presidential election as a Whig and defeated Lewis Cass. Taylor was the last president to keep slaves while in office, and the second and last Whig to win a presidential election.

He was known as "Old Rough and Ready," due to having a forty-year military career in the United States Army, in which he served in the War of 1812, the Black Hawk War and the Second Seminole War. He achieved fame by leading American troops to victory in the Battle of Palo Alto and the Battle of Monterrey during the Mexican-American War. Taylor was widely respected for his military exploits, but had extremely little political knowledge. For a long time he showed no interest whatsoever and had never even voted in his life. With his increasing fame, however, both the Democrats and the Whigs smelled opportunity, and they tried to bring him in. Eventually he joined the Whigs, but he felt little need to serve the party. He had fought for the country and wanted to do the same in politics. However, he soon found out that his leadership in politics was not working. Partly because of little political experience and his early death, he is known as a fairly unimportant president. However, he was honored for his strong principles and honorable integrity, although some saw this more as naiveté.

As president, he angered many Southerners by taking a moderate stance against slavery. He urged the settlers in New Mexico and California to bypass the territorial stage and make constitutions to become a state, paving the way for the Compromise of 1850. Incidentally, he himself was radically opposed to this compromise. He believed that compromise would not improve the situation and that it would be better if California joined as an independent state. He did not take a radical stance on slavery, but mainly tried to keep the country together. The effects of the 1850 compromise are still debated today. Some argue that it postponed the war, while others believe that it reinforced the differences between the North and South of the US at the time.

Taylor died just 16 months after taking office, the third shortest tenure of any president. It is believed that he died from the effects of stomach flu. After his death, there were many people who did not believe this, and a conspiracy theory arose. The Whigs thought he could have been killed by southern pro-slavery groups. In 1991, his body was exhumed and examined for some poisonous compounds. However, no evidence of poisoning was found here. The most common theory is that his drinking water was contaminated by the open sewers of Washington at the time. Former President William Henry Harrison is also thought to have lost his life as a result. Only Presidents William Henry Harrison and James Garfield served shorter terms. Taylor was succeeded by his vice president, Millard Fillmore.

13. Millard Fillmore (1850-1853)

Whig party | Vice president: None (vacant)

"And honorable defeat is better than a dishonorable victory."

Millard Fillmore (Summerhill (New York), January 7, 1800 - Buffalo (New York), March 8, 1874) was an American Whig Party politician and lawyer and the 13th President of the United States from 1850 to 1853. Fillmore was the "Running mate" of Zachary Taylor during the 1848 presidential election and was elected as the 12th Vice President of the United States. After the death of President Taylor from the effects of an infectious disease in, Fillmore succeeded him as President of the United States and completed Taylor's term.

Biography

Fillmore was born into poverty in 1800; his parents were Nathaniel Fillmore (1771-1803) and Phoebe Millard (1781-1831). He had a relatively difficult childhood. Unlike many US presidents, his family was not wealthy and he could not attend school. Without having had any education, he set out to educate himself. He read books and took an internship at a law firm. He worked his way up within the Whig party to its choice as *running mate* (vice-presidential candidate) of Zachary Taylor. It was assumed that the obscure, self-effacing candidate from New York would complement Taylor well in his persona of slave-holding, Southern soldier. Nevertheless, the two came to be diametrically opposed on the issue of slavery in the new territories in the West that had been captured from Mexico in the Mexican-American War. Taylor wanted these territories to become free states; Fillmore was in favor of making them slave states to appease the South. In his own words, "God knows I am disgusted with slavery, but it is an existing evil.... and we must endure it and give it that protection which is granted to it by the Constitution."

Fillmore chaired the Senate during the months of nerve-wracking debates over the Compromise of 1850. He did not comment publicly on the merits of the proposal but, a few days before Taylor died, he did let it slip that, in the event of a tie vote on Henry Clay's proposal, he would vote for it.

Presidency

He was successor to Zachary Taylor, who, it is suspected, died of acute gastroenteritis or sunstroke. Thus it was that Fillmore's sudden arrival as president brought about a major change in political relations in the government. Taylor's cabinet resigned and Fillmore promptly appointed Daniel Webster as Secretary of State - thus allying himself with the moderate Whigs, who were for the Compromise.

A proposal for California to join the Union stoked the heated debate once again without bringing the parties one step closer together.

Clay, who was exhausted, left Washington to recover. Senate leadership passed to Senator Stephen A. Douglas of Illinois. At this turning point, Fillmore spoke out in favor of the Compromise. He sent a message to the Senate suggesting that Texas should be paid to relinquish its claims to the new territories.

As a result, a critical number of Whig senators from the North allowed themselves to be persuaded to waive the Wilmot proviso-the condition that all territories captured in the Mexican War were to be safeguarded from slavery.

Douglas' strategic moves in Congress and Fillmore's pressure from the White House gave a huge boost to the Compromise movement. Douglas went further and split Clay's bill into five parts:

- Admission of California as a free state

- Fixing the Texas border and compensating Texas for it

- The granting to New Mexico of territorial status

- Providing federal marshals to slave owners who were looking for escaped slaves

- Abolishing the slave trade in the District of Columbia (where Washington D.C. is located)

Each proposal obtained a majority and by September 20 Fillmore had signed them into law. Webster wrote of them, "Now I can sleep at night.

Another success of Fillmore's administration was the opening of the trade mission to Japan under Commander Matthew Perry.

However, some of the more militant Whigs were inconsolable and never forgave Fillmore for signing the Fugitive Slave Act. Partly because of them, he was not nominated as a presidential candidate in 1852. The Fugitive Slave Act meant that escaped slaves had to be returned to their rightful owner. A slave owner only had to inform the police about the escaped slave and the process would be initiated. When someone encountered a suspected escaped slave, he had to report it immediately. Failure to do so was punishable by a fine of one thousand dollars (equivalent to about thirty thousand dollars today). Helping fugitive slaves could even lead to a prison sentence. A caught slave was, without any form of trial, sent back to his owner. Because there was no interference from the courts, this law caused the kidnapping of many free Afro-Americans, who were then enslaved as well.

Within a few years, it became clear that the Compromise, intended to calm minds around slavery, had been nothing more than a temporary pause.

Fillmore is generally considered "the least memorable" president. The later President Harry S. Truman once accused him of weak leadership and complicit in the American Civil War. It is absolutely true that Fillmore was unable to calm the tension between North and South, but many biographers feel he deserves more credit. In some ways, Fillmore did show himself to be a strong leader. During his presidency there was the possibility of another war between America and Mexico, but through constant attention Fillmore managed to avert this crisis without losing face. Also, his open attitude towards the Compromise of 1850 is named by many people. By cooperating with this act, Fillmore performed his duty as president and refused to stand in the way of democracy.

After his presidency

After leaving the White House, Fillmore returned to Buffalo. Here he joined the University of Buffalo as rector. When the Whig party broke up later in the 1850s, Fillmore refused to join the Republicans. Instead, he became a candidate of the American party (also called the Know-Nothing party) in 1856. During the American Civil War he opposed Abraham Lincoln and during Reconstruction he supported Andrew Johnson. Fillmore died, aged 74, at 11:15 p.m. on March 8, 1874. His last words - spoken after being administered some soup - were "The food is edible."

So far, Fillmore is the last president who was neither Republican nor Democrat.

The story that Fillmore had the first bathtub installed in the White House comes from a joke by H. L. Mencken in a December 28, 1917 column in the *New York Evening Mail*.

14. Franklin Pierce (1853-1857)

Democratic party | Vice president: William R. King (Vacant later)

"If your past is limited, your future is boundless."

Franklin Pierce (Hillsborough (New Hampshire), November 23, 1804 - Concord (New Hampshire), October 8, 1869) was the 14th president of the United States from 1853 to 1857.

Franklin Pierce became president during a seemingly peaceful time. The United States seemed to have resisted the threat of secession, thanks to the Compromise of 1850. By following the recommendations of Southern advisers, Pierce, who hailed from New England, hoped to avoid another threat of secession. But his strategy, which failed to keep the peace, hastened the breakup of the union.

Biography

Pierce was born in Hillsborough (now Hillsboro), New Hampshire, in 1804. He went through "high school" at Bowdoin College. After graduating, he went to law school, after which he entered politics. At 24, he was elected to the New Hampshire 'legislature'; two years later he became 'Speaker'. In the 1930s he went to Washington, first as a member of the House of Representatives, later as a Senator.

After serving in the Mexican War, Pierce was nominated by friends in New Hampshire as a candidate for the presidential nomination in 1852. At the Democratic Convention, there was enough support to support the "Compromise of 1850" and not to raise the issue of slavery. But a vote had to be taken 48 times, until Pierce finally prevailed.

Probably because the Democrats supported the "Compromise" more strongly than the "Whigs" and because their candidate General Winfield Scott was not trusted in the South, Pierce won the election by a narrow margin.

Two months before the start of his presidency, on January 6, 1853, the family was traveling by train from Andover, Massachusetts to Lawrence, Massachusetts when their car derailed. Franklin and Jane were only slightly injured but their eleven-year-old son died before their eyes. The entire nation shared in the grief. The inauguration on March 4 took place without Jane's presence. Sad and mentally exhausted, Pierce began the presidency. Much has been written about the impact of his son's death on his presidency. Many argue that his son's death was such a blow to his mental state that it was impossible for him to function properly as president anymore. As a result of his son's death, Pierce developed a serious alcohol problem.

Presidency

In his inaugural address, he proclaimed an era of domestic peace and progress and strong policies in relations with other countries. The United States might have to acquire further assets for its own security, he argued, and would not be deterred by "any tacit prohibition of evil."

Pierce had only to tend to expansion to arouse the wrath of the North, who accused him of being a tool of the South, in their desire to spread slavery. Therefore, he aroused fear of this when he pressured the United Kingdom to give up its special interest in part of the coast of Central America, and even more so when he tried to persuade Spain to sell Cuba.

But the most serious flare-up in the struggle was caused by the "Kansas-Nebraska Act," which repealed the Missouri Compromise, and brought the issue of slavery back into the West. This measure, the work of Senator Stephen A. Douglas, stemmed from his desire to promote a railroad from Chicago to California through Nebraska. Secretary of War Jefferson Davis, an advocate of a southern transcontinental route, had convinced Pierce to send James Gadsden to Mexico to buy land for a southern railroad. He bought the area that today includes southern Arizona and part of New Mexico for $10,000,000.

Douglas' proposal to mobilize the western territories, through which the railroad could run, caused enormous problems. Douglas proposed in his laws that the people of the new territories could decide the issue of slavery for themselves. As a result, many moved to Kansas as southerners and northerners sought control of the area. Shootings broke out, and "Bleeding Kansas" became the prelude to the American Civil War.

At the end of his reign, Pierce could claim that a "peaceful situation" prevailed in Kansas. But to his disappointment, the Democrats refused to nominate him again for the presidency, choosing instead to replace him with the less controversial Buchanan.Pierce returned to New Hampshire, leaving to his successor the emerging secessionist storm.

Inheritance and death

Pierce is usually ranked among the least memorable, or worst functioning, presidents. Biographies portray him as an incredibly charismatic man who tried to please everyone. Partly because of this trait, he was not very decisive as president and is usually seen as a puppet of the Democratic Party. Partly because of his poor leadership, the American Civil War arose a few years later. Pierce saw slavery not as a moral issue, but as an issue of property. He was therefore opposed to abolitionism. The historian Larry Gara wrote the following in a biography of Pierce:

He was president at a time that called for superhuman skills, these skills he did not possess, however, and he never grew into the presidency. He never fully understood the depth of sentiment in the North. Pierce was hardworking and his administration largely untouched, but the legacy of those four turbulent years contributed to the tragedy of secession and civil war.

Franklin Pierce died, aged 64, on October 8, 1869, of liver trouble. All his life he struggled with drinking problems due to the death of his son. He had two more sons who both died before they were four years old. His wife, Jane Pierce, suffered from severe depression all her life and so their family life was severely disrupted. In the last years of his life he became increasingly spiritual and was socially active.

15. James Buchanan (1857-1861)

Democratic party | Vice president: John C. Breckinridge

"Whatever the result may be, I shall carry to my grave the consciousness that I at least meant well for my country."

James Buchanan Jr. (Mercersburg (Pennsylvania), April 23, 1791 - Lancaster (Pennsylvania), June 1, 1868) was the 15th president of the United States from 1857 to 1861.He was (and remains to this day) the only bachelor president in the list of presidents of the United States.

In the cabinet of President James Knox Polk, he was Secretary of State from 1845 to 1849. He settled disputes with England over Oregon and attempted to buy Cuba from Spain. He has been criticized for his lack of positive action to prevent the country from sliding into a downward spiral, which eventually resulted in the American Civil War.

Buchanan died in 1868 at the age of 77.

Lifetime

Buchanan was the son of Irish immigrants. He studied law and then went to work as a lawyer. Buchanan was a staunch federalist and initially opposed the War of 1812 because he did not see the need for it. When Britain invaded nearby Maryland, he enlisted anyway and helped defend the city of Baltimore.

His political career began in 1814 in the House of Representatives of the state of Pennsylvania. There he served two years on behalf of the Federalist Party until he was elected to the U.S. House of Representatives. After four terms, he no longer stood for election. President Andrew Jackson appointed him as U.S. ambassador to Russia in 1832. A year later he was back in the United States and running for the Senate. As the Federalist Party was on its last legs, Buchanan made the switch to the newly formed Democratic Party.

The Senate left Buchanan in 1845 to become Secretary of State under President James Polk. Polk had wanted Buchanan to serve on the Supreme Court, but he turned down that nomination because he wanted to finish negotiations with Britain over the exact course of border between the state of Oregon and Canada. Those negotiations culminated in the Oregon Treaty a year later. Buchanan served four years as Secretary of State, despite objections from Vice President George Dallas.

Under President Franklin Pierce, he was ambassador to Britain from 1853 to 1856. He was involved in drafting the infamous Ostend Manifesto. This document described the motivations of the United States to buy Cuba from Spain and made it clear that the United States would declare war if Spain refused. The manifesto was fairly widely regarded as a blunder and limited the ability of the Pierce administration to function.

President

The Democratic Party designated Buchanan as their candidate for president in 1856. In fact, during the heated debate over the Kansas-Nebraska Act, he was in England and had therefore remained neutral in the discussion. The Democrat defeated the Republican candidate John C. Fremont. At the age of 65, he is the fifth oldest person ever to be elected as president of the US. Because of his age, he let it be known in his inaugural address that he would not seek a second term.

At the time Buchanan took office as president, the discussion surrounding slavery dominated national politics. The Kansas-Nebraska Act provided for the organization of the territories of Kansas and Nebraska. The residents of the newly formed territories would be allowed to choose whether or not slavery was introduced. The Act also repealed the carefully negotiated Missouri Compromise of 1820 that had ensured that the number of states where slavery was and was not allowed remained balanced.

Opponents of slavery, known as abolitionists, proclaimed Topeka as the capital of Kansas, while supporters proclaimed Lecompton as the new seat of government. Buchanan appointed Robert J. Walker as territorial governor and tasked him with ending the conflict and drafting a new constitution. Kansas needed its own constitution to be admitted to the United States as a state. Walker, who was from Mississippi was assumed to support the pro-slavery faction to get their version of the constitution passed. Their concept was indeed put to the people of Kansas for approval in a referendum, but the abolitionist movement boycotted the referendum. Walker subsequently resigned from office. Nevertheless, President Buchanan tried to get the U.S. Congress to admit Kansas to the Union on the basis of the "Lecompton Constitution." The House of Representatives did indeed agree to the admission, but the proposal was rejected by the Senate.

The driving force behind that rejection was Senator Stephen Douglas, leader of the Northern Democrats. The battle around Kansas broadened into a battle for leadership within the Democratic Party. Buchanan could count on the support of a large number of southern Democrats, while Douglas had most northern Democrats and a number of "Southerners" behind him. Buchanan disposed of many of his opponents in Washington D.C. and Illinois, Douglas' home state, during the following period. Douglas' term expired in 1859 and Buchanan did everything he could to avoid being re-elected. That scheme failed. In this election, the president lost much of his following in Congress and was winged for the rest of his reign.

Buchanan received conflicting reports in March 1857 that in the Territory of Utah federal judges had been removed from office by Mormons. The government of his predecessor President Pierce had refused to recognize Utah as a state. The wildest rumors circulated. For example, the Mormons were said to have openly rebelled against the United States. Buchanan sent the army to replace Governor Brigham

Young with non-Mormon Alfred Cumming. Because the previous administration had cancelled the mail contract regarding Utah, Young never received notice of his replacement. He therefore resisted by force of arms. Only after Buchanan sent a mediator did Young step down and peace was signed.

The Republican Party won a majority in both houses in the Congressional elections. They blocked many of Buchanan's proposals, including the purchase of Cuba and plans that were to lead to greater influence in Central America. In turn, he presidentially vetoed six bills passed by the Republicans. In March 1860, the House of Representatives convened a committee to investigate a number of offenses that could have caused Buchanan to be deposed, including bribery and blackmail. Although there were indications, the committee could not substantiate the suspicions.

During the National Convention of the Democratic Party in 1860, a schism occurred. During the convention, the Democrats had to nominate a presidential candidate. The southern wing of the party left the convention and nominated the incumbent Vice President John Breckinridge as its candidate. His opponents nominated his archenemy Stephen Douglas, while another faction put forward former Speaker of the House of Representatives John Bell. He took no position on slavery and his main goal was to save the Union. Buchanan supported Breckinridge. When the Republicans put forward Abraham Lincoln as their candidate, it was almost certain that he would be elected because of the divisions within the Democratic Party.General and Chief of the Army Winfield Scott warned Buchanan as early as October 1860 that an election of Lincoln would almost certainly lead to the secession of at least seven states. Scott recommended moving much of the federal army to these states. Buchanan ignored the advice. When Lincoln was indeed elected, calls for secession increased in the southern states. In his final speech to Congress, Buchanan said that while it was not legally possible to leave the Union, the federal government could not prevent it either. He blamed the conflict entirely on northerners who wanted to abolish slavery in the South. His speech was criticized by both the South and the North because he forbade secession but at the same time would not act against it. Five days after the speech, Treasury Secretary Howell Cobb resigned because he no longer supported the president.

South Carolina seceded on December 20, 1860, followed by six other slave states. In February 1861, they proclaimed the Confederate States of America. They seized federal government buildings in their territories, and Buchanan did not act against them. In late December

1860 Buchanan replaced a number of ministers in his cabinet who sympathized with the Confederate States and substituted them for a number of nationalists who believed in the unity of the United States.

Personal life and death

Buchanan's personal life is characterized by the absence of a wife. Thus, this made him the only president of the US who was single. This fact has caused increased historical interest in his life. There are historians who attribute the absence of a woman in his life to a celibate lifestyle, or the possibility that Buchanan was asexual. However, many more historians believe that it is quite possible that Buchanan was homosexual.

In 1818 Buchanan met Anne Caroline Coleman. By 1819 the two were engaged, although they saw little of each other. Buchanan was busy with his law firm and could not be with her much. Coleman broke off their engagement and died a few weeks later on December 9, 1819. Buchanan wrote to her father to request permission to attend the funeral. His request, however, was denied. After her death, he never had another relationship with a woman and also showed little interest in women.

Buchanan had an intimate personal relationship with William Rufus King, an Alabama politician who had briefly served as vice president under Franklin Pierce. They lived together for many years and thus spoke to each other a lot. Others also noticed their intimacies and much gossip broke out about their possible sexual relationship. In 1853, King died of tuberculosis, four years before Buchanan's presidency.

In May 1868, Buchanan caught a cold. The illness worsened rapidly, due to his advanced age, and on June 1, 1868, he died. He lived to be 77 years old.

16. Abraham Lincoln (1861-1865)

Republican party and National Union party | Vice presidents: Hannibal Hamlin and Andrew Johnson

"I am not bound to win, but I am bound to be true. I am not bound to succeed, but I am bound to live up to what light I have."

Abraham Lincoln (Hodgenville (Kentucky), February 12, 1809 - Washington, April 15, 1865) was the 16th president of the United States. He served from 1861 until his death in 1865. Lincoln was the first President of the United States to be assassinated while in office.

Lincoln is considered one of the greatest American presidents. He is praised for his leadership during the American Civil War, the abolition of slavery, the strengthening of the national government, and the modernization of the economy.

Biography

Abraham Lincoln was the son of Thomas and Nancy Hanks Lincoln. He was named after his grandfather on his father's side. His father was a carpenter and farmer. Both his parents were Baptists.

When Lincoln was seven, his parents moved to Indiana. He attended school with his older sister Sarah, who died in 1828 while giving birth to her child. Lincoln's younger brother died shortly after giving birth. A self-taught student, Lincoln mastered reading, writing, and speaking to a level that school could not provide.

In 1818, his mother died from drinking milk contaminated with *Ageratina altissima*. A year after her death, his father remarried Sarah Bush Johnston. She already had three children. In 1851, his father died.

In 1831 Lincoln moved to Illinois where he lived in New Salem from 1837. He held various jobs there, from letter carrier to store owner and was nicknamed *Honest Abe* here. Lincoln also competed in elections for the Illinois state House of Representatives. He won four times, in 1834, 1836, 1838 and 1840, as a member of the *United States Whig Party* while later joining the Republicans. During this time he also studied law in his spare time, and in 1836 he became a lawyer.

In 1839 Lincoln met Mary Todd, in Springfield. After three years they married and over the next eleven years had four children: Robert, Edward, William and Thomas. During this time, Lincoln was a successful lawyer.

In 1846 Lincoln was elected to the House of Representatives after which he gained fame for his views on the Mexican-American War and slavery. After his term in office, he returned home and resumed his law practice.

Lincoln's interest in politics was sparked by the *Kansas-Nebraska Act*. He began to give occasional speeches, which were very successful because of their logic and humor.

Presidency

In 1860, Lincoln ran for president for the Republicans, and was elected the 16th president of the United States. He took the oath of office as president on March 4, 1861.

The Southern States saw a threat in Lincoln because he wanted to prevent the expansion of slavery. Lincoln had been elected exclusively with votes from the Northern States (and California and Oregon). The Southern states then seceded from the United States and formed the Confederate States of America. As a result, in his first term, Lincoln immediately experienced the greatest internal crisis the United States would know: the American Civil War. With conciliatory words in his inaugural address as president, he could not prevent this war. Despite the great loss of life, Lincoln stuck to his uncompromising stance against the South. He did emphasize, however, that his concern was the preservation of the Union, not the abolition of slavery. For example, on Aug. 25, 1862, he wrote in the New York Times, "If I could save the Union without freeing any slave, I would do it; and if I could save it by freeing all the slaves, I would do it; and if I could do it by freeing some and leaving others alone, I would also do that." On April 9, 1865, Southern General Lee signed the surrender, virtually ending the resistance of the breakaway Southern States.

After his re-election in 1864, Lincoln was shot on Good Friday, April 14, 1865, at *Ford's Theatre* (a theater in Washington) by John Wilkes Booth, a fanatical supporter of the Confederate States. The president was struck in the back of the head by a bullet and died the next day on Silent Saturday, April 15, at the *Petersen House* at the age of 56.

His death shocked America violently, including the southern states. At least 100,000 people in Washington and 600,000 in New York said goodbye to the assassinated president. A special funeral train took Lincoln in several days from Washington via New York, Detroit, Buffalo and Chicago to Springfield. Mourners lined the route everywhere. It is estimated that some seven million people attended the various mourning ceremonies.

On May 4, 1865, Lincoln was buried in Springfield. He was interred in the family vault at Oak Ridge Cemetery.

Legend has it that a few days before the assassination Lincoln had dreamed that he saw someone laid out in the White House. When he asked what had happened, a soldier is said to have replied that the president had been assassinated.

Andrew Johnson, his vice president, succeeded Abraham Lincoln as president. As a gesture of reconciliation, Lincoln elected this Democrat as vice president. This later caused problems with the Republican majority in Congress and Senate resulting in (unsuccessful) impeachment proceedings.

Cabinet members under Lincoln

Beard

Abraham Lincoln grew his beard in 1861, partly on the advice of eleven-year-old Grace Bedell. She wrote him in a letter that it would look better on him, since he had such a thin face. When Lincoln passed through Bedell's hometown on the train to Washington after his election, thousands of residents had gathered to see the new president. In his speech, Lincoln told of Bedell's letter and stated that partly at her suggestion he had grown his beard. He asked if she was present and invited her to come forward.

17. Andrew Johnson (1865-1869)

National Union party and Democratic party | Vice president: None (vacant)

"If you always support the correct principles then you will never get the wrong results!"

Andrew Johnson (Raleigh (North Carolina), December 29, 1808 - Elizabethton (Tennessee), July 31, 1875) was the seventeenth president of the United States (1865-1869). Before that in 1865 he was vice president under Abraham Lincoln. After his death on April 15, 1865, he became president.

Biography

Andrew Johnson was born in Raleigh, North Carolina, and was self-taught. He moved to Tennessee in 1826, where he worked as a tailor. He was an alderman in Greeneville from 1828 to 1830 and mayor from 1834 to 1838. From 1835 to 1837 and from 1839 to 1841 he was a member of the Tennessee House of Representatives. In 1841 he was elected as a Democrat to Congress, of which he was a member from March 4, 1843 to March 3, 1853. He did not aspire to a subsequent term and became governor of Tennessee, a position he held until 1857. He then served as a member of the Senate from October 8, 1857 to March 4, 1862.

In 1864, Republican Abraham Lincoln elected him vice president. He was sworn in on March 4, 1865. After Lincoln's assassination, on April 15, 1865, he succeeded him as president.

Presidency

Johnson governed during the *Reconstruction* period, the period just after the American Civil War, during which the southern slave states were brought back into the union. He continued the policy that Lincoln had initiated, but wanted to reinstate the states with the former slaveholders much sooner. However, this was structurally opposed by Congress, which was dominated by the Republicans. Congress wanted assurances regarding the civil rights of the black population before they would admit the states. With Congress he was constantly at odds. As he criticized Congress, this only got worse.

Deposition procedure

The House of Representatives eventually initiated impeachment proceedings because Johnson had fired Edwin Stanton, the Secretary of War, in violation of the Constitution. The procedure fell just short, falling one vote short of a two-thirds majority in the Senate by 35 votes to 19. Johnson thus legitimately retired at the end of his term, on March 4, 1869. He was the first president against whom the House of Representatives instituted impeachment proceedings.

After his presidency, Johnson participated in elections to the Senate (1869) and the House of Representatives (1872), both of which he lost. On March 4, 1875, he was still elected to the Senate and served until his death on July 31, 1875. He died at the age of 66 in his daughter's home.

18. Ulysses S. Grant (1869-1877)

Republican party | Vice presidents: Schuyler Colfax and Henry Wilson

"In every battle there comes a time when both sides consider themselves beaten, then he who continues the attack wins."

Ulysses Simpson Grant (Point Pleasant (Ohio), April 27, 1822 - Wilton (New York), July 23, 1885) was an American general and commander-in-chief of the Northern forces during the American Civil War. He was the 18th president of the United States from 1869 to 1877.

Youth

Grant was born in Point Pleasant, Clermont County in Ohio. His parents were Jesse Root Grant and Hannah Simpson and they named him **Hiram Ulysses Grant**. His father and grandfather on his mother's side had been born in Pennsylvania. His father was a tanner. In the fall of 1823, they moved to Georgetown in Brown Country, Ohio. Grant spent most of his time here until his seventeenth birthday.

When he was 17, he was nominated by his deputy as a cadet in the U.S. Army. He was admitted to the army's elite academy, West Point in New York. However, the delegate mistakenly signed him up as Ulysses S. Grant, and that is how he was henceforth known (which did not reflect badly on him later; the abbreviation of his name contributed firmly to his popularity). He graduated in 1843, 21st in a class of 39 cadets.

On August 22 of that year he married Julia Boggs Dent, with whom he had four children: Frederick Dent, Ulysses Simpson Jr., Ellen Wrenshall and Jesse Root.

Military career

Before the Civil War

Grant served during the Mexican-American War under Generals Zachary Taylor and Winfield Scott and fought in the battles of Resaca de la Palma, Palo Alto (in present-day Texas), Monterrey and Vera Cruz. He received citations twice for bravery displayed: at Molino del Rey and Chapultepec. The following summer, on July 31, 1854, he went on a major leave of absence. Seven years of civilian life followed, during which Grant was about as unsuccessful in everything he tackled. With his pay from the army he bought a farm, which promptly went bankrupt. In St. Louis he worked as a real estate agent for a while, but was fired for lack of success. Eventually he went to work in his father's and brother's tannery as an assistant.

Tennessee

When Southern troops captured Fort Sumter on April 14, 1861, Grant assembled a company of volunteers and reported to Springfield, Illinois, as a company captain. The governor felt that a West Point alumnus could be better employed and appointed him colonel of the 21st Illinois Infantry Regiment effective June 17, 1861. His first mission was not a great success and he continued to get an office job. Nevertheless, promotion followed and he became brigadier general of volunteers as of August 7.

Through a detour, Grant was returned to the field at the head of a battalion. On February 6, 1862, he and his men won the North's first, major victory in the American Civil War by capturing Fort Henry in Tennessee. The following week, he took Fort Donelson, demanding unconditional surrender, which inspired North and South to adopt a nickname (based on his initials): *Unconditional Surrender* Grant.

Soon he established a reputation as a tenacious leader who relentlessly pursued the Confederate army and never let go of his enemy. Because of these qualities, he won a number of great but costly victories in various battles. One famous - and infamous - victory he won was the battle of Shiloh, where over two days more Americans (around 5,000) died than in all previous American wars combined. Grant spent the evening between the two days of this battle with his friend and sub-commander William T. Sherman. In his memoirs, Sherman left a portion of their conversation that typifies Grant greatly. Sherman remarked that the first day had been very hard. Grant responded by saying "Yep - but tomorrow we roll them up".

Vicksburg

After the victory at Shiloh, Grant was ordered to take the city of Vicksburg. This city was the last on the Mississippi River in Southern hands and the last obstacle to the Union taking control of the entire river. Grant led his troops on a long march around the city, surrounded it and began a siege of several months. During this siege, two more of Grant's traits became apparent. First, his use of many men and heavy weapons to win battles - a huge change from existing military tactics. In doing so, Grant demonstrated an understanding of the changing nature of warfare that not many of his peers followed and helped define the picture of warfare up until the introduction of *Blitzkrieg* by German armies in 1940. The second trait was less flattering, namely, Grant's habit of getting through periods of boredom (such as long sieges) with the help of large amounts of liquor. Grant's oft-mentioned (but largely undeserved) reputation as a drunkard has its origins here. Grant, however, was by no means an alcoholic. During periods of action during the war and later - in the company of his wife, when she could provide distraction - there was rarely, if ever, any liquor in his vicinity.

Vicksburg held out for months, but on July 4, 1863, the city surrendered to Grant. He presented the city to President Abraham Lincoln in celebration of American Independence Day, with which the nation celebrated its birthday in grand fashion - by coincidence, the day before, Robert E. Lee's Army of Northern Virginia had been defeated at the Battle of Gettysburg and withdrawn back toward the South. It would be until 1943 before the 4th of July would be celebrated again in Vicksburg.

Chattanooga

After his victory at Vicksburg, Grant was given field command of the troops on the Western Front, and in this capacity he assumed command of Major General William S. Rosecrans' forces, which had been cornered at Chattanooga. Grant immediately went on the attack, driving the Southern army to the defensive around Lookout Mountain. This slope was thought impregnable, but Grant had it stormed by surprise the next day -- thus arriving at one of the great insights that would also be horribly borne out in World War I, namely that a position defended by heavy firearms can be taken if you are willing to take enormous losses. The losses here were not too bad because of the element of surprise, but Grant would later experience this differently.

Because of Grant's tenacious nature, willingness to go all out to conquer, and total unwillingness to give up until the last man on his side was dead, Lincoln began to see in him the man who could lead the American Union to victory (this is in contrast to a number of previous generals Lincoln had tested, all of whom had proved disappointments against Lee). On March 2, 1864, Grant was promoted to lieutenant general and as of March 17, he was given command of all United States troops.

Army of the Potomac

Grant left the war in the West to the one man he trusted blindly - William Tecumseh Sherman. A brotherhood had formed between them (which Sherman described in his autobiography as "Grant stayed loyal to me when I was mad and I to him when he was drunk himself silly") and Grant knew that Sherman would handle things the way Grant wanted. Grant himself took command of the huge Army of the Potomac, which had been facing the Army of Northern Virginia and Robert E. Lee since 1861 - with a complete lack of success.

Lincoln and Grant set as their unwavering goal the capture of Richmond, Virginia (the capital of the Confederate States of America), and Grant marched south. His first battle against the invincible Lee was the Battle of the Wilderness, a bloodbath that Grant lost thickly. To this he reacted as no commander of the Army of the Potomac had ever done: instead of retreating and regrouping, he gave chase to Lee. This placed Lee for the first time face to face with a commander who was unconditionally willing to bring the superiority of his army to bear on Lee's, to which Lee was already commenting that he was "probably losing the war now."

The Battle of the Wilderness became the Wilderness Campaign, which included such battles as the Battle of Spotsylvania Court House (a close tie between Grant and Lee) and Cold Harbor - a bloodbath in which Grant spent two days trying to take a fortified riverbed by storming it. In his memoirs, Grant called the Battle of Cold Harbor (which he lost) "The one, really big blunder I made as a commander." In the end, Grant had his troops pull around Lee's army across the river. Lee, flanked, hastily pulled his army around Richmond, and when Grant ran into this wall of men, the nine-month war of attrition of the Siege of Petersburg began - another great drinking moment for Grant.

Victory

By March 1865, Grant had succeeded in severely weakening Lee's army and extending his lines by 35 miles. Exhausted by starvation, bombing, and bad weather, Lee's soldiers deserted in large numbers. After the Confederate government evacuated from Richmond, the Confederacy collapsed like a house of cards. Lee led his troops into the woods until they were finally surrounded by Grant's army at Appomattox Court House. On April 9, 1865, Lee surrendered and on May 26, 1865, the war was over.

As a reward for services rendered, Grant was promoted by the U.S. Congress on July 25, 1866, to an entirely new rank in the U.S. Army: General of the Army.

Presidency

Grant decided, in part because of the tumultuous presidency of Andrew Johnson, to enter politics. On May 20, 1868, he was nominated, almost unopposed, as a candidate for president by the Republican party. He won the election that same year, with 3,012,833 of the total 5,716,082 votes cast. This made him the 18th president of the United States.

His presidency was dominated by corruption scandals. In particular, the Whiskey Ring fraud in which $3 million in taxpayer money was misappropriated is infamous. Orville E. Babcock, private secretary to the president, was involved and only a presidential pardon from Grant kept him out of jail. The Whiskey Ring was followed by a scandal involving Secretary of War William W. Belknap, who was investigated for taking bribes in exchange for selling free-trade posts from American Indians - Belknap was found guilty. Although it was never proven that Grant himself did anything wrong or benefited from the actions of his ministers, he has been blamed for not being decisive enough in combating the misdeeds of his associates, in stark contrast to his ruthless actions as a general during the Civil War. Even when guilt was proven, he took little or no action against his associates.

Later life

After his second term, Grant made a two-year world tour. In Sunderland, England, he opened England's first public and free library.

In 1883, Grant was elected as the eighth president of the National Rifle Association.

Grant also went into business as a senior partner in the firm Grant and Ward. Perhaps somewhat predictably, this firm went bankrupt, dragging Grant's family capital with it. Meanwhile, Grant was dying of throat cancer and needed to find a way to provide money for his family after his death. Desperate, he worked to write down his memoirs, which he completed a few days before his death. This time, his last "business" intention succeeded: these memoirs provided his wife and children with a generous income.

Grant died on July 23, 1885, only 63 years old, at Mount McGregor in Saratoga County, New York State. He is buried with his wife in Grant's Tomb in New York City, the largest mausoleum in the United States.

During his lifetime, Grant was a Methodist. Today, his portrait appears on the U.S. $50 bill.

19. Rutherford B. Hayes (1877-1881)

Republican party | Vice president: William A. Wheeler

"One of the tests of the civilization of people is the treatment of its criminals."

Rutherford Birchard Hayes (Delaware (Ohio), October 4, 1822 - Fremont (Ohio), January 17, 1893) was the 19th president of the United States from 1877 to 1881.

Early political career

Before becoming president, Hayes was a delegate for the state of Ohio. Born at Delaware, Delaware County in that state in 1822; his parents were Rutherford Hayes and Sophia Birchard. He received his education at the normal schools (no private education), the Methodist

Academy in Norwalk, Ohio, and the Webb Preparatory School in Middletown, Connecticut. He graduated from Kenyon College in Gambier, Ohio in August 1842 and from Harvard Law School in January 1845. He was registered as an attorney on May 10, 1845 and started an office in Lower Sandusky (now called Fremont). In 1849 he moved to Cincinnati and started an office there. Between 1857 and 1859 he was city attorney. On June 27, 1861, he enlisted and was appointed major of the 23rd Regiment of Ohio Volunteer Infantry. On October 24 he was promoted to superior, on October 24, 1862 to colonel, and on October 9, 1864 to Brigadier of Volunteers. On March 3, 1865, he was appointed Major General of the Volunteers.

Hayes was elected as a Republican to the 39th and 40th Congresses and served there from March 4, 1865 to July 20, 1867, when he left the House of Representatives after running for governor of Ohio. He was governor from 1868 to 1872 and a candidate for the 43rd Congress (but he lost that election). He was re-elected governor in 1875 and served in that role from January 1876 until March 2, 1877, when he bid farewell to the governorship-he had been elected president of the United States. Because March 4, 1877, was a Sunday, he took the oath of office on March 3 in the Red Room of the White House. On March 5, he did it all over again on the East Balcony of the Capitol, this time with an audience in attendance. He was president until March 4, 1881.

His presidency

Hayes became president after the tumultuous and scandal-ridden years of the Newman administration. Since his service in the American Civil War, he had a reputation as an honest man when, as Major General, he refused to campaign for a seat in the House of Representatives on the stated reason that "any officer who abandons his men to go on election races should be scalped." As governor of Ohio, his scruples could sometimes drive even his political allies to despair, earning him the nickname "Old Granny" ("Old Grandma"). Nevertheless, his opponent in the race for the White House, Democrat Samuel J. Tilden, was the favorite and he also won the popular election by a margin of some 250,000 votes (out of 8.5 million voters).

The elections of 1876

However, the President of the United States is not directly elected, by the Council of Electors - in which the Electors of four states could not make a decision. To win, a candidate needed 185 votes. Tilden had

184, Hayes 165, and 20 votes (of those four states) were undecided. And to complicate matters further, three of those states (Florida, South Carolina and Louisiana) were Southern states and therefore under military occupation.

After months of deliberation and negotiation, Southern Democrats were assured that if Hayes were elected he would withdraw Federal troops from the South and end Reconstruction. In return, the Democrats agreed to serve on a committee to determine the final outcome. That committee, consisting of eight Republicans and seven Democrats voted 8 to 7 to award all open votes to Hayes. The Republicans gave this as an excuse that the problem in those four states had been an issue of who could and could not vote. The Democrats, however, felt robbed of the presidency and further called Hayes "Rutherfraud."

Key legislation

During his presidency, Hayes signed a number of laws, including one on February 15, 1879 that gave women lawyers the right to argue cases before the U.S. Supreme Court.

After his presidency

Hayes died in Fremont, Ohio on January 17, 1893, aged 70. He was buried in Oakwood Cemetery. After his house was given as a gift to the State of Ohio as land for the Spiegel Grove State Park, he was reburied there in 1915.

20. James A. Garfield (1881-1881)

Republican party | Vice President: Chester A. Arthur

"The truth will set you free, but first it will make you miserable."

James Abram Garfield (Moreland Hills, Ohio, November 19, 1831 - Long Branch, New Jersey, September 19, 1881) was the 20th president of the United States and the second president to be assassinated.

His tenure was one of the shortest in the history of U.S. presidents; six months and 15 days (the shortest-serving president was William Henry Harrison).

Garfield was born in what was then Orange Township, Cuyahoga County, Ohio, a suburb southeast of Cleveland. His father died in 1833, and he was raised by his mother and an uncle. He became a teacher, teaching classical languages, and later became head of the Eclectic Institute where he taught. On November 11, 1858, he married Lucretia Rudolph, and they had five children. His son James Rudolph Garfield also became a politician and later served as Secretary of the Interior under Theodore Roosevelt.

Garfield studied law on his own, but decided that academic life was not right for him and he became a politician. He was a passionate Republican all his life. In 1859, he became a senator from Ohio.

His military career began with the American Civil War when he enlisted in the 42nd Ohio Volunteer Infantry in the Union Army. Among other things, he participated in the battles of Shiloh in April 1862 and Chickamauga in September 1863. He was eventually promoted to major general. Still in 1863, he resigned from the army to run for his home state seat in the House of Representatives.

Until 1878, Garfield was re-elected to the House of Representatives every two years. In 1880, at the Republican convention, he was designated as his party's presidential candidate on the 36th ballot. In November 1880 he won the presidential election by a narrow margin over Winfield S. Hancock, and was installed as president in March 1881. During his short term, Garfield was primarily concerned with arguments over appointments with New York Republican Party boss Roscoe Conkling.

On July 2, 1881, Garfield was shot with two bullets in a Washington D.C. train station by Charles J. Guiteau. One of the bullets could not be found or removed, and an infection resulting from the use of unsterilized medical instruments made Garfield increasingly ill. He was taken to the coastal town of Long Branch in hopes that the sea air would strengthen him. However, Garfield developed a severe lung infection there and died at the age of 49 on September 19, 1881.

Garfield was succeeded by his vice president. His assassin Guiteau could not stomach the fact that he himself had not been elected consul in Paris. Guiteau was found guilty of Garfield's murder and sentenced to death. On June 30, 1882, he was hanged.

21. Chester A. Arthur (1881-1885)

Republican party | Vice president: None (vacant)

"Be fit for more than the thing you are now doing. Let
everyone know that you have a reserve in yourself;
that you have more power than you are now using."

Chester Alan Arthur (Fairfield (Vermont), October 5, 1829 - New York,
November 18, 1886) was the 21st U.S. president from 1881 to 1885.
He was a member of the Republican Party.

Arthur was born the son of a Baptist preacher who emigrated from
Ireland. In 1848 he graduated from Union College in Schenectady.
Thereafter he was active in teaching and law. As a 24-year-old lawyer,
in 1854 he defended Elizabeth Jennings, a young black woman who
had been denied access to New York's new streetcar on Sunday
morning because of her skin color. Arthur won the lawsuit the woman

had filed. She was awarded damages and segregation on New York's streetcars was abolished.

During the American Civil War, he served in a logistics unit from his hometown of New York. He attained the rank of quartermaster general. From 1871 to 1878 he was tax collector in New York Harbor. In 1881 he became vice president, alongside President James Garfield. It was Arthur's first elected office. Garfield died on September 19, 1881 after an assassination attempt, leaving the inexperienced Arthur unexpectedly president.

Arthur's presidency was characterized by important social reforms, such as the calling of open and fair examinations for important appointments. As a result, Arthur was quite well regarded as president. In 1884 he tried unsuccessfully to be nominated by his party for a second term, although he knew by then that he was suffering from a fatal liver disease. Arthur died in 1886 at his home in New York. He is buried in the Albany Rural Cemetery, also in New York.

22 & 24. Grover Cleveland (1885-1889, 1893-1897)

Democratic party | Vice president: Thomas A. Hendricks

Grover Cleveland served as the 22nd and the 24th president.

"I know that I am honest and sincere in my desire to do well; but the question is whether I know enough to accomplish what I desire."

Stephen Grover (Grover) Cleveland (Caldwell (New Jersey), March 18, 1837 - Princeton (New Jersey), June 24, 1908) was an American Democratic Party politician and jurist and the 22nd and 24th Presidents of the United States from 1885 to 1889 and from 1893 to 1897.

Cleveland was a self-taught law student, working as a lawyer and prosecutor from 1860 to 1871. Cleveland was a former mayor of Buffalo and governor of New York, when he defeated James Blaine in the 1884 presidential election. During his reign he was praised for his courage, honesty, and incorruptibility. He was less popular because of his attempts to reduce import duties, his frequent vetoes of Congressional decisions, and his systematic ignoring of the press. Consequently, he lost the 1888 election to Benjamin Harrison, although he won the most votes nationally.

In 1892, however, he defeated that same Benjamin Harrison; his second term ran from 1893 to 1897. During that entire term he was confronted with a deep economic crisis, which had started just before he took office. He did not succeed in bringing it under control, mainly because of the lack of a Central Bank to regulate the money supply. He did succeed in repealing the controversial Sherman Silver Purchase Act of 1890, enacted by Harrison, which henceforth placed gold rather than silver at the basis of the money supply. A measure that was just as controversial.

In 1894 he sent federal troops to break the Pullman strike, which many considered a blot on his record.

Cleveland is the only president of the United States to have served as president in two nonconsecutive terms. He was also the only president to marry within the walls of the White House. On June 2, 1886, he married Frances Cleveland (Frances Clara Folsom), 27 years younger and at that time 21 years old, the youngest, and in the opinion of many also the most beautiful first lady to this day. She thus replaced Rose Cleveland, the president's sister, who served as first lady during the period when he was not yet married.

He died of a heart attack on June 24, 1908. His last words were, "I have tried everything to do well." Cleveland lived to be 71 years old.

Lifetime

Early years

Cleveland was born the fifth in a family of nine children. His father Richard Falley Cleveland was a Presbyterian minister. In 1844, the family moved to Fayetville, New York State. Nine years later the family moved again, this time to Clinton, New York, where the head of the family became secretary of the American Home Missionary Society. Financially, the family was not well off, forcing Cleveland to drop out of school. Shortly after the family moved to Holland Pattent, his father died as a result of a stomach ulcer.

Through his brother William, Cleveland found work as an assistant teacher in an institution for the blind. In 1854 he returned to Holland Pattent where an elder of his church offered to pay for Cleveland's education if he became a minister. Cleveland declined the offer and moved to Buffalo, where his uncle Lewis Allen gave him a job as a clerk. Allen worked at an influential law firm where President Millard Fillmore had previously worked. Cleveland received in-house training and was admitted to the New York Bar in 1859.

Attorney

Cleveland worked for his uncle for three years, after which he started his own practice. In 1863 he became a prosecutor in Erie County. That same year he was called up for military service. However, he was also permitted to send a replacement. Cleveland paid Polish immigrant George Benninsky $150 to take his place. Benninsky survived the American Civil War.

As a lawyer, Cleveland was known as a hard worker. He had a frugal lifestyle, but was also much to be found in the social life of the city, so his network grew rapidly. As a lawyer, Cleveland defended several participants in the Fenian raids, which were Irish-Americans who invaded Canada from the United States in protest against the British occupation of Ireland. He became really famous when he won a libel case against the publisher of the newspaper *Commercial Advertiser*.

Sheriff

Cleveland was a Democrat at heart. He wanted nothing to do with Republicans John Fremont and Abraham Lincoln. In 1865 he ran for prosecutor in Erie County, but lost the election to Lyman Bass. In 1870 he was elected sheriff in the same county.

Probably the biggest advantage of this job was the salary: $40,000, which converts to almost a million dollars today. Cleveland's most startling operation during this period was the execution of Patrick Morrisey who had murdered his mother. Cleveland, as sheriff, was allowed to pay a deputy to carry out the execution, but chose to do it himself. When his three-year term was up, Cleveland returned to the legal profession.

During this period, Cleveland dealt with the widow Maria Halpin. She later accused him of rape. Cleveland then accused Halpin of being an alcoholic who was not careful about contact with men. He had her locked up in an institution, where the staff soon realized that she did not belong there. She was therefore released. The child Cleveland fathered with Halpin would play another important role during the 1884 presidential election.

Mayor of Buffalo

The Buffalo City Council had a bad reputation. Many council members were associated with corruption, both Democrats and Republicans. The Democratic party leadership approached Cleveland, who had an impeccable record, whether he was available for the mayoralty. He agreed and was subsequently elected.

Cleveland came to be known during this period as someone who was willing to tackle corruption within the public administration. A good example of this was the tenders for city cleaning. Parties could bid for these. The city council, for political reasons, chose the most expensive bidder asking for over $400,000, rather than the lowest bid asking for only $100,000. Cleveland vetoed this and the City Council still agreed to the cheapest bid.

Governor of New York

Leading up to the 1882 gubernatorial election, Cleveland was seen as a potential contender. The Democratic state convention initially seemed to want to favor either Roswell Flower or Henry Slocum. Cleveland emerged as a compromise candidate when the convention could not make a choice from either man. Cleveland defeated Republican candidate Charles Folger by a wide margin. This was partly because Folger had to deal with a split in his own party.

Also as governor, Cleveland placed an emphasis on stopping unnecessary government spending. In the first two months, he vetoed the bill eight times. His veto of a proposal to lower train ticket prices was controversial. The proposers wanted to hit unpopular train owner Jay Gould in the wallet. Cleveland opposed this because Gould had made the train tracks in question profitable again after the takeover. In addition, Cleveland feared that the proposed law violated the contract clause in the Constitution. Despite the initial opposition, the veto was upheld.

Cleveland's actions made him an enemy of Tammany Hall, a major Democratic organization in New York. Their opposition grew after Cleveland thwarted the re-election of one of their leaders Thomas F. Grady in the state senate. After that, he increasingly clashed with his own party colleagues. On the other hand, Cleveland was able to count on the support of reform-minded Republicans, including Theodore Roosevelt, which allowed him to still gain a majority for several important laws.

Presidential election of 1884

Samuel Tilden initially enjoyed the most support within the Democratic Party, but he declined the honor due to poor health. There was then no outright favorite. Each candidate had his objections. Thomas Bayard had spoken out in favor of seceding from the southern states in 1861, Benjamin Butler was hated in the South for his performance during the American Civil War, and Allen Thurman was seen as too old. Cleveland had opponents within Tammany Hall, but that did not prevent him from winning a majority on the second ballot at the Democratic Convention. His running mate became Thomas Hendricks of Indiana.

Old accusations against Blaine of corruption were revived when letters from him surfaced, making the stories seem true. Cleveland instead portrayed himself as the anti-corruption candidate. During the campaign, it was revealed that Cleveland had an illegitimate child and was financially supporting the mother. Cleveland confirmed this story.

The election seemed to be going to be decided in New York, Indiana, New Jersey and Connecticut. Tammany Hall eventually sided with Cleveland because the alternative, a Republican president, was always worse. Blaine had an Irish mother and hoped to rely on the support of the American-Irish population. Shortly before the election, Republican Samuel Burchard made a speech about the Irish in which he spoke of "rum, Roman and rebellion." The Democrats skillfully exploited the incident and spread the phrase to the Irish people of New York. Cleveland eventually won in all four swing states, including New York by a difference of twelve hundred votes. In doing so, he garnered 219 electoral votes compared to 182 for Blaine. In absolute votes, the difference was a quarter of a percent in Cleveland's favor.

First term as president

Reforms

It was customary for a new president to appoint his party members to key positions in government. Cleveland initially waived that right and kept Republicans who functioned well in office. He did, however, reduce the number of federal officials. Only later in his term did he replace several partisan Republicans with Democrats.

Cleveland established the Interstate Commerce Commission that oversaw railroads. Along with Secretary of the Navy William Whitney, he reformed the Navy. He cancelled several construction contracts with companies responsible for a number of poor quality ships. Secretary of the Interior Lucius Lamar demanded large tracts of land back from several railroad builders because they had not fulfilled a promise to further expand the railroad network.

The Senate, through the Tenure of Office Act, had the power to block any resignation of an officer by the president. Cleveland refused to cooperate with this because he felt it violated the president's independent position. His attitude led to the repeal of the Act in 1887.

Veto's

As president, Cleveland had to deal with a Senate where Republicans were the majority. He frequently used his veto. For example, he blocked the granting of pensions to hundreds of Civil War veterans. According to Cleveland, the Pension Office had already rejected their pension application and it was not the job of Congress to review that decision.

His most famous veto was over the Texas Seed Bill. A drought had destroyed crops in several counties in Texas. Congress made available ten thousand dollars to buy new seeds for farmers. Cleveland was in favor of a restrained government. Moreover, it would weaken solidarity among citizens if they looked to the government for help every time.

Import tariffs

During the American Civil War, the U.S. government had implemented import tariffs as a temporary measure to protect its own industry. After the war, however, the tariffs had never been reduced, let alone eliminated. It made the government a lot of money, so much so that it led to a budget surplus in the 1980s. Cleveland, like most Democrats, favored lowering tariffs. Many Republicans and Democrats from the northern states, where most manufacturing sat, feared that lowering tariffs would harm their own industries. The House of Representatives passed a bill in 1887, reducing tariffs from 47 percent to 40 percent. In the Senate, a majority opposed it, so the bill died a quiet death. The issue became a major topic in the 1888 presidential election.

Indians

A month before Cleveland's appointment, his predecessor Chester Arthur opened more than sixteen thousand square miles of land in Dakota Territory for the settlement of white land movers. The land had previously been allocated to the Winnebago and Crow Creek Indians. Cleveland felt that Arthur's executive order violated a number of treaties with the tribes. On April 17, 1885, he ordered that the land movers leave the area. He sent eighteen companies to see that his order was obeyed.

Cleveland felt that Native Americans were under the tutelage of the state, which was responsible for improving living conditions and enforcing their rights. Cleveland supported the idea of cultural assimilation. Under the Dawes Act, the federal government was allowed to subdivide Native American lands. Until that point, the land had been managed by the tribe as a whole. Now the land was allocated to individual tribal members with the idea that this would allow them to engage in agriculture. However, the pieces allocated to each person were too small to be profitable. After allotment, much land remained which was then opened up for the settlement of non-Indians. The area available to Indian tribes decreased by two-thirds in fifty years.

Foreign Policy

Cleveland was a non-interventionist and opposed further expansion of the United States. His foreign minister, Thomas Bayard, negotiated with Briton Joseph Chamberlain over fishing rights in the waters around Canada. Cleveland's predecessor had sent delegates to the Colonial Conference in Berlin. There agreements had been made to protect American interests in the Congo region. The treaty was before the Senate for approval, but Cleveland withdrew the proposal when he became president.

Judicial appointments

Cleveland successfully nominated two justices to the Supreme Court in his first term. The first was Lucius Lamar, a former senator from Mississippi and at that time his Secretary of the Interior. He replaced the late William Bunham Woods. Lamar was popular as a minister. Two decades earlier, he had fought along under the Confederate flag, which caused many Republican senators to vote against it anyway. In the

Senate vote, he received 32 votes in favor and 28 against. Chief Justice Morrison Waite died in March 1888. Cleveland nominated Melville Fuller as his replacement. He was appointed without much difficulty.

Military Policy

At the request of Secretary of War William Endicott, a program worth 127 million was set up to improve coastal defenses. A total of 70 forts were built at 27 sites to defend important ports and river mouths. There was also a substantial investment in the navy. Sixteen steel warships were built, for example, which later played a crucial role in the Spanish-American War of 1898.

Civil Rights

Cleveland considered Reconstruction a failed experiment and refused to use his power to guarantee African-American voting rights. He condemned violence against Chinese immigrants. At the same time, he considered immigration from China undesirable. He made a case to Congress for the passage of a law that would have made Chinese immigrants returning to their homeland unwelcome in the U.S.

Getting married

Cleveland entered the White House as a bachelor. He was assisted for the first two years by his sister Rose who performed the duties of hostess. In 1885 he was visited by Frances Folsom, the daughter of a friend. She was 28 years younger than Cleveland. He obtained permission from her mother to correspond. In no time, they were engaged and ready to marry. On June 2, 1886, that was the day. Cleveland was the second president to marry while in office. Frances Folsom, at 21, was the youngest First Lady ever. In the public eye, the age difference did not play a major role. Folsom was well received thanks to her warm personality. Five children resulted from the marriage.

Presidential election of 1888

The Republicans nominated Benjamin Harrison as their presidential candidate in 1888 and Levi Morton as his running mate. Cleveland's vice president Thomas Hendricks died in 1885. The Democratic Party slid Allen Thurman from Ohio into the new election as his deputy. The Republicans attacked Cleveland mainly for his desire to lower import tariffs. In doing so they won many voters in the northern, industrial states. The Democrats in New York State were also divided over the incumbent Governor David Hill, causing Cleveland to lose crucial votes. A show of support from the British ambassador did not work in his favor either.

In the election four years earlier, gains in the states of New York, New Jersey, Connecticut, and Indiana had been crucial. In 1888 Cleveland lost in Indiana and New York, in the latter state only by a difference of fifteen thousand votes. In total, Cleveland garnered the most votes (48.6 percent against 47.8 percent for Harrison), but he garnered fewer electoral votes so the incumbent still lost the election.

Burger

After the transfer of the presidency, the Clevelands left for New York, where the former president took a position with a law firm. At first, Cleveland was reluctant to comment on his successor's policies. Harrison introduced a law that raised many import tariffs to fifty percent. Also, because of his actions, more money was backed by silver. Cleveland resented both policy changes and criticized President Harrison in an open letter in 1891. This put him back in the spotlight toward the 1892 presidential election.

Presidential election of 1892

Cleveland's biggest rival within the Democratic Party was Senator David Hill. He managed to unite a number of opponents of the former president, but their support proved insufficient. Cleveland was chosen as the Democratic presidential candidate in the first vote at the party convention in Chicago. His running mate was Adlai Stevenson.

The general election was overshadowed by the death of first lady Caroline Harrison two weeks before going to the polls. Both Harrison and Cleveland shut down their campaigns. Four years earlier, the debate over import tariffs had cost Cleveland many votes. In the meantime, however, they were so high that many voters had changed their minds about this. Moreover, many Republicans were turning to James Weaver, the candidate of the newly formed Populist Party. Cleveland won the election by a wide margin, both in terms of electoral votes and absolute vote totals.

Second term as president

Adjustment of import tariffs

Cleveland felt it was important to reduce import tariffs. On the initiative of Delegate William Wilson, a bill was passed in the House of Representatives in December 1893 to do just that. The revenue lost to the government would be compensated by the introduction of an income tax of 2 percent for amounts over four thousand dollars. In the Senate, the bill met with more resistance. Many Democrats stood up for the interests of their own state. Six hundred amendments were passed, nullifying most of the reforms. Cleveland was furious about the final result, although at the same time he thought the law was an improvement over the status quo.

Growing discontent

The Panic of 1893 had worsened the working conditions of many workers. A group led by Jacob Coxey attracted much attention with a march toward Washington D.C. in protest of President Cleveland's policies. Of greater impact was the so-called Pulmann strike. This strike began at the Pulmann Company in protest against low wages and long workdays. On the initiative of American trade unionist Eugene Debs, the strike quickly spread. In June 1894, one hundred and twenty-five thousand railroad workers laid off work, which had its effect on business.

The railroads carried the mail and some lines were under federal control. Cleveland received court approval to break the strike. He sent federal troops to Chicago and about twenty railroad centers, ending the strike. Most governors, with the exception of John Altgeld, governor of Illinois, supported the president, as did much of the media. However, the rift with the union movement was growing.

There was much dissatisfaction with Cleveland's policies. In the 1894 midterm elections, the Republican Party won its largest victory in decades. It obtained a majority in the House of Representatives, as well as in many state parliaments.

Foreign Policy

Upon taking office, Cleveland faced the question of whether or not to annex Hawaii. During his first term, he had promoted trade with the island state and obtained permission for a naval base at Pearl Harbor. In the next four years, Queen Liliuokalani was deposed at the hands of some white businessmen. Hawaii became a republic. The new government led by Sanford Dole wanted to join the United States. President Harrison's government agreed and entered into a treaty that was submitted to the Senate for approval. Cleveland withdrew the proposal five days after taking office.

Cleveland asked former Congressman James Henderson Blount to travel after Hawaii and investigate the situation there. Blount's report showed that much of the native population was against annexation. Cleveland himself was not in favor of annexation either. Initially he pushed for the return of Queen Liliuokalani, but abandoned his attempt after opposition from the Senate. He established diplomatic ties with the new republic. It was not until Cleveland's successor William McKinley that Hawaii was incorporated into the United States.

As president, Cleveland championed a broad interpretation of the Monroe Doctrine, which opposes European interference in the Americas. He lodged a protest with Britain when the country became embroiled in a dispute with Venezuela over the precise boundary with British Guiana. The crisis dragged on until it dawned on British Prime Minister Lord Salisbury how important the issue was to the United States. The matter was referred to an independent arbitration tribunal, which awarded most of the disputed territory to British Guiana after all.

Judicial appointments

Clevelands had a difficult relationship with the Senate and this affected his nominations of Supreme Court candidates. After the death of Samuel Blatchford, William Hornblower nominated himself as a candidate. Hornblower headed a New York law firm, but had incurred the wrath of Senator David Hill by campaigning against one of his candidates. The Senate rejected Hornblower's candidacy. Wheeler Hazard Peckham was the second candidate nominated by Cleveland, but he faced exactly the same problems. Peckham's candidacy was also voted down. Cleveland's third nomination was a safe choice: Senator Edward Douglass White. In 1896, another vacancy arose. Cleveland nominated Rufus Wheeler Peckham. Unlike his brother, Rufus Wheeler was admitted to the Supreme Court.

23. Benjamin Harrison (1889-1893)

Republican Party | Vice President: Levi P. Morton

"Prayer steadies one when he is walking in slippery places - even if things asked for are not given."

Benjamin Harrison (North Bend (Ohio), August 20, 1833 - Indianapolis (Indiana), March 13, 1901) was the 23rd president of the United States (1889-1893). He was a grandson of President William Henry Harrison.

Harrison studied law in Cincinnati and settled as a lawyer in Indianapolis in 1854. In 1856 he joined the newly formed Republican Party. During the American Civil War, Harrison served in the 70th Indiana Regiment from 1862 to 1865 and rose from lieutenant to brigadier general. He was among the troops under General William T. Sherman who took the city of Atlanta in September 1864. After the war,

Harrison resumed his law practice. From 1881 to 1887 he served in the U.S. Senate for his home state.

In 1888, Harrison was elected president. Although he garnered fewer votes than his opponent, incumbent President Grover Cleveland, he managed to secure more electoral votes (233 versus 168). Harrison was inaugurated on March 4, 1889, and remains the only president with Indiana as his home state. His presidency has been especially important because of the economic legislation introduced. During his tenure, the annual budget of the national government reached one billion dollars for the first time. Also, six new western states were admitted to the Union: North Dakota, South Dakota, Montana, Washington, Idaho and Wyoming. Harrison was defeated in turn by his predecessor Cleveland in the 1892 presidential election. He remained president until March 4, 1893.

Harrison settled in Indianapolis after his retirement, resumed his law practice, lectured, and wrote articles in newspapers and magazines. He died on March 13, 1901, at the age of 67. He is buried in Indianapolis. His second wife Mary survived him by more than 46 years and died on January 5, 1948 at the age of 89.

25. William McKinley (1897-1901)

Republican party | Vice presidents: Garret Hobart and Theodore Roosevelt

"In the time of darkest defeat, victory may be nearest."

William McKinley Jr. (Niles (Ohio), January 29, 1843 - Buffalo (New York), September 14, 1901) was the 25th president of the United States from 1897 until his death in 1901. On September 6, 1901, he was the victim of an assassination attempt. He died on September 14 at the age of 58 and was succeeded by Vice President Theodore Roosevelt.

Political career

In 1876 he became a Republican member of Congress, where he remained, with a brief interruption, until 1891. He made himself popular by advocating higher import duties (McKinley Tariff Act 1890), among other things. He was elected governor of Ohio in 1892 and president of the United States in 1896. He allowed himself, albeit reluctantly, to be carried away by the imperialist currents of his day, thus bringing the country to war with Spain in April 1898. After the successful conclusion of this struggle, he advocated the annexation of the Philippines and partial independence for Cuba under strong American control. He also approved the annexation of Hawaii. In 1900 he was re-elected with an even larger majority. He served as president of the US from 1897-1901.

In November 1900, the government of the Ottoman Empire had decreed that Jews could only visit the country (Palestine) for 3 months at a time. This prompted Theodor Herzl to write to American Jews and ask members of the Senate and Congress and President McKinley to do everything in their power to have this discrimination (non-Jewish US citizens were not affected by this measure) ended. When the American ambassador complained in the spring of 1901, Turkish Porte replied that individual Jewish visitors were not the problem, but groups of Jewish settlers. Immigration of Zionist Jews, land acquisition and building of the first kibbutzim in Palestine had been happening for over 20 years and Palestinian notables had expressed concern about this in 1895 Istanbul.

Murder of McKinley

During a visit to the Pan-American Exhibition at Buffalo, New York, on September 6, 1901, McKinley became the victim of an assassination attempt. Polish immigrant Leon Czolgosz, a fanatical anarchist who showed signs of feeble-mindedness, fired twice with a pistol at the president. The first bullet went into his shoulder, the second pierced his guts and lodged in his back. The first bullet was easily found and removed, but the second bullet the surgeons could not find. McKinley seemed to be recovering, however, so the decision was made to leave the second bullet in place, since searching for It might cause more damage. The newly developed X-ray machine, which was presented at the exhibition, was not yet dared to be used on the president. McKinley was on the mend for a week, but eventually went into shock and died on September 14, 1901, eight days after the attack, from the effects of the gangrene that had affected his injuries. He lived to be 58 years old.

Three quarters of an hour after McKinley's death, the rushing Vice President Theodore Roosevelt was sworn in as the new president. At 42, Roosevelt was the youngest man to ever become president of the United States, albeit without a direct election.

26. Theodore Roosevelt (1901-1909)

Republican party | Vice President: Charles W. Fairbanks

"Do what you can, with what you have, where you are."

Theodore (Teddy) Roosevelt (New York, October 27, 1858 - Oyster Bay (New York), January 6, 1919) was an American politician of the Republican Party. He served as the 26th president of the United States from 1901 to 1909.

Roosevelt, a historian and author by trade, was Deputy Secretary of the Navy in President William McKinley's cabinet from 1897 to 1898 and the 33rd Governor of New York from 1899 to 1900. For the 1900 presidential election, he was President William McKinley's running mate and was elected as the 25th Vice President of the United States. On September 14, 1901, President William McKinley died after an assassination attempt and Roosevelt succeeded him. In the 1904 presidential election, he became the first former vice president to be elected to his own term after the death of his predecessor. In 1906, Roosevelt became the first American to receive the Nobel Peace Prize.

After his presidency, Roosevelt went on safaris through Africa and South America. Roosevelt unsuccessfully attempted during the 1912 presidential election for another term as a Progressive Party candidate. Roosevelt died, aged 60, on January 6, 1919 from the effects of an embolism.

Before his presidency

Theodore Roosevelt suffered from asthma and other ailments in his youth. Because of his temperament, he felt no need to live a life of idleness. In 1880 he completed his studies at Harvard University. Shortly thereafter he was elected to the New York State House of Representatives as a Republican. A worsening of his asthma and the death of his first wife made Roosevelt decide to go west. There he worked for two years as a rancher. After Roosevelt returned east, he held several positions. Among other things, he was Deputy Secretary of the Navy. In 1898, the Spanish-American War broke out. Roosevelt came out from behind his desk to throw himself into the fray. He became commander of a unit of volunteer cavalry and fought in Cuba. From 1895 to 1897, he served as commissioner of police of New York.

Then Roosevelt got involved in the political fray. He was elected governor of New York State and began a campaign against corruption in politics. The Republican leaders arranged for Roosevelt to run in the presidential election under William McKinley as a vice presidential candidate. They hoped that Roosevelt would be forgotten as vice president, so they would have no more trouble with him. It turned out differently: in 1901, six months after being sworn in for his second term as president, McKinley was shot by an anarchist. At 42, Roosevelt became the youngest president ever.

Presidency

During the two Roosevelt administrations, achievements included the following:

Domestic:

- Strengthened government control over large corporations, through legal attacks on corporate monopolies. He created a Department of Commerce and Labor that was given the power to investigate violations of existing antitrust laws.
- Pure Food and Drug Act. It was the first government measure to protect consumers.
- National Parks.

In 1901, African-American front man Booker T. Washington was invited to the White House for a dinner by Roosevelt. This dinner provoked outrage in the southern states.

Abroad:

- His motto for foreign affairs was *speak softly but carry a big stick* ("speak softly but carry a big stick"). He laid the groundwork, despite Colombia's refusal, for the construction of the Panama Canal. Panama was a Colombian province at the time. Roosevelt supported a Panamanian rebellion and was able to purchase the Canal Zone from the new Panamanian regime in 1904 for the sum of $10 million.
- For his mediation between Russia and Japan and the creation of the Treaty of Portsmouth that ended the Russo-Japanese War, he received the Nobel Peace Prize in 1906. Roosevelt was the first politician to receive this award. The award was controversial, leftists in Norway pointed to his military role during the Spanish-American War that made the Philippines an American colony.
- Between December 1907 and February 1909, a fleet of 16 American battleships, the Great White Fleet, made a round-the-world voyage at Roosevelt's behest. He wanted to show the world the power of his navy, partly for the purpose of protecting overseas territories and enforcing treaties.
- The following year, Roosevelt sent an American representative to the conference on the crisis that had broken out between France and Germany over Morocco. America made a significant contribution to the drafting of the agreement that resulted from the conference.
- During his presidency he was attentive to the problems of Jews in North Africa. And when 49 Jews died in a pogrom at Kishinev in Russia, he wrote a letter to the Czar in 1903, reproaching him severely for this .

Later life

Roosevelt was succeeded as president by William Howard Taft. When he left the White House he was, 50 years old, the youngest ex-president ever. A short time later he went on a safari through Africa, a great desire of Roosevelt.

In 1912 Roosevelt wanted to run for president again, but the Republican Party nominated incumbent William Howard Taft, who had been nominated for president by Roosevelt himself in 1908. After this he founded his own party: the *Progressive Party* also called the *Bull Moose Party*. He was nominated with Hiram Johnson as vice presidential candidate.

Roosevelt lost the election to Democrat Woodrow Wilson, but did finish second in the race, ahead of incumbent President William Howard Taft. It was the first time a sitting president had finished third in the election.

In 1913 he went on another safari, this time through South America. During the trip, Roosevelt became seriously ill and nearly succumbed to malaria. Roosevelt recovered, but was severely weakened; he himself stated that the trip had taken half his life.

In 1918 (a year after the British Balfour Declaration) he wrote that in his opinion it seemed entirely right to establish a Zionist state around Jerusalem. In another letter he stated that there could be no peace unless the Armenians and Arabs were given independence and the Jews were given control of Palestine.

He died, aged 60, on January 6, 1919, of an embolism.

27. William Howard Taft (1909-1913)

Republican party | Vice president: James S. Sherman

"Don't write so that you can be understood, write so that you can't be misunderstood."

William Howard Taft (Cincinnati (Ohio), September 15, 1857 - Washington, March 8, 1930) was an American politician of the Republican Party. He served as the 27th president of the United States from 1909 to 1913. He then served as the Chief Justice of the United States from 1921 to 1930.

Taft, a lawyer by profession, was the Attorney General of the United States from 1890 to 1892 under President Benjamin Harrison. He served as Governor General of the Philippines from 1901 to 1904 under Presidents William McKinley and Theodore Roosevelt and subsequently served as Secretary of War under President Roosevelt.

Lifetime

Youth

His father Alphonso Taft was a judge and later served as Secretary of War and Secretary of Justice under President Ulysses S. Grant. He himself went to study at Yale. Intellectually he could keep up, but he had to rely mainly on his dedication. In 1878 he graduated as the second best of his year. After Yale he continued his studies at the Cincinnati Law School. During this time he also worked as a court reporter for a local newspaper. Shortly before graduation, he was admitted to the Bar and was able to work as an attorney.

Employed as an attorney and judge on the Ohio Supreme Court

Taft's managing editor offered him a full-time job at the paper if he was willing to give up his work as a lawyer, but Taft declined. Instead, in October 1880, he was appointed assistant prosecutor in Hamilton County. He served one year in that position, but stepped down after President Chester Arthur wanted to appoint him to another position. He declined because he would have to fire people who were competent for their positions but out of political favor. In 1884, Taft campaigned for Republican presidential candidate Senator James Blaine, but lost to Grover Cleveland.

Around 1880, Taft met his wife Helen Herron. Four years later they saw each other regularly. After a rejected first proposal, Herron and Taft still got married. They had three children. The oldest son, Robert, would make it to the Senate.

By Ohio Governor Joseph Foraker, Taft was appointed in 1887 to fill a vacant seat on the Ohio Supreme Court, which sat in Cincinnati. After one year, he was re-elected to a five-year term. He probably made his most startling ruling in the case of *Moores & Co. v. Bricklayers' Union*. In this case, bricklayers refused to work for any company that did business with a company called Parker Brothers. Taft stated in his ruling that there was an illegal boycott.

Attorney General and Federal Judge

The Supreme Court had a vacant seat in 1889. Governor Foraker suggested to President Benjamin Harrison that he appoint Taft, who was aspiring to the seat. The president did not. Instead, Harrison appointed him attorney general. This was not an undeserving promotion either, for in that position Taft represented the interests of the U.S. federal government before the Supreme Court in cases in which it was a party. He won 15 of the 18 cases heard by the Supreme Court.

The U.S. Congress decided in March 1891 that each federal Court of Appeals would be expanded by an additional seat, i.e., an additional judge. Harrison appointed Taft to the Court of Appeals for the 6th Circuit in Cincinnati in March 1892. This was an appointment for life and seemed a nice stepping stone to the Supreme Court. Taft's older half-brother Charles was a successful businessman and supplemented his "modest" judge's salary, allowing Taft and his wife to live on stand.

As a judge, he was seen as conservative, although he defended the right to unionize and the right to strike (two major issues in the last decade of the 19th century). In 1896, in addition to his work as a federal judge, he began teaching at the Cincinnati Law School. As a judge, he could not get directly involved in politics, but Taft did follow closely developments within the Republican Party. He watched with some disbelief the rise of Ohio governor William McKinley, but supported him when it became clear that he had the best chance of winning the Republican presidential nomination in 1896. Under McKinley's presidency, only one seat on the Supreme Court became vacant. The president chose Joseph McKenna.

Governor General in the Philippines

President McKinley had an appointment with Taft in January 1900. The latter hoped it would be about an impending Supreme Court vacancy. Instead, the president wanted Taft to serve on a committee to set up a civilian government in the Philippines. It would then be necessary for Taft to step down as a judge, but McKinley promised that he would appoint him to the Supreme Court in return as soon as a position became available.

The American seizure of power in the archipelago led to the Philippine Revolution which then turned into the Philippine-American War. By 1900, the Americans under the leadership of Governor General Arthur MacArthur Jr. were on the winning side. MacArthur saw little point in self-government for the Philippines, but was forced to cooperate because the commission was over the military budget. On July 4, 1900,

Taft succeeded MacArthur as governor general. Taft wanted to work with the Filipinos on an equal footing toward self-government, but full independence he saw as something for the distant future.

McKinley was assassinated in 1901. With his successor President Theodore Roosevelt, Taft had been friends since the 1990s. They met again in January 1902 when Taft was in Washington recovering from two operations resulting from an infection. Later that year he traveled to Rome for negotiations with the Vatican. This was because he wanted more farmland made available to Filipino farmers, but much of the land was owned by various Spanish Roman Catholic priestly orders. Taft wanted them to sell most of their land, then leave the country and be replaced by American priests. The visit helped reach an agreement on that a year later.

At the end of 1902, Taft heard from Roosevelt that Judge George Shiras' seat on the Supreme Court would become available. Roosevelt offered him the seat, but Taft declined because, in his opinion, his duties in the Philippines were not yet completed. One of the reasons Roosevelt offered the seat to Taft was because it was the chance to neutralize a potential rival for the presidency. Indeed, Taft's success in the Philippines had not gone unnoticed in the American press. Another year later, Roosevelt asked Taft to be Secretary of War. This time Taft did agree, also because the Philippines fell under the management of the War Department. That way he could stay involved.

Minister of War

As Secretary of War, Taft had to deal with President Theodore Roosevelt, who himself was heavily involved in military affairs. Roosevelt had made it known publicly in the run-up to the 1904 presidential election that he would not seek a third term, and wanted to keep that promise. Taft strongly considered that he could become the next Republican presidential candidate. Toward that end, he twice thanked himself for a position on the Supreme Court.

After Panama's secession from Colombia in 1903 and with the conclusion of the Hay-Bunau Varilla Treaty, the United States had obtained the right to build a canal in Panama that would connect the Atlantic Ocean with the Pacific Ocean. Roosevelt had determined that the War Department would be responsible for the construction. In 1904 Taft visited Panama and in 1907 appointed George Washington Goethals as chief engineer after John Frank Stevens resigned.

Spain had lost Cuba as a colony to the United States after the Spanish-American War in 1898. After a period of occupation, Cuba had become independent in 1902. The first years after independence were turbulent with many internal conflicts. In September 1906, Cuban President Tomás Estrada Palma asked the United States to intervene. Taft traveled to Cuba with a small army and proclaimed himself temporary governor. Two weeks later he was succeeded by Charles Edward Magoon.

Taft remained involved with the Philippines. He demanded in 1904 that Filipino agricultural products be admitted to the U.S. market freely - that is, without paying import duties. This led to protests among American sugar and tobacco producers. President Roosevelt raised the issue with Taft, but the latter threatened to resign if the president changed his policy. Roosevelt thereupon abandoned the subject. In 1905, Taft led a congressional delegation to the Philippines. He returned again in 1907 when the first Philippine Assembly was installed.

Both times after his visit to the Philippines, Taft traveled on to Japan. His first visit was in July 1905, a month before the end of the Russo-Japanese War. Taft met with Japanese Prime Minister Katsura Tarō. They struck a deal in which they agreed that the United States had no objection to the Japanese occupation of Korea and that Japan had no ambitions regarding the territory of the Philippines. There were concerns in the United States about the large number of Japanese workers coming to America. During the second visit, Japanese Foreign Minister Hayashi Tadasu promised that fewer passports would be issued to Japanese who wanted to emigrate to the United States.

Presidency

Presidential Elections 1908

Roosevelt did everything in his power to get Taft the Republican nomination. For example, he demanded that his cabinet members support Taft, or at least not support any other candidate, on pain of resignation. Several politicians, such as Treasury Secretary George Cortelyou, explored whether they would stand a chance, but ultimately did not get involved in the race. Governor of New York Charles Evans Hughes ran for office, but on the day of his announcement, President Roosevelt sent an extensive message to Congress warning against corruption in business. As a result, Hughes' announcement that he was running was relegated to the inside pages of newspapers.

At the Republican Convention in Chicago in June 1908, Taft had no serious competitors and to his own satisfaction was elected on the first ballot. He was less pleased with the Convention's choice of his running mate for the vice presidency. He had hoped for a progressive, such as Senator Jonathan Dolliver, instead the choice fell on conservative Delegate James Sherman. Taft resigned on June 30 to devote himself entirely to his campaign.

In the general election, Taft ran against the Democrat, William Jennings Bryan, who represented his party for the third time as a presidential candidate. Many of Roosevelt's reforms came from Bryan's proposals, leading many Democrats to argue that he was Roosevelt's true successor.

Taft gave fuel to the criticism that he was only Roosevelt's slipstream by traveling to the president's home in New York for advice before his acceptance speech. Taft supported many of Roosevelt's policies anyway. For example, he was in favor of the right to unionize but against instituting a corporate boycott. Also, unlike Bryan, he felt that the railroad network could be just fine in the hands of private companies, overseen by a government commission that could set the maximum fare. During a vacation in August 1908, photos of Taft on the golf course appeared. President Roosevelt warned him that it would appear to the outside world that he had close ties to business.

Whether or not to institute a nationwide alcohol ban suddenly became a major issue in the campaign in mid-September. Carrie Nation demanded that Taft make his views known, but the Republican candidate had already decided in advance not to comment on it because his supporters thought differently. Thus, there was only something for him to lose by taking a stand. In the end, Taft won the election by a safe margin. He obtained 321 electoral votes against 162 for Bryan. He obtained a total of 51.6 percent of all votes.

The inauguration took place inside the Capitol because of a winter storm. Taft had a more difficult relationship with the press, simply because he was less available for interviews or photo opportunities than his predecessor.

Foreign Policy

Key Principles

Taft reformed the State Department, the U.S. Department of State. The Department was organized into geographic divisions, including sections for the Middle East, Latin America, and Western Europe. Taft and his Secretary of State Philander Knox intended not to become involved in Europe's internal conflicts and were prepared to use force if necessary when the Monroe Doctrine was violated (the doctrine instituted by President James Monroe that any form of European interference in the Western Hemisphere was taboo). The protection of the Panama Canal, which opened in 1914, was leading in terms of foreign policy in the Caribbean and Central America. Taft encouraged U.S. diplomats to actively support U.S. companies abroad. He hoped that international trade would contribute to world peace.

Latin America

Taft's government used a so-called Dollar diplomacy towards Latin America. They believed that all involved would benefit from American investment in the region, and that it would also reduce the influences of the former European rulers. The policy met with little support both at home and abroad. Many members of Congress felt that the United States should engage as little as possible with foreign countries, and many Latin American countries had no desire to continue as a protectorate of the United States.

When Taft took office, unrest in Mexico, which had been under the rule of the dictator Porfirio Díaz for decades, was growing. Many Mexicans supported Diaz's main opponent Francisco Madero. There were several incidents in which Mexican rebels crossed the border into the United States for weapons and horses. Taft wanted to prevent that and sent the U.S. military toward the border region. He was the first American president to travel to Mexico. He met Diaz first in El Paso, Texas and then in Ciudad Juárez, Mexico. Frederick Russell Burnham, along with a Texas Ranger, disarmed a man who was planning an attack on both presidents and had approached them within a few feet. Shortly before the elections in Mexico, Diaz imprisoned Madero, upon which his followers unleashed an armed rebellion. This led to Diaz's resignation and also ushered in the Mexican Revolution, which would continue for ten years. In Arizona, two people were killed and a dozen wounded by gunfire from the other side of the border. Taft ordered the territorial governor to strike back hard.

Nicaragua's President José Santos Zelaya wanted to withdraw all commercial concessions to U.S. companies, while U.S. diplomats secretly supported Juan Estrada's insurgents. Nicaragua had large foreign debts, and the United States wanted to prevent European powers from using those debts to obtain permission to dig a second canal that could connect the Atlantic and Pacific Oceans. That would negate the advantage the Americans had with the Panama Canal. Zelaya's successor José Madriz failed to put down the rebellion because Taft had sent American troops to support the insurgents. Estrada's troops took the capital in August 1910. The United States forced the new government to take out a loan to refinance the national debt. Things remained unsettled in the years that followed which led to Taft sending more U.S. troops in 1912. The U.S. occupation of Nicaragua lasted until 1933.

In its final days, the Roosevelt administration had signed another agreement with Colombia and Panama. Colombia, however, refused to ratify the treaty. U.S. Secretary of State Knox offered ten million dollars in late 1912, later increased to twenty-five million, if Colombia would ratify the treaty. The Colombians felt that was too little and the issue would not be resolved under Taft's presidency.

Far East

Through his stay in the Philippines, Taft followed with close interest all developments in the region. He was very attached to good relations with China and replaced Roosevelt's ambassador William Rockhill, as he had little interest in trade with China. His successor was William Calhoun.

The Xinhaire Revolution took place in 1911. This marked the end of the Chinese Empire and precisely the beginning of Republic of China. Sun Yat-sen was elected as the first president. Taft was reluctant to recognize the new regime, despite a majority of the American public being in favor. The House of Representatives passed a resolution in February 1912 urging recognition. Taft preferred that the various Western powers act together. In his last annual message to Congress in December 1912, Taft let it be known that he was pushing for recognition, but because he had lost the election, it never came to pass.

Taft continued his policy of limiting immigration from China and Japan. In 1911, a revised friendship agreement between Japan and the United States was signed, giving much greater rights to Japanese living in the United States. This led to unrest on the West Coast, but Taft informed several local influential politicians that there was no change in immigration policy.

Europe

President Taft was in favor of resolving international conflicts through arbitration He negotiated an agreement with France and Britain to resolve mutual conflicts in this way. These agreements were signed in August 1911. Both Taft and Knox, a former senator, had not involved the Senate in the whole process. There was considerable opposition, especially among Taft's own party. The Senate passed several amendments that were unacceptable to Taft, which prevented the accords from going into effect.

The U.S. government did manage to resolve a number of conflicts with Britain. For example, clear agreements were made about the boundary between Maine and New Brunswick, and a long-running dispute that concerned whaling in the Bering Strait - in which Japan was also involved - was resolved. A similar dispute that concerned fishing rights around Newfoundland was also settled.

Domestic Policy

Competition Law

Roosevelt policy of breaking up large business combinations through legal pressure was continued and intensified by Taft. Under Sherman's Competition Act ("Sherman's Antitrust Act"), seventy cases were presented to the court in four years. In 1911, two major cases against Standard Oil Company and American Tobacco Company were decided in favor of the government.

The Democrat-controlled House of Representatives began an investigation in June 1911 against U.S. Steel, President Roosevelt had supported in their choice to buy the *Tennessee Coal, Iron, and Railroad Company.* In doing so, Roosevelt wanted to prevent the economic crisis of the day - the so-called Panic of 1907 - from worsening. Taft, Secretary of War at the time, had praised the president for his decision. In retrospect, Roosevelt had probably been misled by U.S. Steel who pretended to have little interest in the company, but instead made a great purchase at a far too low price.

Taft's Department of Justice filed a lawsuit against U.S. Steel in October 1911 demanding that hundreds of subsidiaries be made independent. Several key businessmen and financiers within and around the company were also indicted. The indictments claimed that Roosevelt had contributed to the monopoly power of U.S. Steel and that he had been duped by clever industrialists. Roosevelt was unhappy that he was being put all the blame and that Taft was getting away with a statement that he was only remotely involved.

Another case that had political ramifications was the lawsuit against International Harvester Company, a manufacturer of farm implements. Roosevelt's government had investigated the company but had taken no further action against any abuses found. Taft's government picked up the case at a time when Roosevelt was competing with Taft for the Republican nomination for the 1912 presidential election. Taft's supporters blamed Roosevelt for doing nothing, while the latter in turn blamed Taft for doing nothing for three and a half years and only taking action when it was politically convenient.

Ballinger-Pinchot Affair

Roosevelt was a strong advocate of conservation, as were several of his political supporters, such as Secretary of the Interior James Garfield. Taft agreed with the need for conservation, but believed it should be done through legislation, not presidential decrees. He replaced Garfield as Secretary of State for early Seattle Mayor Richard Ballinger. Roosevelt was surprised by this as he believed that Taft had promised to keep Garfield in office. This was one of the events that made Roosevelt realize that Taft was pursuing a different course than he was.

During his presidency, Roosevelt had taken a relatively large amount of land out of the public domain through presidential decrees, especially by declaring large tracts of land as national parks, including large areas in Alaska that were rich in coal. Clarence Cunningham had discovered many coal deposits in the ground there in 1902 and claimed these pieces of land for mining. The government investigated the legitimacy of these claims. This was done by Louis Glavis. In 1909, the new Home Secretary Ballinger agreed to the claims making mining possible. Glavis then sought out the press and disclosed that Ballinger had acted as Cunningham's lawyer in the past, creating a conflict of interest. Instead of taking on Ballinger, Taft fired Glavis based on a report by Attorney General George Wickersham.

Gifford Pinchot was the head of the United States Forest Service, a federal agency responsible for managing the nation's forests. He was a supporter of Glavis and had still been appointed by Roosevelt. Taft had instructed his subordinates not to comment on the matter, but in January 1910 he sent a letter reporting on the course of events to Senator Jonathan Dolliver. Pinchot was subsequently fired, but an investigation was launched by Congress. In the end, Ballinger was able to count on a majority vote, exonerating him, but the investigation was embarrassing for the Taft administration. For example, Glavis attorney Louis Brandeis showed that Secretary Wickersham's report on the basis of which Glavis had been fired was antedated. The whole affair also caused a rift between Taft and Roosevelt's supporters.

Civil Rights

In his inauguration speech, Taft announced that he would not appoint African-Americans to federal positions because doing so would only contribute to racial tensions. His policies differed from Roosevelt's in that Taft actively replaced black government officials who came into contact with burdened white citizens who wanted nothing to do with African-Americans. This left very few dark-skinned people in appointed positions in the federal government in the South. In the North, only a single African-American was appointed. The Republican Party - Abraham Lincoln's party - was originally the party that stood up for the rights of African Americans, but Taft's policies contributed to them beginning to move toward the Democratic Party.

Judicial appointments

President Taft appointed six justices to the Supreme Court, more than any other president except George Washington and Franklin Delano Roosevelt. The death of Rufus Peckham provided him with his first opportunity. The president nominated an old friend and colleague from the Court of Appeals for the 6th Circuit, namely Horace Lurton. Earlier he had tried to persuade Roosevelt to appoint Lurton. Justice Secretary Wickersham objected that Lurton, a former Confederate soldier and Democrat, was already 64, but Taft cared little.

After the death of David Josiah Brewer in March 1910, he nominated New York Governor Charles Evans Hughes. He promised Hughes that he was his most likely choice for the position of chief justice, should that position become vacant. When that position did indeed become available after the death of Chief Justice Melville Fuller on July 4, 1910, it took Taft five months to find a successor. His choice fell on Edward Douglass White, the first sitting Supreme Court justice to advance to the position of chief justice. Possibly the choice fell on White and not Hughes because Taft himself still had ambitions to become chief justice. Hughes was a lot younger than White and the chance that the seat would become available again in a relatively short period of time was therefore much greater.

For White's seat, Taft nominated Federal Judge Willis of Devanter. At that time, a replacement for William Henry Moody also had to be found, as he had stepped down due to illness. Taft appointed Joseph Lamar, a Democrat he had met while golfing and who had a good reputation as a judge. His last appointment was that of Mahlon Pitney after the death of John Marshall Harlan This was the last time that someone who had not attended law school was appointed to the Supreme Court. It was also the most controversial nomination. Pitney had little affinity for labor unions and therefore faced more opposition in the Senate than other candidates. The Senate finally voted with 50 votes for and 26 against Taft's choice.

Presidential Elections 1912

Former President Theodore Roosevelt made an extensive trip between March 1909 and June 1910. He went on safari in Africa and then visited Europe. Taft and he had little contact during this time, although they met twice after Roosevelt's return to the United States. In private correspondence, Taft's predecessor expressed disappointment with the sitting president.

At the beginning of the fall of 1910, Roosevelt made a series of speeches in which he accused the Supreme Court of undermining democracy. In the case of *Lochner v. New York,* the Supreme Court had ruled in 1905 that the government could not limit the number of maximum working hours. That, in fact, fell under the freedom of contract. The Supreme Court reached its opinion based on the Fourteenth Amendment to the Constitution. As a result, Roosevelt felt that the Supreme Court should be stripped of the power to declare laws unconstitutional. Although Taft also had to have little of the judgment of America's highest court in the case of *Lochner v. New York*, he did not share Roosevelt's further opinion.

In the 1910 midterm elections, the Republican Party lost the majority in the House of Representatives and a number of seats in the Senate, although they retained their majority there. After the election, Roosevelt became increasingly progressive in his remarks. He argued that Taft was not guided by the principles of Lincoln, but by those of the Gilded Age. To be clear, that was not right.

Leading up to the 1912 presidential election, it became increasingly clear that Roosevelt was going to run. Responding to the unwritten rule that presidents do not run for a third term, Roosevelt said it was about three consecutive terms. There was no question of that now. In addition to Roosevelt, Senator Robert La Follette also ran for the Republican nomination.Roosevelt won the Republican primaries, although they were much less decisive at the time than they are today and were only held in fourteen states. Roosevelt won 278 of the 362 delegates. However, Taft controlled the party apparatus and thus still managed to bring in many delegates, more than Roosevelt. At the Republican Convention, Roosevelt's allies tried to have these delegates declared invalid. Some Republicans still went looking for a compromise candidate when it became clear that Roosevelt would leave the party if he was not elected, but were unsuccessful. Taft was eventually elected in the first round of voting.

Indeed, the former president left the Republican Party and formed the Progressive Party with his followers. Taft went into the general election with little confidence, as he was headed for almost certain defeat. The Democrats had nominated New Jersey Governor Woodrow Wilson. This one saw Roosevelt as his main opponent and so attacked him in particular. Taft adhered to the custom that sitting presidents do not actively campaign and only gave an acceptance speech in early August. He had hoped that his cabinet members would run for him, but they were very reluctant. To complete the fiasco, his running mate, the incumbent vice president, James Sherman died six days before the election. He was still replaced by Nicholas Murray Butler, the president of Columbia University, but that made little difference. Wilson won the election easily with 435 electoral votes behind him against Roosevelt's 88. Taft won only in the states of Utah and Vermont and thus obtained 8 electoral votes.

Return to Yale

Taft had appointed judges at every federal level. A return to the legal profession did not actually seem an option, as it would make him susceptible to charges of conflict of interest when he appeared before a federal court. Instead, he accepted a professorship from Yale Law School. In 1913, he served one year as president of the American Bar Association (ABA).

During his presidency, Taft had been appointed chairman of the committee responsible for the construction of the Lincoln Memorial. Several Democrats wanted to replace him for a party colleague. Taft argued that the loss of the presidency did not hurt, in contrast to attempts to remove him from the commission. He was subsequently allowed to stay on and was allowed to dedicate the monument himself as Chief Justice in 1922.

His successor Wilson had little to do with Taft in his first term. The former president spoke out publicly only about U.S. policy toward the Philippines, although in private he rejected Wilson's policies. He also had little to say about Wilson as a person. In a private letter, he called him "a reckless hypocrite" and an opportunist "who had no convictions that he would not be willing to give up for more votes." Taft was most troubled by Wilson's nomination of Louis Brandeis to the Supreme Court. Brandeis had, in fact, antagonized him in the Ballinger-Pinchot affair.One When Brandeis passed the hearings, Taft and several former ABA presidents wrote a letter claiming that Brandeis was not qualified for the Supreme Court. However, the Democrat-controlled Senate agreed to Wilson's nomination.

As president of the League to Enforce Peace, an organization formed after the outbreak of World War I, Taft spoke out in favor of Wilson's foreign policy in 1915. Rather than focusing on mediation between the fighting parties, the League to Enforce Peace reflected on the establishment of the international legal order after the war. It expressed the importance of international arbitration and felt that it should be housed in a permanent organization, with a court and a Council of Conciliation. The organization should also have the ability to implement economic and military sanctions. This was a rough outline for the League of Nations, which was to be established later. The League to Enforce Peace did not consist of idealistic fringe figures, but rather of people close to the center of power, such as Senator Henry Cabot Lodge Jr. In May 1916, President Wilson spoke at a League meeting.

Taft was supportive of Charles Evans Hughes' choice to step down from the Supreme Court to compete for the presidency on behalf of the Republicans in the 1916 presidential election. Hughes in turn tried to reconcile Taft with Roosevelt, but it did not come to more than one handshake. This was unfortunate for Hughes, as he needed a united party to win the election. He now lost by a narrow margin to Wilson.When President Wilson declared war on Germany in April 1917, he could count on Taft's support. He was president of the American Red Cross at the time and that required so much time that he temporarily stopped working at Yale.

In February 1918, Taft was approached by Republican Party Chairman Will Hays about another attempt at reconciliation with Roosevelt. When Taft dined at the Blackstone Hotel in Chicago shortly thereafter, he learned that Roosevelt was present with a party. He sought out his predecessor and both men embraced, leading to applause in the room. Their renewed friendship did not continue as Roosevelt died in January 1919.

After the war, when Wilson proposed creating a League of Nations, and agreeing to the Treaty of Versailles, Taft again supported him. In doing so, he went against many of his party colleagues who did not want to ratify the treaty. On the other hand, Taft also expressed his reservations. In doing so, he annoyed both camps and thus lost whatever influence he still had with the Wilson administration. In the end, the Senate did not ratify the Treaty of Versailles.

Chief Justice of the Supreme Court

Leading up to the 1920 presidential election, Republicans chose Senator Warren Harding as their presidential candidate and Governor of Massachusetts Calvin Coolidge as his running mate. After their election victory, Taft visited President-Elect Harding at his home in Ohio and advised him on a number of appointments. At this meeting, Harding asked if Taft would be available when a seat on the Supreme Court became vacant. Taft said he was only available for the position of Chief Justice. Chief Justice White reportedly informed Taft that he would remain in office until a Republican entered the White House. At the time Harding was appointed, White had not given any signal that he would resign. Nor would White resign, for he died on May 19, 1921.

President Harding still considered nominating William Day, at that time a member of the Supreme Court for 18 years. Day would then step down after six months, but it would be the crowning achievement of his career. Taft heard about the proposal and did not think it was a good idea because a short-term appointment would jeopardize continuity of work. After Harding also rejected this proposal, Justice Minister Harry Daughtery urged Taft to nominate him quickly. Harding did just that. The former president was appointed by the Senate even without a hearing. Only four senators voted against, including three progressive Republicans (supporters of Roosevelt). Taft thus became the only U.S. president to also become a member of the Supreme Court.

Individual Rights

The Bill of Rights, the name of the first ten amendments to the Constitution, provided citizens with many rights that protected them from the federal government. The Supreme Court laid the groundwork in 1925 to ensure that those same rights also protected citizens vis-à-vis individual states and local governments. In the case of *Gitlow v New York*, Taft agreed with a majority that upheld the conviction of Benjamin Gitlow. He had called for the overthrow of the government, citing freedom of speech. Although he was convicted, the Supreme Court went along with the reasoning that the First Amendment also provided protection over state-level governments.

In the *Pierce v. Society of Sisters* case, the Supreme Court decided the same year that the state of Oregon had the right to regulate private schools, but not to ban them. This affirmed the right of educational freedom for parents.

Power of government

In the case of *Balzac v. Porto Rico,* the Supreme Court reached a unanimous verdict in 1922. The case revolved around a newspaper publisher on Puerto Rico who had been denied the right to a trial by jury, a right guaranteed in the Sixth Amendment. The Supreme Court ruled that Puerto Rico was a territory and that Puerto Rican citizens did not necessarily have the same rights as American citizens under the Constitution.

Taft wrote the opinion in the 1926 case *Myers v. United States* and concluded that the president did not need the consent of the Senate to remove an appointed official from office. According to Taft, who was supported by a majority of the justices, the Constitution imposed no restrictions on the president in this regard. Taft saw this as his most important decision as chief justice.

In the following year, the Court dealt with the case of *McGrain v. Daughtery.* A parliamentary committee was investigating a scandal where former Attorney General Harry Daugherty and his brother may have been at fault. Daugherty was subpoenaed to turn over some of his brother's documents, but refused to do so because, in his view, Congress did not have that authority at all. The Supreme Court disagreed with him.

Role of Chief Justice

As chief justice, Taft was keen for decisions to be unanimous. He advised the various presidents whom they should - in his opinion - appoint as judges. At first Taft got along well with President Calvin Coolidge, but he became disappointed when he saw who all nominated Coolidge as judge. The same was true of Coolidge's successor Herbert Hoover.

Also, Taft believed it was responsibility as chief justice to get involved in the lower federal courts. He wished for a staff that could support him in this regard. In his view, many courts were undermanaged. Congress debated a bill in late 1921 that would appoint 24 new federal judges and give the Chief Justice the authority to transfer judges for a specified period of time to courts that were struggling with temporary backlogs. Not everyone was undividedly enthusiastic about this law.

Therefore, it was stipulated that the Chief Justice could only do so with the consent of the senior judge of the courts concerned.

The Supreme Court itself also had to deal with a sharply increasing workload and a substantial delay in handling cases. That was because at the time it was possible for any party in a case heard by one of the federal appellate courts to appeal to the Supreme Court. Taft felt that in most court cases the final word was up to the various federal appeals courts. The Supreme Court, he said, should only hear cases in which a ruling would have far-reaching consequences. Taft and several of his colleagues pushed for a law that gave the Supreme Court the power to decide for itself which cases it would and would not accept. To Taft's frustration, it took three years for that law (in February 1925) to become law.

When Taft became Chief Justice, the Supreme Court did not yet have its own building, but sat in the Capitol. There it was bursting at the seams. Taft pushed for a building of his own. Congress agreed and a piece of land south of the Capitol was purchased. Taft hoped to still see the new building with his own eyes, but construction was not completed until 1935, five years after his death.

During Herbert Hoover's inauguration as president, Taft, who as chief justice was responsible for administering the oath, misquoted part of the oath. It would also happen to his distant successor John Roberts at the inauguration of Barack Obama eighty years later.

Death

His brother Charles died on December 31, 1929. Taft attended his funeral, but was in poor health himself. When the Supreme Court returned from its Christmas recess a week later, he had not recovered enough to take office. His health deteriorated rapidly and by the end of January he could barely speak. He was concerned that Harlan Stone would be designated as his successor and did not step down as chief justice until he received assurances from Hoover that he would nominate Charles Evans Hughes. Taft then stepped down on February 3. He died a month later. Taft is the first president and the first chief justice to be buried in Arlington National Cemetery. Harlan Stone, after Charles Evans Hughes retired, was still appointed chief justice by Franklin Delano Roosevelt on June 30, 1941.

28. Woodrow Wilson (1913-1921)

Democratic party | Vice president: Thomas R. Marshall

"Friendship is the only cement that will ever hold the world together."

Thomas Woodrow Wilson (Staunton (Virginia), December 28, 1856 - Washington D.C., February 3, 1924) was the 28th president of the United States from 1913 to 1921.

A Democratic Party politician, Wilson served as the 34th Governor of New Jersey from 1911 to 1913. As a Democratic Party candidate, Wilson won the 1912 U.S. presidential election. He defeated the divided Republican Party of incumbent President William Howard Taft and former President Theodore Roosevelt. For his commitment to world peace, Wilson received the Nobel Peace Prize in 1919. He was a proponent of racial segregation.

Woodrow Wilson died at the age of 67 after suffering a stroke.

Before his presidency

Born to an Ulster Scottish family, Wilson grew up in a religious and academic family; his father was a Presbyterian minister. He studied law at the University of Virginia, served a year as a lawyer in Atlanta, and then studied political science at Johns Hopkins University, where he received his doctorate in 1886. In 1885 he married Ellen Louise Axson and published his dissertation analyzing the separation of the legislative and executive branches of government in the U.S. Constitution (Congressional government). To date, Wilson is the only U.S. president with a doctoral degree obtained by doctoral dissertation.

In 1890 Wilson became professor of jurisprudence and political economy at Princeton University, where he was a popular lecturer and respected scholar. After being elected president of the university in 1902, he became nationally known and, without applying, was nominated for the governorship of New Jersey in 1910. He was a presidential candidate on behalf of the Democratic Party in 1912. The Republicans were divided; they had two candidates: William Howard Taft and Theodore Roosevelt, so Wilson won this election.

Presidency

In 1913, Wilson introduced the Federal Reserve System, following a financial crisis. The commercial banks wanted protection, structure and help in the form of self-regulation. Wilson wanted the federal government to have a say in capital. A compromise was reached and they settled on a system of twelve regional Federal Reserve Banks, which the banks in that region would run themselves. In contrast, the seven members of the overarching Board of Governors would be appointed by the president. The Governors would also have overlapping terms of fourteen years, to ensure independence.

Wilson's colored voters were disappointed as he continued and expanded the policy of racial segregation. He included segregationists in his cabinet, allowed black officials to be separated from whites in ministries, and defended this policy as a rational, scientific way to reduce social friction (July 1913 letter to Oswald Garrison Villard).

Universal suffrage was one of the issues Wilson had to deal with during his presidency. Wilson himself was progressive and a supporter of universal suffrage, but he faced strong opposition on this issue. In addition, shortly after his inauguration, World War I broke out.

In 1915 the United States, under the presidency of Wilson, invaded Haiti; it would remain occupied until 1934. According to the Wilson administration, this was done to thwart a German invasion: the German Empire, in fact, had major economic interests in Haiti. Under U.S. envoy Franklin Roosevelt, the later Democratic president, a constitution was drafted and a general "corvée" introduced, which had previously been imposed only on the black underclass. Much was done to the island's infrastructure, but the administrative reforms did not work out well. Disagreements with Mexican dictator Victoriano Huerta led to the U.S. occupation of Veracruz in 1914. Under Wilson's presidency, the United States also intervened in Panama, Cuba, and Nicaragua.

Initially, Wilson succeeded in keeping the United States out of the world war, although he did provide material support to France and Britain. His neutrality policy led to his re-election in 1916. He then won over Republican Charles Evans Hughes. In 1917, the pressure to participate in the war increased. The interception of the Zimmermann telegram, which showed that Germany wanted to set up Mexico against the U.S., and the torpedoing by the Germans of the passenger ship Lusitania, as part of the unlimited submarine war, led to a declaration of war to Germany and the other central powers on April 6, 1917. This gave the U.S. the deciding vote in favor of the Western Allies; the Russian empire had now collapsed and made a separate peace with Germany.

After the war, Wilson dedicated himself to world peace with varying degrees of success. On January 8, 1918, Wilson uttered his famous *Fourteen Points*, in which he advocated, among other things, an alliance of nations, the right of peoples to self-determination, and an organization to guarantee the territorial integrity and political independence of countries large and small.

Wilson signed the 19th Amendment to the United States Constitution on January 9, 1918. This included universal suffrage, including for women. Previously, Wilson had opposed this amendment because his party was divided on it. In August 1920, the amendment went into effect after being ratified by Congress and two-thirds of the states.

Wilson brought his Fourteen Points to the Paris peace talks in 1919. The proposal to create an alliance of nations (the League of Nations) was included in the Versailles Peace Treaty, but most of the other points fell or were not fully implemented.

On June 18 and 19, 1919, Wilson made a visit to Belgium. This visit by Woodrow Wilson to Belgium was the first visit by an American president to Belgium.

For his commitment to world peace, Wilson received the Nobel Peace Prize in 1919. To his great disappointment, the United States itself did not become a member of the League of Nations.

Wilson sent a commission of inquiry headed by Herbert Churchill King and Charles Crane to Palestine that same year to investigate the opinions of the Palestinian-Arab population living there as to who they thought should receive the League of Nations mandate. The King-Crane Commission , officially called the "(Inter-)Allied Commission on Mandates in Turkey of 1919", was a commission of inquiry concerning the division of territories within the former Ottoman Empire . The Commission began as an outgrowth of the Paris Peace Conference in 1919. It visited areas in Palestine, Syria, Lebanon and Anatolia , interviewed local public opinion and assessed its opinion on the best course of action for the various regions.It thus also traveled through Palestine and found that the majority of the Arab population was opposed to the Balfour Declaration and that people wanted the U.S. to have the mandate and not the British. That the Bedouins in the desert also shared this opinion: let the US do for us what they did for the Philippines! After all, the British wanted to give the land to the Zionists to establish a Jewish National Home in it and the people already saw how they were advancing the Zionist cause in their country.President Wilson, however, never saw the commission's report and its recommendations. He became ill and could no longer function as president. The report disappeared into a drawer and was not published (by a newspaper) until 1922.

On October 2, 1919, Wilson suffered a stroke. This left him barely able to function; the details regarding his limitations were not revealed until after his death. His second wife, Edith Bolling Galt Wilson, made a selection of the topics to be brought to Wilson's attention. The other topics were handled by his ministers. Wilson's term ended in 1921.

After his presidency

Wilson continued to live with his wife in Washington, D.C., where he died on February 3, 1924, at the age of 67. His wife lived in the same house for 37 more years, where she died on December 28, 1961.

In 2020, Princeton University decided to remove Wilson's naming rights to two institutions because of his racist views and racially segregated policies.

29. Warren G. Harding (1921-1923)

Republican party | Vice President: Calvin Coolidge

"Honesty is the great essential. It exalts the individual citizenship, and, without honesty, no man deserves the confidence of the people in private pursuit or in public office."

Warren Gamaliel Harding (Marion (Ohio), November 2, 1865 - San Francisco (California), August 2, 1923) was an American politician of the Republican Party. He was the 29th president of the United States, from 1921 to 1923.

Harding, an entrepreneur by trade, was publisher of the local newspaper *The Marion Star* in his hometown of Marion, Ohio. In 1904, Harding became the lieutenant governor of Ohio under Governor Myron Herrick. In 1914, Harding was elected as a senator for Ohio. In the 1920 U.S. presidential election, Harding was the candidate on behalf of the Republican Party. Together with running mate Calvin Coolidge, he defeated Democratic candidate James Middleton Cox and his running mate Franklin Delano Roosevelt.

His tenure became infamous for the heavy corruption that permeated the highest echelons of government (including the Teapot Dome scandal). Harding, like his successor, was a staunch Republican who believed that the government should intervene as little as possible in the economy. He also opposed foreign interference, including American participation in the League of Nations. Despite corruption allegations, Harding was praised for his commitment to civil rights for African Americans.

He signed a joint resolution of both houses of the U.S. Congress on September 21, 1922 (House Resolution 360) expressing their approval of the British mandate regarding Palestine and the intention to establish a Jewish homeland in it, in which religious freedom would prevail. The Arab (Palestinian) inhabitants could choose to accept and remain in Jewish authority or to settle elsewhere in Arab territory. Harding appointed some Jews to his advisory board . The resolution states, among other things: *The land we know as Palestine was populated by Jews from the beginning of history until Roman times. It is the ancestral homeland of the Jewish people.*

Harding became ill during a tour of Alaska and the trip was cut short. Harding traveled on to San Francisco where he soon suffered from respiratory problems. He probably contracted pneumonia. Although Harding seemed to recover he died suddenly on August 2, 1923 at the age of 57. Historians are unsure of the exact cause of death; heart failure or stroke are considered the most obvious cause of death. Harding was succeeded by his vice president Calvin Coolidge.

30. Calvin Coolidge (1923-1929)

Republican party | Vice President: Charles G. Dawes

"Nothing in the world can take the place of
persistence. Talent will not; . . Genius will not; . .
Education will not; . . Persistence and determination
alone are omnipotent."

John Calvin Coolidge Jr. (Plymouth (Vermont), July 4, 1872 - Northampton (Massachusetts), January 5, 1933) was the 30th president of the United States, a position that came to him as the then 29th vice president due to the death of President Warren G. Harding in 1923. Coolidge was president from 1923 to 1929. Coolidge died of a heart attack at the age of 60.

Biography

Coolidge was born in Plymouth, in Windsor County in the state of Vermont, the son of John Coolidge and Victoria Moore. After graduation, he dropped the name *John*. He studied at Amherst College in Massachusetts and graduated in 1895. He settled as a lawyer in Northampton in the same state and became a member of the town council in 1899. Furthermore, he was town attorney from 1900 to 1902, court clerk in 1904, and member of the Massachusetts state House of Representatives (not to be confused with the national House of Representatives) from 1907 to 1908.

He was elected mayor of Northampton for the period 1910-1911 and was a member of the Massachusetts Senate between 1912 and 1915, the last two years as president of that body. He served as lieutenant governor of the state from 1916-1918 and as governor from 1919-1920. He gained national fame when the Boston police went on strike with his statement "There is no right to strike against public safety for anyone, anywhere, anytime."

In 1920 Coolidge competed for the nomination for the presidency of the Republican Party, but he lost to Senator Warren G. Harding of Ohio. The popular candidate for the vice presidency was Senator Irvine Lenroot of Wisconsin, but the party chose Coolidge. The Harding-Coolidge team won over Ohio Governor James M. Cox and his *running mate* and Secretary of State for the Navy Franklin Delano Roosevelt.

Coolidge took the oath of office as vice president on March 4, 1921, and served until August 3, 1923. On that day he was sworn in as President of the United States, following the death of Warren Harding. Coolidge was sitting at home - a family visit - where there was no electricity or telephone when news of Harding's death reached him. His father, a notary public, administered the oath to him in their living room by the light of a kerosene lamp; later, in Washington, D.C., he was administered the oath again by an official of the Federal Government.

Coolidge was - unusually for a prominent politician - a man of few words; this earned him the nickname "Silent Cal" ("Silent Cal"). The story goes that at an official dinner at the White House, a guest made a bet with her friends that she could get the president to say at least three words during the meal. When Coolidge learned of this wager from her, he simply replied "You lose."

On June 2, 1924, he signed the Indian Citizenship Act, which granted Native Americans citizenship.

Coolidge won the 1924 presidential election for the term until March 4, 1929. His election slogan was *Keep Cool with Coolidge*. He took advantage of the then new medium of radio and made radio history several times: his inaugural address was the first to be broadcast by radio, on February 12, 1924, he was the first president to deliver a political speech on the radio, and on February 22, the first to have such a speech broadcast from the White House.

Coolidge was the last president who did not try to intervene in free market forces and let the economic cycle run its course. There was relatively little reason to do so during his presidency, as the United States was experiencing tremendous economic growth: the so-called "Roaring Twenties". Because of this, Coolidge is sometimes referred to as "the president when America was at play. Coolidge was not only able to cut taxes, he also paid off $1 billion in national debt.

For foreign policy he showed little interest.He did receive a visit on April 15, 1924 from Rabbi Abraham Yitzchak Kook , who was then Ashkenazi Chief Rabbi in Palestine. He headed a delegation of rabbis who had been in the U.S. for months starting in March of that year to raise funds for Talmud schools (Yeshivot). He thanked the president for American support for the Balfour Declaration and said that the return of the Jewish people to their ancient land of Israel (Palestine) would be good not only for the Jewish people, but even for all of humanity. Coolidge replied that the U.S. government would be pleased to assist the Jews whenever possible .

Only once did he travel abroad: on January 16, 1928, he addressed the Sixth Pan American Conference in Cuba. His presidency fell during the period of Prohibition, and alcohol was taboo at receptions in Washington. The reporter for the Saturday Evening Post was curious what would happen when, at a reception in Havana, a large tray of Cuban rum approached the president. "Cal himself, of course, was the cynosure of the drama. As the tray approached from his left, he wheeled artfully to the right, seeming to admire a portrait on the wall. The tray came closer. Mr. Coolidge wheeled right another 90 degrees, pointing out to President Machado the beauties of the tropical verdure. By the time he completed his 360-degree turn, the incriminating tray had passed safely beyond him. Apparently he had never seen it. His maneuver was a masterpiece of evasive action."

The growing era of the United States in the 1920s brought about many social changes, the *jazz-era*, not only because of the breakthrough of jazz music as entertainment for the large white audience, but also because of the rise of electronic mass media (radio and film and their associated advertising) and of a mass consumer culture, with which America would fill the rest of the world with a mixture of envy, rejection and imitation. Coolidge no longer felt at home in his own time. He therefore did not run again. He communicated this in the succinct style typical of him: "I choose not to run for president in 1928."

He became president of the Nonpartisan Railroad Commission and honorary president of the Foundation for the Blind. He died at the "Beeches," at Northampton, Massachusetts on January 5, 1933. He was buried in the Notch Cemetery in his hometown, Plymouth, Vermont.

31. Herbert Hoover (1929-1933)

Republican party | Vice President: Charles Curtis

"Be patient and calm; no one can catch fish in anger."

Herbert Clark Hoover (West Branch (Iowa), August 10, 1874 - New York, October 20, 1964) was the 31st president of the United States from 1929 to 1933. Before that, Hoover was famous for his humanitarian actions during World War I, particularly through food aid to occupied Belgium. From 1921 to 1928 he was Secretary of the Economy under President Warren G. Harding and, after his death, under successor Calvin Coolidge. As president, he faced a severe economic crisis that would become known as the Great Depression. As a result, Hoover lost his re-election in 1932.

Family and background

Herbert Hoover was born in West Branch, Iowa. His family belonged to the Quakers. His parents were Jesse Hoover and Hulda Minthorn. His father died in 1880, his mother in 1884.

In November 1885, 11-year-old "Bert" Hoover boarded a train heading west to Newberg, Oregon. He had twenty cents with him, sewn into his clothes, and also a basket full of goodies from his Aunt Hannah. Upon arrival, he was met by his uncle John Minthorn, a doctor and school superintendent whom Hoover later remembered as "a stern man on the face of it, but like all Quakers, a rough diamond with a white stone." As an errand boy at his uncle's *Oregon Land Company*, he learned bookkeeping and typing and took evening classes in business administration. Thanks to a teacher, Mrs. Jane Grey, he became attentive to writers such as Charles Dickens and Sir Walter Scott. Dickens' "David Copperfield," the story of an orphan who also had to fend for himself in the world, would always be a favorite.

Training

In the fall of 1891, Hoover went to study geology at the new Stanford University in Palo Alto, California. He did more outside the lecture hall than in it, managing baseball and American football teams, starting a laundry and running a speakers' agency. He sought the support of other underprivileged boys against campus administrators and was reluctantly elected student treasurer of the "Barbarians" program - a position in which he cleaned up a $2,000 student union debt.

Hoover earned his tuition by doing typing work for Professor John Casper Branner, who also got him a summer job as a cartographer of the Ozark Mountain region of Arkansas. In Branner's geology lab, he also met Lou Henry, the daughter of a banker born in 1874. Lou, like her fellow Iowa native, loved the outdoors and was as independent as he was. "What others think about you is not as important as what you feel inside," she told friends from college.

Hoover graduated in May 1895, three months before his 21st birthday. He left Stanford with $40 dollars in his pocket and no job prospects. He took with him more from his farmland alma mater than a college degree; Stanford had given Hoover an identity, a profession, and a future wife. Stanford became, for the orphan from West Branch, primarily a surrogate family, a place to return to.

In 1899, he married his Stanford sweetheart Lou Henry. They left for China, where he worked for a private company as China's premier mining engineer. In June 1900, the Hoovers were trapped in Tianjin by the Boxer Rebellion. For over a month, the town was under siege. While his wife worked in the hospital, he led the raising of barricades and once risked his life to save some Chinese children.

After this adventure, the couple left for Australia. There Hoover went to work setting up mining in Western Australia and developed a system of mining that is still in use today. He made a considerable fortune there. In 1912 he and his wife translated the classic Renaissance work on mining by the German scholar Georgius Agricola, "De Re Metallica" from the Latin. To this day, this work is considered one of the standard works on mining and his translation is still reprinted.

Hoover's philanthropic years

Hoover then felt that he had made enough money; from his Quaker faith he sought a way to be of service to fellow men. In August 1914, a good opportunity came up. The outbreak of World War I left 120,000 Americans stranded in Europe, penniless.

On August 3, Hoover received an urgent request for help from the U.S. Ambassador to London, Walter Hines Page. Within 24 hours, 500 volunteers were drummed up and the Grand Ballroom of the Savoy Hotel was converted into a canteen and distribution center for food, clothing, tickets for the steamboat and cash. "I didn't realize it at the time, but on August 3, 1914, my career as an engineer was over; I had stepped onto the slippery slope of public life."

During the following weeks, Hoover provided help to get home to everyone from Chief White Feather from Pawhuska, Oklahoma, to jewel-encrusted widows. When one lady angrily demanded a written statement that her ship would not be torpedoed in the middle of the ocean by a German U-boat, he immediately signed.

Along with nine engineer friends, Hoover loaned desperate travelers a total of one and a half million dollars. All but $400 was repaid, solidifying the Great Engineer's confidence in the American character. "The difference between dictatorship and democracy," Hoover was fond of saying, "is simple: dictators organize from the top down, democrats from the bottom up."

In the fall of 1914, Belgium - stuck between German bayonets and British blockades - was threatened by famine. During his stay in China, Hoover had befriended the Belgian diplomat and entrepreneur Emile Francqui, who was now in charge of the General Company of Belgium. He asked Hoover to set up an unprecedented humanitarian aid operation for the tiny kingdom, which depended on imports for 80 percent of its food supply. To do so, he would have to give up a career as the world's most substantial mining engineer. He mulled over the request for several days and finally told a friend "let the fortune go to hell." He accepted the immense task on two conditions: that he would receive no pay, but full freedom in the organization and administration of what was to become known as the Commission for Relief in Belgium.

The Commission became, in effect, an independent republic of humanitarian aid, with its own flag, navy, factories, and railroads. Its budget of $12 million a month came from voluntary donations and government support. More than once Hoover made public pledges for far more money than he actually had. He practiced a kind of shuttle diplomacy, as he crossed the North Sea 40 times to persuade the warring powers in London and Berlin to let emergency aid through for war victims. He taught the Belgians, who considered cornstarch to be cattle feed, to eat corn bread. In all, the Commission saved some ten million people from starvation.

Each day brought new crises. The British investigated allegations that Hoover was spying for the enemy. Germany deported youthful Commission employees, including a Salvation Army major, for the same reasons. In the U.S., Senator Henry Cabot Lodge wanted to prosecute Hoover for conspiring with the enemy. Theodore Roosevelt, however, promised to keep Lodge in check. He informed Hoover that "the courage of a politician is greater in his office than in the newspaper."

Despite the obstacles, Hoover persisted, purchasing rice from Burma, Argentine corn, Chinese beans, and American flour, meat, and fat products. Long before the 1918 Armistice, Hoover was an international hero who, according to Ambassador Walter Hines Page, "began his career in California and will end it in heaven."

When the United States entered the war, President Woodrow Wilson appointed Hoover to head the Food Administration. He succeeded in reducing domestic consumption of food that was also needed overseas without putting it on sale in America and thus still provided the Allies with a good meal.

After the armistice, Hoover, a member of the Supreme Economic Council and head of the American Relief Administration, organized food shipments for the millions of hungry in Central Europe. He offered aid in 1921 to famine-stricken Russia, which was now in the power of the Bolsheviks. When a critic asked whether he was thus not supporting Bolshevism, Hoover angrily replied, "Twenty million people are dying of hunger. Whatever their politics, they will be fed!"

Presidency

Summary

As a Republican president, he had to deal primarily with the Great Depression, the result of the New York Stock Exchange crash, on October 24, 1929, during his time in office. He tried to get the economy out of the doldrums by establishing government funds, where businessmen and farmers could easily take out loans. These and other measures did not have the desired effect.

Commencement

After serving very capably as Secretary of the Economy under Presidents Warren Harding and Calvin Coolidge and taking the lead in emergency relief after the great floods of the Mississippi River in 1927, Hoover became the Republican Party's candidate for President of the United States in 1928. He said then, "We here in America are now closer to the final victory over poverty than any country ever in the history of the world." He encouraged the population to take an active part in economic growth as much as possible, and especially to invest in stocks ("A small amount every month," was his advice). Within a few months of his taking office, the stock market crash of 1929 followed and the economy collapsed, ushering in the Great Depression. His candidacy for the presidency turned out to be his worst career move for Herbert Hoover, who up to that point seemed incapable of making mistakes.

After the crash, Hoover announced that while he would balance state spending, he would cut taxes and increase spending on public works. However, he signed the Hawley-Smoot Tariff Act, which increased import duties on 20,000 taxable products. This law is often seen as the cause for worsening the Depression and is also often seen as Hoover's greatest political blunder. The Hoover administration's curbing of the amount of money in free circulation (for fear of inflation) is also seen by modern economists as a tactical error.

Hoover's finance minister, by the way, was Andrew Mellon, who had defected from the Coolidge government.

Hoover and the economy

Herbert Hoover is one of the least understood and most reviled presidents in the history of the United States. Politically colored allegations that he was a "laissez-faire" president who would not get off his chair to do anything about the economy continue to this day, despite clear evidence to the contrary. Thanks to Hoover's experiences in World War I, he firmly believed that government had the means to positively affect people's lives. As a result, Hoover not only sought rapprochement with the U.S. Congress to address the economy, but he also used his executive power to establish various programs and implement reforms.

The following list is a summary of some of the steps Hoover, also known as "the forgotten progressive," took to shore up the economy and remedy the suffering of the American people.

1. He signed the Emergency Relief and Construction Act, the federal government's first welfare law

2. He increased spending on public works, including:

    o   a request to Congress for an additional $400 million for the federal construction program

    o   a directive to the Department of Commerce in December 1929 to establish a Public Construction Division

    o   Additional subsidies for shipbuilding by the Federal Maritime Council

    o   urging the governors of the states to step up their public works (although few complied)

3. He signed the Federal Home Loan Bank Act that created the Federal Home Loan Banking System to assist citizens in obtaining loans to purchase their own homes

4. He increased subsidies for farmers (who were struggling greatly)

5. He set up the *President's Emergency Relief Organization* to organize local, private relief organizations resulting in over 3,000 emergency response committees throughout the U.S.

6. He urged bankers to set up the National Credit Corporation to assist banks that were in financial distress in order to secure the funds of people with bank accounts

7. He actively encouraged businesses to keep wages high during the Great Depression. Many businessmen, most notably Henry Ford, raised workers' wages (or kept them the same) at the

beginning of the Depression in the hope that providing workers with lots of money would halt the economic malaise.

8. He signed the Reconstruction Finance Act. This act created the Reconstruction Finance Corporation that provided loans to states for public works and emergency relief. It also provided loans to banks, railroads, and farm loan banks.

9. He raised import tariffs to preserve American jobs. After hearings by the Ways and Means Committee, Congress agreed to legislation that Hoover signed, despite some hesitation. The effect of this Hawley-Smoot Tariff Act was a global trade war, often seen as the reason for worsening the Depression. Today, this is seen as a classic example of well-intentioned government action having a severely negative impact.

To pay for all these measures, Hoover agreed to the steepest tax increase ever in the United States. The Revenue Act of 1932 increased the income tax for the highest earners from 25% to 63%; property taxes and business taxes went up by nearly 15%. Hoover also urged Congress to scrutinize the New York Stock Exchange; this pressure resulted in a number of reforms.

Despite these measures and rigorous intervention by Hoover's successor FDR, the economy did not improve. A severe recession took place in 1937-38 (which some economists even refer to as a depression) and the economy struggled until the 1940s (unemployment did not fall below 9.9% until 1942).

Palestine

Hoover had an isolationist stance during the pogroms of 1929 , the first serious foreign policy crisis of his presidency. He did not intervene to protect Palestinian Jews, nor did he pressure the British to do so. He did remain "steadfast in his support for the building of Zionist-Jewish Palestine." In 1928 Hoover had praised the work of Zionist settlers in transforming Palestine, which, in his words, had remained "abandoned and neglected for centuries." As president, he sent letters of support to the Zionist Organization of America and to the American Palestine Committee, a Christian-Zionist organization, when it was founded...

The Bonus Army Incident

In July 1932, World War I veterans and their families demonstrated in Washington, D.C., to have a "bonus" immediately paid to them promised by the Bonus Act of 1924, to be paid out in 1945. Hoover deployed the military to remove the uninvited guests from the Capitol and faced stiff criticism that this was likely a violation of the Posse Comitatus Act of 1878.

After his presidency

Hoover's political opponents in Congress, whom he suspected of opposing his programs for political reasons, painted him as a cruel and unfeeling president.

Hoover suffered a heavy defeat in the 1932 election and was succeeded by Democrat Franklin D. Roosevelt in March 1933. Although he expressed immediate support for the president in his efforts to revive the economy, Hoover did become a fierce critic of the New Deal and repeatedly warned against an excessive role for government. He laid out his fears in his book *The Challenge to Liberty*, in which he described fascism, communism, and socialism as enemies of traditional American freedoms.

In March 1947, Hoover turned against the Morgenthau Plan and, using economic arguments for the time being, sounded the alarm about the famine in occupied Germany. Then, slowly, a change occurred: CARE packages for starving German children were put together. According to Hoover, the reduction of Germany to an occupied isolated agricultural state would cost "25 million of them [Germans]" their lives.

He was in a way mindful of the plight of the Palestinians and in December 1945 he had presented a plan he had devised for Palestine to the Anglo-American Committee of Inquiry on Palestine Hoover argued that his plan would be beneficial to both Jews and Arabs. It would resolve "the Palestinian question" and greatly enhance the possibilities of Palestine as a haven for Jews. His proposal amounted to this: the Arab population of Palestine would be moved to Iraq with the implicit assumption that this transfer would be voluntary. The committee agreed that the plan deserved careful study.In 1949, with the emergence of the problem of hundreds of thousands of Palestinian refugees, this Hoover plan took on special urgency for him. Hoover wrote to the White House that the refugees were "in a deplorable situation" and could be taken into Iraq. His Iraq plan would be the final solution for these unfortunate people, he believed, and it would strengthen the economy of that country The U.S. government did not adopt the plan.

Also in 1947, President Harry S. Truman appointed Hoover as a member of a commission (which chose him as chairman) to reform the presidential departments. By President Dwight D. Eisenhower, he was appointed to a similar commission in 1953. Many cuts resulted from the proposals of both commissions. Over the years Hoover wrote many articles and books; he was working on one of these when he died of colon cancer in New York in October 1964 at the age of 90. He was buried in the grounds of his presidential library, which had opened two years earlier in his hometown of West Branch, Iowa. Next to him was reburied his wife Lou, who had already died in 1944.

32. Franklin D. Roosevelt (1933-1945)

Democratic party | Vice presidents: John Nance Garner, Henry A. Wallace, and Harry S. Truman

"We cannot always build the future for our youth, but we can build our youth for the future."

Franklin Delano Roosevelt, also known by his initials **FDR**, (Hyde Park (New York), January 30, 1882 - Warm Springs (Georgia), April 12, 1945) was an American politician of the Democratic Party. He was the 32nd president of the United States from 1933 to 1945.

Roosevelt was a lawyer by profession. He was Deputy Secretary of the Navy from 1913 to 1920 under President Woodrow Wilson. During the

1920 U.S. presidential election, he was the running mate of presidential candidate James Middleton Cox. Cox lost the election to Republican candidate Warren Harding. Roosevelt was the governor of New York from 1929 to 1932.

During the 1932 U.S. presidential election, Roosevelt was the Democratic Party candidate. Due to the poor economy, he defeated the incumbent President Herbert Hoover. As president, Roosevelt made extensive use of the media to win over public opinion and explain his policies. His informal *off-the-record style* of press conferences and his popular *fireside chats*, "talk by the fireside" on the radio before and during World War II, are examples. With the *New Deal*, he initiated a program against the social and economic consequences of the Great Depression.

Roosevelt is the only President of the United States to have been elected four times, a record that cannot be bettered because since Amendment XXII of 1947 the President can only be re-elected once. On April 12, 1945, Roosevelt died of a stroke at the age of 63.

President Theodore Roosevelt (1858-1919) was a distant cousin of his.

Youth and marriage

Franklin Delano Roosevelt was born on January 30, 1882, the only child of wealthy parents and distant descendant of Dutch American Claes Maertensz van 't Rosevelt, born on the Hyde Park estate in upstate New York. The Roosevelts had made fortunes in sugar refining and had invested that money in land. James Roosevelt, Franklin's father, remained active in commerce and tried to build monopolies in mining and in the railroad system in the South, among other things. He also invested considerable money in building a canal through Nicaragua.

Franklin enjoyed a privileged upbringing in which his mother Sarah in particular took strict care of him. He was given ample opportunity to pursue various hobbies. He rode ponies, collected stamps, loved to fish and put up birds he had shot. His great passion, however, would remain sailing throughout his life. He was educated at home by governesses. They taught him the basics of French, German and English. The bond with his mother was so strong that the moment when he would be sent to *Groton School*, a reputable boarding school in Massachusetts, was always postponed. At that school Franklin showed himself to be a moderate and quiet student. After Groton, he went to *Harvard University* and took classes in economics, constitutional studies, and history. Again, his study results were rather moderate, possibly, because he spent more time making social contacts than studying. During this period Franklin fell in love with Eleanor, a distant cousin of his and uncle-sister of Theodore Roosevelt. After their engagement in the fall of 1904, they married on March 17, 1905. Meanwhile, Roosevelt had completed his education at Harvard and he enrolled in law school at *Columbia Law School* in New York. In 1907 he was sworn in as a lawyer and from then on worked as a civil lawyer.

New York State Senate

In 1910, he made his debut in American politics when the Democratic party asked him to run for a seat in the New York State Senate. In his election campaign, he made combating the corruption of party bosses of both the Democratic and Republican parties the main theme. What also helped to increase his popularity - even among Republican voters - was the fact that he was related to Theodore Roosevelt and he did not fail to remind them of this.

Roosevelt ran his campaign *above the parties*. He financed his own expenses and drove around in a red, flag-draped Maxwell (the only car available) to shake hands and chat with everyone. After his election, he campaigned fiercely as a Democrat for Woodrow Wilson, who was a presidential candidate in 1912.

From 1913 to 1920, Roosevelt served as Deputy Secretary of the Navy.

Childhood Paralysis

In 1921, Roosevelt was stricken with poliomyelitis (infantile paralysis). This disease paralyzed his entire lower body. In 1927 he founded an association at a health resort in Georgia to help other victims of this disease. Around that time, Roosevelt was back in politics. A 2003 U.S. study stated that FDR probably did not have polio, but rather Guillain-Barré syndrome, which can have similar symptoms. It has further been documented that Roosevelt suffered from hypertension; at the time still a difficult-to-treat disease that is believed to have contributed to his heart condition and his rather early death from a stroke. It has also been suspected that he had melanoma, but the latter has never been proven.

Governor of New York

He was elected governor of New York in 1928. Immediately he began a vigorous social reform program. In 1932 he chaired a commission that investigated corruption in the Democratic administration in New York and forced Mayor Jimmy Walker to resign. Of more national importance was the "Brain Trust" (brain bank, think tank) of advisers, brought together by Roosevelt to help New York recover from the horrific aftermath of the malaise that followed Stock Market Crash of 1929.

Presidency

In 1932, Roosevelt ran for president and won easily. His speech at the swearing-in ceremony earned him a great reputation. He proclaimed that it was his firm belief that *the only thing to be feared was fear itself*. He also announced his New Deal. This program involved government control of industry and agriculture and was intended to revitalize the economy through large injections of public funds, which was, however, financed with large tax increases until 1938. Roosevelt continued to strive for a balanced budget until 1938, which he promised, leading to a depression recession in 1936. It was not until 1938 that an expansionary fiscal policy was implemented on the advice of John Maynard Keynes, which produced very strong economic growth.

First term

The phenomenon of presidential press conferences dates back to the early 20th century, starting with President Theodore Roosevelt. However, not all of his successors used them equally. Franklin Delano Roosevelt announced at his first press conference as president that he wanted to change his style. The journalists were no longer required to submit questionnaires in advance and gradually these conferences took on a very informal character. In addition, he demanded that the journalists present not quote the things he told them *off the record*, but only use them as a kind of inspiration. The press, especially in the first years of his policy, was charmed by his approach. This good relationship with journalists was of great importance to Roosevelt so that his program of the *New Deal* would not be portrayed in an unfavorable light in the press. In addition to these press conferences, Roosevelt also held occasional *Sunday Suppers* at the White House on Sunday evenings, to which the press was welcome. Roosevelt also turned his attention to the communication possibilities of radio. While still governor of New York State, he had already given his first radio speeches in March and April 1929 to defend his policies. In his much-lauded *fireside chats*, he now aimed to connect with the American people. Roosevelt captivated his audience by talking about politics in words that everyone could understand and also managed to evoke a sense of intimacy with his "fireside chats. However, he prepared these speeches extremely well and on the day of the broadcast he knew the *chat* by heart. The fireside chats took on particular importance during World War II when Roosevelt sought to uplift the American people and give them hope for the future. This is strongly reflected in his December 8, 1941 speech following Japan's attack on Pearl Harbor.

An indication of the importance Roosevelt placed on reputation advocacy is the increasing number of staff members who worked under the press secretary during those years. *First lady* Eleanor Roosevelt also played an important role by preparing Franklin's speeches, publishing her own columns (*My day*), and giving lectures.

Second term

In 1936, Roosevelt won the election for the second time-the largest victory in electoral history. In total, he got 523 electoral votes behind him, and only the states of Maine and Vermont had supported Governor Alfred L. Landon and Frank Knox, respectively. However, the *Literary Digest poll* had predicted a very different result, with Landon winning the argument. However, it was clear that a large segment of the population wanted to continue supporting Roosevelt and believed in his social reform plans. Roosevelt kept his word and when the unemployment rate reached ten million, he signed the *Emergency Relief Appropriation Act* on June 21, 1938, providing a $3 billion fund to help mitigate the effects of the recession. A few days later, on June 25, the *Fair Labor Standards Act* was signed, providing for a minimum wage (from 25 to 40 cents an hour) and capping total hours of labor to be performed (44 hours, eventually to be reduced to 40 hours). He also succeeded in gaining Congressional approval in June 1939 to pledge $1.5 billion in aid to one of his New Deal administrations, the *Work Projects Administrations* (W.P.A.).In foreign policy, Roosevelt posed as a "good neighbor" to Latin America and called for peace with Hitler and Mussolini.

Third term

On November 5, 1940, Roosevelt became the first president in American history to be elected to a third term. He is the only president in the history of the United States to have been elected more than twice (four times, see below). Today, this is no longer possible, as a president may now stand for re-election only once, under the 22nd Amendment to the U.S. Constitution, adopted in 1947.

He had convincingly defeated his Republican opponent Wendell Willkie
by getting 38 states with a total of 449 electoral votes behind him. It
was a less delineated victory than the previous one, which probably
had to do with the uncertainty surrounding possible U.S. participation in
the war now raging in Europe. Franklin also did not have the support of
major union leader John L. Lewis of the C.I.O. who had even
threatened to resign if Roosevelt was re-elected. In the end, however,
most voters were convinced that Roosevelt should be given a chance
to continue his program of reversing the effects of the Depression.
Roosevelt had promised to work on social security for older Americans,
banking reform, crop control, and rural electricity.

He also wanted the United States to help Europe in World War II. In his
State of the Union, of January 6, 1941 he held out to Congress in his
famous Four Freedoms speech that there were Four Freedoms at
stake in the war. For everyone, everywhere in the world: freedom of
speech and of religion, and freedom from fear and from want.

In August 1941, Roosevelt met Winston Churchill on a warship just off
the coast of Newfoundland, where they signed the Atlantic Charter, a
declaration of common objectives. It became the founding document
for the United Nations, signed by 26 countries in 1942. Meanwhile, the
United States itself had been engaged in war for about a month, due to
the Japanese attack on Pearl Harbor on December 7, 1941.

While he left the conduct of military operations to military personnel,
Roosevelt spent much time negotiating and conferencing with Allied
leaders.

A Jewish state?

He preferred to postpone interference in the question of Palestine and
the formation of a Jewish National Home there until peace talks would
be held at the end of the war. The Zionist movement, however, was not
going to sit idly by during that time. It decided to work hard. Especially
in the United States, that emerging promising power. American Zionist
organizations took the initiative. They joined forces, after the necessary
discussions, and formed the American Zionist Emergency Council
(AZEC).With the members of World Zionist Organization , who were in
the U.S. from May 9 to 11, 1942, including David Ben Goerion and
Chaim Weizmann, AZEC convened a conference at the Biltmore Hotel
in New York to draw up a plan of action. The starting points were: the
condemnation of the British White Paper of 1939; Palestine to become
a Jewish state (commonwealth); unlimited immigration and settlement
of (one million) Jews in the (entire) land of Palestine under the

leadership of the Jewish Agency for Palestine (read: WZO), so that the Jews would form the majority of the population as soon as possible. This plan became the program of action for the Zionist movement, with the exception of the Zionist revisionists, a militant minority.When it was adopted, people brought up the point that it should then also be brought out into the open. To this the American Jewish Committee and the Jewish Labor Committee - two non-Zionist Jewish groups - disagreed and left the conference. Morris D. Waldman, the executive vice-president of the American Jewish Committee, later testified, "President Roosevelt and the State Department convinced us that a resolution at the conference involving a Jewish state (commonwealth) would likely arouse the hostility of the Arab world toward the Allies and thus throw that crucial region into the lap of the Nazis. On June 11, 1943, Deputy Secretary of State Sumner Welles had accompanied Dr. Chaim Weizmann, president of the Jewish Agency for Palestine, to the White House for a meeting with President Roosevelt. The President noted in passing that Prime Minister Churchill and he had decided to invite a representative group of Jews and Arabs to confer with them in an effort to reach mutual understanding about the future of Palestine.Lieutenant Colonel Harold B. Hoskins of the U.S. Army, "an ...Arabist and expert on the Arab-Jewish problem" was nevertheless sent to King Ibn Saud of Saudi Arabia to gauge his opinion.His report was very unfavorable to the Zionist cause.

Fourth and final term

In 1944, with Harry S. Truman as vice president, he won the presidential election for the fourth time.

At the Yalta Conference in February 1945, Roosevelt, by then seriously ill, Churchill and Stalin made vital decisions regarding postwar Europe. Agreement was reached on the four zones of occupation in conquered Germany. Agreements were also made with the Soviet Union regarding territory in Asia. Even before Roosevelt died, some agreements were violated by Stalin, about which Roosevelt reacted with great bitterness.

Two months later, on April 12, 1945, Roosevelt died. After his death, he was succeeded by Vice President Harry Truman.

In his memory, the Franklin Delano Roosevelt Memorial was built in Washington, D.C.

Four Freedoms legacy

Already during his lifetime, Roosevelt commissioned the Four Freedoms Monument to inspire a larger audience for the concept of the four freedoms: freedom of speech, freedom of religion, freedom from want, and freedom from fear. After his death, two more sculptures bearing this name were also unveiled in Cleveland (Ohio) and Evansville (Indiana). Furthermore, painter Norman Rockwell was inspired to paint four works on this concept: *Freedom of Speech*, *Freedom of Worship*, *Freedom from Want* and *Freedom from Fear*.

Since 1982, five Four Freedoms Awards have been presented annually, in the even years in Middelburg by the Roosevelt Foundation and in the odd years by the Franklin and Eleanor Roosevelt Institute in New York. The connection with Zeeland lies in the town of Oud-Vossemeer on the island of Tholen, where Roosevelt's ancestors are believed to have come from. Since 1986, the Roosevelt Study Center, which conducts research into American (political) history, has existed in the capital city of Zeeland. Middelburg also has the University College Roosevelt, which provides a bachelor's program in Liberal Arts and Sciences for Utrecht University, since 2004.

33. Harry S. Truman (1945-1953)

Democratic party | Vice president: Alben W. Barkley

"In reading the lives of great men, I found that the first victory they won was over themselves.... self-discipline with all of them came first."

Harry S. Truman (Lamar (Missouri), May 8, 1884 - Kansas City (Missouri), December 26, 1972) was the 33rd president of the United States from 1945 to 1953. Before that, he served for several months as the 34th Vice President of the US under Franklin D. Roosevelt. When the latter died as incumbent president, Truman took over the office. He was a member of the Democratic Party.

Truman did not have a second first name, but only the middle initial "S." In southern states, including Missouri, this was not unusual. The initial "S" was a compromise between the names of his grandfathers Anderson Shippe Truman and Solomon Young.

Biography

Early life

As a child of farmers, Harry S. Truman did not attend regular schools until he was eight years old; before that, he attended a Calvinist Sunday school in Independence, Missouri, among other places. After attending school at *Independence High School,* he was a supervisor with the *Santa Fe Railroad* and also worked as a volunteer with the Democratic National Convention. He also worked as an office clerk and a typist at the *Kansas City Star* newspaper.

Truman enlisted in the Missouri National Guard in 1905. His eyesight was inadequate, being 50% left and 40% right, but he reportedly rolled through the inspection by secretly studying the letter chart. He served until 1911.In 1917, after being a member of the Missouri reserve troops for several years, he became active in World War I. He was a member of the Missouri National Guard. He made it to colonel in battles in the Vosges Mountains, which became the basis of his future political career in the Democratic Party.

Ecclesiastically, he belonged to Baptism. Truman became a Freemason in 1909. In September 1940, he became Grand Master of the Metropolitan District of Missouri.

In 1922, Truman wanted to join the Ku Klux Klan (KKK), popular at the time among white men, through a friend, but renounced after some time, after which he requested a refund of his registration fee. During his presidency, Truman championed equal rights for black citizens and introduced legislation to improve the position of black Americans.

In 1919, Truman married Bess Wallace, whom he had known since childhood. It was not easy for them to have children: there were two stillborn children and several miscarriages. In 1924, their only daughter Margaret was born.

Presidency

In the 1944 presidential election, Harry Truman was elected the 33rd Vice President of the US. When incumbent President Roosevelt died on April 12, 1945, Truman became his successor in office. His main task at the beginning of his presidency would be to end World War II.

Truman's presidency was eventful: he was president during the end of World War II, the beginning of the Cold War, the creation of the United Nations, and most of the Korean War. Truman was an informal president, with many familiar stop words and slogans, such as "The buck stops here," by which he meant that he was the one who made the decisions and was and should be responsible for them. (*To pass the buck* means to shift blame; so by *the buck stops here* he meant "blame me.")

Atomic bombs on Japan

After the German surrender on May 7, 1945, the war continued to rage in full force in the Far East. To bring the conflict to a swift end, Truman decided to use nuclear weapons against Japan. Truman only learned of the existence of the atomic bomb when he became president, because his predecessor Roosevelt had not informed him of it.On August 6, 1945, the crew of the Enola Gay dropped an atomic bomb on the city of Hiroshima, and three days later, on August 9, the city of Nagasaki was also the target of an atomic attack. More than 150,000 people were killed in these bombings (80,000 in Hiroshima and 75,000 in Nagasaki), and another that number died of their injuries and from radiation-related diseases in the weeks that followed. The immediate consequence of the deployment of atomic weapons was the Japanese surrender on August 15, 1945, and thus the end of World War II.

The use of atomic weapons against Japan is still a sensitive topic that can lead to heated discussions. Proponents argue that by deploying the atomic bomb and thus shortening the war, many lives were saved of civilians in the Japanese-occupied territories and of soldiers by avoiding a prolonged extremely bloody invasion of the Japanese islands. Opponents, however, argue that the killing of hundreds of thousands of innocent civilians through the targeted use of atomic weapons against civilian targets is a war crime and cannot be justified in any situation, partly because of the disastrous long-term consequences. Moreover, they question the necessity of throwing the atomic bombs before the Japanese capitulation, since Japan would have already signaled its willingness to surrender conditionally before August 6, 1945. However, the Potsdam Declaration on July 26, 1945, which threatened Japan with "immediate and total destruction" if it did not surrender, was rejected by the Japanese government with what it itself called a "deadly silence. On August 9, just hours before the second bomb fell, the Soviet Union declared war on the Japanese puppet state of Manchuria and invaded it. This may have contributed to Japan's decision on August 15 to capitulate to the U.S. anyway.

After the Second World War

After the war, Truman was known as a fervent anti-Communist who attached importance to keeping Europe outside the sphere of influence of the then Soviet Union. Incidentally, Truman showed himself to be a proponent of international cooperation, and in 1945 he co-founded the United Nations. In 1947, Truman also supported the creation of the state of Israel (although his Secretary of State George C. Marshall and most foreign policy experts opposed it). The Baptist Truman felt a religious calling to support modern Zionism, which was strengthened by his contacts with the religious Jew Chaim Weizmann , who played an important role in the World Zionist Organization.Truman had also participated in an intense lobbying effort to help UN Resolution 181 of November 29, 1947 regarding the partition of Palestine into a Jewish and an Arab state gain a majority. Together with American senators, he won over several Latin American countries. 11 minutes after the declaration of independence on May 14, 1948, he recognized the de facto right of the State of Israel to exist. Followed immediately by Joseph Stalin of the USSR .

In 1947, the Marshall Plan, devised by George Marshall, was approved by Truman, mainly because it corresponded to his Truman Doctrine. This plan involved allowing Europe to rebuild itself through American subsidies. For many countries, the Marshall Plan was a significant help in post-war reconstruction. In the same year, Truman devised the containment policy. This meant that if any country threatened to become communist, the U.S. had the right to intervene.

In the 1948 presidential election, the Democratic Party was very divided over declaring Truman as its candidate for reelection. The post-war realignment of the U.S. war economy, which involved a massive downsizing of the armed forces (especially the Navy), and the passage of a law on labor unions (the Taft-Hartley Act), with Congress overriding a presidential veto, had been fraught with difficulty. In the end, Truman did become a compromise candidate. Thanks to his intensive campaign with a whistle-stop tour of rural America and the weakness of his Republican rival Thomas Dewey, Truman was re-elected against all odds. In fact, the Chicago Tribune had already declared Dewey the winner.

At the outbreak of the Korean War in 1950, Truman made the decision to come to South Korea's aid militarily.

In 1951, the 22nd Amendment to the U.S. Constitution was adopted. This amendment ensured that the U.S. president would henceforth be eligible for re-election only once or, in the case of a mid-term replacement, be president for a maximum of 10 years. (Franklin D. Roosevelt, Truman's predecessor, had been re-elected three times.) However, this rule did not yet apply to the incumbent president, but after Truman lost the 1952 Democratic primary for the state of New Hampshire he withdrew his candidacy for a third term. Subsequently, Truman began searching for a suitable successor for the Democratic Party. He had his eye on former General Dwight D. Eisenhower, but he preferred to run for the Republican Party. Chief Justice Fred M. Vinson also refused, while Truman's Vice President Alben Barkley was considered too old. Eventually Truman found a suitable presidential candidate in Adlai Stevenson, the governor of the state of Illinois, who was held in high esteem by intellectuals. After some urging, Stevenson declared his willingness to stand for the Democratic party. In the 1952 presidential election, however, Stevenson was defeated by Eisenhower, who took over the presidency from Truman on January 20, 1953.

Later life

After leaving the White House, Truman returned to Missouri. There he ran into financial difficulties fairly quickly. He had little savings and only a meager pension from his time in the military. He turned down commercial offers, but he did sign a contract to write his memoirs. For this he received $670,000, of which $37,000 remained after paying taxes and personnel. The memoirs appeared in two volumes and became a success. In 1958 the US Congress passed the *Former Presidents Act*, which entitled former presidents to a pension of $25,000 per year. It was suspected that Truman's difficult financial situation in particular prompted this. The only other former president alive at the time, Herbert Hoover, did not actually need the money, but accepted it so as not to embarrass Truman.

In the summer of 1957, Truman's presidential library opened in Independence, Missouri. He had raised a lot of money for this himself and also had his office there, where he wrote articles and books. In 1965, the library was the site of the signing of the Medicare Act by President Lyndon B. Johnson, honoring the efforts Truman had made during his presidency for social care. Truman continued to campaign for the Democratic Party into old age. On December 26, 1972, he died in a Kansas City hospital at the age of 88 from complications of pulmonary edema. His wife Bess did not advocate a state funeral in

Washington D.C., but rather a sober funeral in private. Truman was buried on the grounds of his presidential library. Bess Truman was also buried here after her death in 1982.

34. Dwight D. Eisenhower (1953-1961)

"No man is worth your tears, but once you find one that is, he won't make you cry."

Dwight David Eisenhower (Denison (Texas), October 14, 1890 - Washington D.C., March 28, 1969) was an American general and politician. He was the Commander-in-Chief/General *of the Army (five-star general)* of the Allied Forces in Europe during World War II and the 34th President of the United States (1953-1961).

Lifetime

Dwight grew up in Abilene, Kansas, the third of seven sons in the family of David Jacob Eisenhower (1863-1942) and Ida Elizabeth Stover (1862-1946). He was originally named David Dwight Eisenhower, but the two first names were soon switched because the name David was more common in the family. Dwight, as well as his brothers, were often called Ike as children, a shortening of the Eisenhower surname. Dwight kept that pet name for life and in his election campaign the slogan was "I like Ike." His ancestor Hans Nicolas Eisenhauer, who hailed from Karlsbrunn in what is now Saarland, Germany, had emigrated with his family to Lancaster, Pennsylvania, in 1741. In 1892, Eisenhauer's father and mother moved to Abilene (Kansas), where he graduated from *Abilene High School* in 1909. He received his further education at West Point, the famous military academy, where he graduated in The class the stars fell on. While stationed in Texas he met Geneva Doud (1896-1979), whom he married in 1916. Together they had two children. The oldest son, Doud Dwight Eisenhower (1917-1921), died of scarlet fever as a three-year-old toddler. The youngest, John Sheldon Doud Eisenhower (1922-2013), made it to brigadier general of the reserve and then served as U.S. ambassador to Belgium from 1969 to 1971.

Military career

In World War I, he worked in the leadership of the U.S. tank warfare training camp. During this time, he became very interested in mechanized warfare, including through his discussions with George Patton and other colleagues. However, their ideas were strongly disapproved of by their older, superior generals. After World War I, he held many staff positions as a major. Among others, he worked for Generals John J. Pershing and Douglas MacArthur. He also spent four years in the Office of the Deputy Secretary of War between the two world wars. In the middle of those years he served in the Philippines, where, after serving sixteen years as a major, he was appointed lieutenant colonel in 1936. In June 1941, he was appointed chief of staff of Walter Krueger's 3rd U.S. Army, which was then stationed near San Antonio, Texas. In September 1941, he was promoted to brigadier general. After Pearl Harbor, General George C. Marshall brought him to Washington to head the department that was drawing up plans to defeat Germany and Japan. In 1942, he was appointed commanding general of U.S. forces on the European battlefield. In November 1942, he led the U.S. landing forces in the joint British-American invasion of North Africa, the first major Allied offensive of World War II. The following year, Eisenhower successfully led the invasion of Sicily. Italy came into play later that same year and the fighting there continued into 1945. He was then appointed commander-in-chief of the Allied invasion of northern Europe, which he successfully led to a successful conclusion with English Field Marshal Bernard Montgomery. At the conclusion of the war in Europe, Eisenhower commanded the troops occupying Germany and also served as Chief of Staff of the United States Army. Like Douglas MacArthur, Dwight D. Eisenhower received the Army Distinguished Service Medal five times. A black page in his performance as Commander-in-Chief was his order after the capitulation to designate German soldiers who had surrendered as so-called "Disarmed Enemy Forces." This meant that they were no longer covered by the Geneva Convention and were locked up in the so-called "Rheinwiesenlager", where they did not receive adequate food and medical care. Estimates of the number of deaths vary widely and range from thousands to hundreds of thousands due to malnutrition and lack of medical care.

Degrees and assignments

Dwight David Eisenhower, after college, served in the military from 1915 through 1952 and went through all ranks as an officer in the U.S. Army, taking on a wide variety of assignments.

Civic Life

In 1948, he resigned his military positions and became president of Columbia University in New York. This return to civilian life did not immediately bring Eisenhower into politics. He turned down offers to run for the Republican nomination for president and left college in December 1950 to become the first commander-in-chief of NATO.

In the 1952 presidential election, incumbent President Harry S. Truman would not run for re-election. In the search for a successor, Eisenhower was approached by Truman in the fall of 1951 to ask if he was interested in the Democratic candidacy. Eisenhower responded evasively, but when he registered for the Republican *primary* in New Hampshire a few months later, Truman knew his answer. The general now yielded to the Grand Old Party and won the Republican nomination from conservative Robert Taft. In the meantime, President Truman had found a suitable candidate in Adlai Stevenson, the governor of the state of Illinois, who was held in high esteem by intellectuals. After some urging, Stevenson declared himself willing to stand for the Democratic party. Eisenhower, however, defeated Stevenson by a large majority.

Presidency

Although Eisenhower cut taxes and hoped to curb the role of the federal government, world tensions during the Cold War led him to request large budgets for military purposes. They were the highest ever submitted to Congress in peacetime. Eisenhower also won the 1956 election, with an even bigger victory, if possible, over Stevenson.

Eisenhower was shocked by the Holocaust, but said he would not have supported the establishment of Israel had he been president in 1948. However, once this state was established "we have to live with it." During Eisenhower's tenure, a few incidents strained the U.S.-Israel relationship: the Israeli Jordan River irrigation project, the Qibya massacre, and the Suez War. Gradually the relationship became diplomatically friendly .Eisenhower disagreed with the Israeli project to divert Jordan River water to Israel. There was a beginning of intention to withhold financial aid for that country (without the outside world knowing). Just then in mid-October 1953 came the massacre in Qibya (killing 60/69 ? inhabitants) by an Israeli Unit 101 (led by Ariel Sharon). This was in retaliation for the murder of two residents of the Jewish town of Yehud . It completed Eisenhower's displeasure.Three years later there was the Suez Crisis of 1956: Eisenhower put an end to the conspiracy of the United Kingdom , France and Israel whose armies penetrated Egypt. He forced Israel to leave the Sinai.The fuss in the US over the Qibya massacre prompted friends of Israel in the US and Israelis to start defending Israel in the US. The Israel Lobby (which we now know as AIPAC) came into being. The Eisenhower administration suspected this first lobby club of being paid by Israel and did not want it. Thereupon the group gained dues-paying members....

In 1957, Eisenhower made a momentous social policy decision. He forced a Supreme Court ruling that would have ensured that segregated schools for whites and blacks were abolished. Arkansas State Governor Orval Faubus called in the National Guard to prevent white and black from attending the same school in the state capital of Little Rock. Eisenhower sent in federal troops.

In 1953, following the death of Soviet leader Stalin, Eisenhower sought opportunities for Cold War relaxation with the countries behind the Iron Curtain. He had come to power at the height of the witch hunt against communists led by Senator Joseph McCarthy. Moreover, Eisenhower's Secretary of State, John Foster Dulles, was obsessed with combating what he called the threat to the world posed by revolutionary communism. The United States therefore supported the nationalist-Chinese government of Chiang Kai-shek in Taiwan against Mao

Zedong's China and increased support for the corrupt regime in South Vietnam, came to the aid of dictatorial regimes in the Middle East with military and economic support, and opposed President Nasser of Egypt.

International tension eased when Eisenhower received Soviet leader Khrushchev on a state visit in 1959. An agreed-upon return visit was angrily cancelled by the Russians after an American U2 reconnaissance plane was shot down over Russian territory, capturing pilot Gary Powers. But despite the tensions, Eisenhower's presidency can be seen in retrospect as a period of relative international peace and prosperity in America itself. The Korean War effectively ended in 1951, although the warring factions fought bitterly on until 1953, the year of the armistice.

After the presidency

In 1961, Eisenhower was unable to make himself available for the presidency after two terms (a president in the U.S. may only serve two terms). In his farewell address, he warned of the military-industrial complex. He was succeeded by the Democrat John F. Kennedy. He then devoted himself to writing his memoirs. In the spring of 1969, Dwight D. Eisenhower died at the age of 78 in a Washington D.C. hospital. He is buried on the grounds of his presidential library in Abilene, which opened in 1962. His wife Mamie was buried next to him after her death in 1979.

35. John F. Kennedy (1961-1963)

Democratic party | Vice president: Lyndon B. Johnson

"Those who dare to fail miserably can achieve greatly."

John Fitzgerald ("Jack") **Kennedy** Brookline (Massachusetts), May 29, 1917 - Dallas (Texas), November 22, 1963), also known by his initials **JFK**, was an American politician of the Democratic Party. As of January 20, 1961, he was the 35th and youngest elected president of the United States until he was assassinated on November 22, 1963, at the age of 46, during an official visit in an open limousine, in Dallas.

To the general public, Kennedy became known as the president who announced American plans to put a man on the moon in order to win the space race with the Soviet Union. In addition, his prematurely aborted term was marked by the Cuba crisis and increasingly strong American interference in the Vietnam War and his attempt to stop the arms race. Kennedy, however, was a leader more pragmatic than ideologically inspired.

Lifetime

Young years

Kennedy came from a Roman Catholic family of Irish origin. His mother's name was Rose Kennedy. His father Joseph (Joe) Kennedy was a politician and stone wealthy businessman. The couple had nine children. The family was also jokingly called the *unofficial royal family of the United States* and the *Kennedy clan* after Kennedy's election to the presidency, because so many influential people came from it.

Kennedy proved highly intelligent and had good school records, but he suffered from a lingering gastrointestinal illness early on and later severe back problems that would torment him for the rest of his life. He lived and studied in London for some time and before the war made a trip through Europe, on which he wrote a sharp analytical report containing warnings against Hitler, entitled "Why England Slept" about Britain's part in the Munich Treaty, as his graduate thesis in 1940, a thesis that subsequently became a bestseller as a book published. He graduated cum laude from Harvard with a degree in international relations.

During the war, he served as a lieutenant in the Navy although he was initially physically disqualified. However, thanks to the influence of his family, he managed to be placed in a combat position, something that could be beneficial in later elections.

One day after Japan bombed Pearl Harbor (on December 7, 1941), Kennedy was deployed to the Pacific. There he commanded a motor torpedo boat (the PT-109) that was overrun by the Japanese cruiser Amagiri near the Solomon Islands and sank, after which he still managed to rescue his crew with a courageous action. After the boat sank, Kennedy and the survivors swam for four hours in the sea before reaching an island 5.6 km away (Kasolo Island or Kennedy Island). Kennedy, who had been part of Harvard's swim team, pulled an injured crew member in the process. Because Kasolo Island is only 100 meters in diameter and there was no food to be found, Kennedy and his men swam to another island (Olasana Island). Because Japanese ships passed by regularly in this area, this trip was not without danger. After living on coconuts for 10 days, Kennedy and his men were discovered by local residents and finally rescued. For his demonstrated

courage and perseverance, Kennedy received the Navy and Marine
Corps Medal. To reporters who asked him how he became a war hero,
Kennedy joked "because they sunk my boat."

As a result of injuries sustained in this action and other ailments, such
as Addison's disease (for which no proper medication had been
developed at the time), Kennedy suffered from severe back pain. Out
of public view, therefore, he often walked on crutches. Although
outwardly Kennedy gave the impression of being an extraordinarily
healthy man, in reality he was not. He was under constant medical
supervision and had a body physician.

Kennedy had a lively interest in women early on and had a large
number of mistresses, including longtime Danish journalist Inga Arvad
in Washington in the 1940s, who was suspected of being a Nazi spy. It
is also alleged that Kennedy had a relationship during his marriage with
Marilyn Monroe, who had sung to him so seductively on his forty-fifth
birthday (*Happy Birthday, Mr. President*). However, evidence for this is
lacking. He had been married since 1953 to Jacqueline Bouvier, with
whom he had four children: Arabella (1956, stillborn), Caroline (1957),
John F. Jr. (1960-1999) and Patrick (1963, died two days after his
birth).

Political career

In 1946, Kennedy was elected Congressman for Boston and in 1952 as
a Senator. In 1956 he wrote "Profiles in Courage" about U.S. senators
who, at the risk of their careers, took positions that differed from those
of their party. This book received the journalistic Pulitzer Prize for
biography in 1957.

As a Congressman, Kennedy first visited French Indo-China, where the
First Indochinese War was underway at the time. In 1956, after the
founding of North and South Vietnam, he visited the region again.

Presidency

John F. Kennedy was elected the 35th president of the U.S. in 1960
after a narrow electoral victory (half a percent difference). over the
Republican and incumbent Vice President Richard Nixon. His running
mate was Lyndon B. Johnson, who then became his vice president.
Kennedy's presidency was strongly pragmatic; historian Barbara
Tuchman characterizes Kennedy as "neither progressive nor
conservative (...) a man of quick wit and strong ambition who was able
to articulate many lofty principles convincingly, eloquently, and even

mercifully, while his actions were not always consistent with them. (...) In the Kennedy camp, idealists were usually called 'whiners' or 'sentimental do-gooders.'"

Kennedy was not easily manipulated and showed early on who was in charge. After the failed Bay of Pigs invasion, Kennedy fired two senior CIA bosses and reportedly threatened to "shatter the CIA into a thousand pieces and scatter it in the wind." Kennedy also wanted to fire J. Edgar Hoover, who had been the director of the FBI since time immemorial. He changed his mind when this plan, because of its political ramifications, proved unfeasible. Kennedy's presidency was also characterized by his pursuit of peace and his humanity. All of this earned him supporters, but also created opponents in high places.

Kennedy's presidency began in an economically prosperous time. However, there were many points of conflict in the country. Racism was especially prevalent in the South and there was strict racial segregation in public life, similar to apartheid in South Africa. Resistance to this grew, partly under the influence of the Rev. Martin Luther King. Many civil rights fighters were inspired by Kennedy's message of progress, but in practice received no support from the president. Kennedy believed that the elimination of racial segregation was a matter for the individual states and not for the federal government. Only when federal laws were violated (such as the refusal to serve black travelers on bus trips between different U.S. states) did he intervene. The black population had to wait for President Johnson, Kennedy's successor, to introduce legislation against discrimination based on skin color.

Foreign Policy

From the very beginning, the Cold War predominated in Kennedy's foreign policy, which was co-determined by Republican Secretary of Defense Robert McNamara. The National Liberation Front of South Vietnam had been established in December 1960, and two weeks before Kennedy's inauguration on January 20, 1961, Nikita Khrushchev, the Russian president, had promised full Soviet support for the "national liberation wars" in Vietnam, Cuba, and elsewhere. Kennedy referred to this in his inaugural address as the "hour of greatest danger" to freedom. Already in the first ten days of Kennedy's presidency, a plan was launched to use American money and personnel to expand the South Vietnamese armed forces by 20,000 soldiers and 32,000 paramilitaries. Interference in the Vietnamese civil war intensified; by early 1963, there were 17,000 U.S. military personnel present in South Vietnam.

Vietnam

Congress was kept out of the decision-making process on Vietnam; to accusations from Republican quarters that he was "not forthright" with his people, Kennedy replied in February 1962 that "no combat troops in the usual sense of the word had been sent there." The main activities of the U.S. military in Vietnam were troop transport, training of South Vietnamese men, air support in anti-guerrilla operations, and defoliation of forests by Agent Orange and others (beginning in 1961). The number of American deaths in the area during Kennedy's first year in office was 14, the following year 109. Under American leadership, the odds seemed to be turning for South Vietnam; violent deportation of the South Vietnamese rural population by its own government, incidentally, also played a major role in this, as it allowed the "Vietcong" guerrillas to be denied access to food.

Kennedy played a role in the escalation of the war in Vietnam, having supported a successful military coup against Vietnamese President Ngô Đình Diệm, but not his assassination. Diệm was opposed to greater U.S. military involvement in Vietnam and doubted his country's alliance with the United States.

The Bay of Pigs Invasion

Soon Kennedy had to deal with a legacy of his predecessor, President Eisenhower: a plan to invade Cuba by anti-Castro Cubans led by the CIA and others. Kennedy was informed by his staff and decided to go ahead with this plan. Kennedy assured the American people that the country would not become involved in this itself. At the last minute, the CIA wanted permission to use American forces because the invasion with the anti-Castro Cubans failed. Kennedy refused and the invasion ended in a major fiasco. Hundreds of men died or were captured. For a high ransom, Kennedy was later able to "buy" them from Castro. This incident became known as the Bay of Pigs Invasion and the Bay of Pigs Fiasco. Kennedy gave a televised speech in which he took full responsibility for the blunder.

Journey to the Moon

Kennedy gave space exploration a huge boost during his presidency after the Soviets took a lead in the space race. In 1961, he proposed to the U.S. Congress that money be made available for a trip to the moon. Kennedy, however, questioned whether this trip should be a national issue. In a lecture to the United Nations on September 20, 1963, he indicated that he saw possibilities of making this trip in cooperation with the Soviet Union. Kennedy did not get the chance to elaborate on that proposal; two months later he was assassinated.

Cuba Crisis

In the second half of his presidency, international Cold War tensions intensified and culminated in the Cuba crisis, which could have turned into World War III. Nuclear missiles were involved and Khrushchev had threatened to shoot them down. Kennedy played bluff poker at the highest level, but emerged victorious on October 28, 1962. His diplomatic resolution of the crisis increased his popularity.

Israel

He made it possible for Israel to buy American Hawk anti-aircraft missiles in 1962. The State Department telegram states: "In view of the build-up in the region of offensive air armament and missile systems, we feel compelled to respond positively to Israel's request to be able to buy defensive short-range Ground-to-air interceptor missile systems.After Israel had kept it hidden for years, he got wind of Israeli nuclear activities near Dimona in the Negev . Released documents show that in 1963, President John Kennedy gave Israeli Prime Minister Levi Eshkol a dire warning that U.S. support for the young country would be "seriously jeopardized" if Israel did not allow the periodic inspections of Israel's nuclear reactor that he requested. He insisted on semi-annual U.S. inspections. He was furious, because in the Cold War with two nuclear superpowers facing each other, he was very attached to non-proliferation . However, the agreements that were subsequently made with the Israelis were so weak that, in fact, there were hardly any real inspections. The American inspectors therefore ultimately had only suspicions .

Statements

Kennedy was a gifted speaker with a strong charisma that stood out to people throughout the Western world. He became an icon of the Western camp during the Cold War. On his visits abroad, he always received enthusiastic attention, such as in Berlin, where he stood on the balcony of Rathaus Schöneberg and uttered the legendary words *"Ich bin ein Berliner."* Another of his much-quoted statements is *"Ask not what your country can do for you, ask what you can do for your country"*, which was part of his inauguration speech.

Some other striking and still widely quoted statements related to the early 1960s expressed intention to *"put people on the moon"* within ten years (and bring them back safely). This would also happen with the Apollo program, which was then underway. From his speech to the United Nations General Assembly in September 1961 come the statements that this organization would be *"the only alternative to war"* and that *"mankind must put an end to war, otherwise war will put an end to mankind."*

Murder

On November 22, 1963, at 12:30 CST (18:30 UTC), Kennedy was fatally wounded by two rifle bullets, one through the head and one through his back, while being driven in an open presidential limousine across Dealey Plaza in Dallas, Texas. His driving tour was part of a public tour of Texas, organized in part for his eventual re-election in 1964.

Kennedy was the fourth President of the United States to be assassinated and the eighth to die in the line of duty. Two official investigations led to the conclusion that Lee Harvey Oswald, working in the Dealey Plaza textbook warehouse, was the assassin. According to the Warren Commission investigation, Oswald acted alone; according to the House of Representatives Committee of Inquiry investigation, there was at least one other shooter. Kennedy's assassination is still a subject of speculation and has provided material for many conspiracy theories.

Two days after Kennedy's assassination, Oswald was murdered at the Dallas police station by nightclub owner Jack Ruby, preventing him from being arraigned and from being tried.

The grave of John F. Kennedy is located in Arlington National Cemetery, Virginia, near the Pentagon. With an "eternal flame," it is a place of remembrance for its many visitors.

After Kennedy's assassination, Jim Garrison, the district attorney in New Orleans, led an extensive investigation into the circumstances surrounding it. This eventually led to a trial for conspiracy against the businessman Clay Shaw, who was, however, acquitted.

Honors

Kennedy's name lives on, among other things, in the John F. Kennedy International Airport (formerly *Idlewild*) in the Queens borough of New York, and after his death his successor determined that the launch base at Cape Canaveral in Florida would henceforth be called the

Kennedy Space Center. In the mid-1960s the aircraft carrier the USS John F. Kennedy, the only ship in the John F. Kennedy class, was built in the US. The great impression he had made became clear when, within a few months after his death, major streets and squares were also named after him in Europe. On January 9, 1964, the Rivierenlaan in Amsterdam was renamed President Kennedylaan. In Antwerp, a tunnel under the Scheldt was named after him. In Ghent, a bridge over the Moervaart was named after him.

36. Lyndon B. Johnson (1963-1969)

Democratic party | Vice president: Hubert Humphrey

"Books and ideas are the most effective weapons against intolerance and ignorance."

Lyndon Baines Johnson (also known by his intials **LBJ**) (Stonewall (Texas), August 27, 1908 - there, January 22, 1973) was the 36th president of the United States.

Political career and election as president

Johnson was a Democratic Party politician and was a delegate for the 10th District of the state of Texas from 1937 to 1949. He then served as a senator for Texas until 1961. In the 1960 U.S. presidential election, Johnson was a candidate for the Democratic Party nomination. He lost the nomination to John F. Kennedy, who chose Johnson as his running mate. Together with Johnson, Kennedy defeated Republican candidate Richard Nixon and his running mate Henry Cabot Lodge Jr.

On November 22, 1963, President Kennedy was assassinated during a tour of the city of Dallas. Johnson, himself a Texan, acted as host during this trip; Kennedy still visited his ranch. Johnson rode along in the same parade, but was not hit. He was sworn in that same day as the 36th president of the United States. In the 1964 U.S. presidential election, he and running mate Hubert Humphrey were widely re-elected, defeating Republican candidate Barry Goldwater and his running mate William Miller.

Great Society

In the U.S., Johnson is almost unanimously described as an extraordinarily skilled and shrewd politician who managed to get many of his social plans through the U.S. Congress. He gave these social policies the name Great Society. Among other things, he introduced Medicare, health insurance for the elderly. He also started legislation to combat environmental pollution. In addition, Johnson was active in the field of civil rights. For example, he managed to pass the Civil Rights Act of 1964, which abolished segregation. On August 6, 1965, he signed the Voting Rights Act, which exponentially increased the number of black voters and elected officials. In early 1966, he appointed Robert C. Weaver as Secretary of Planning and Housing, the first black American to become a member of a U.S. government. He also appointed Thurgood Marshall as the first black chief justice.

Vietnam War

Johnson had inherited the Vietnam conflict from John F. Kennedy, but under LBJ's presidency the conflict would derail into an open war. From the Tonkin Incident in 1964 until the end of his presidency in 1969, the war would be stepped up and up. However, the war thus began to cost more and more money, causing the U.S. economy to decline in the late 1960s and preventing LBJ from realizing his *Great Society* in the way he wanted. The war led to much opposition, including within his own party. For the 1968 presidential election, Johnson found a formidable rival in Senator Robert F. Kennedy. On March 31, 1968, Johnson held a live televised press conference in the Grand Ballroom of the Hilton Chicago, in which he announced that he was not running for re-election. He left the White House on January 20, 1969. Johnson's successor Nixon promised an honorable end to the Vietnam War.

Israel

Johnson took over from France as Israel's major foreign arms supplier. In 1964 he gave $52 million in civilian aid, Skyhawk planes and Patton tanks and other military equipment. These weapons would make a difference in 1967 during the Six Day War, for example in the first surprise attack that took out the Egyptian air force. From that year to the present, the U.S. would increasingly play this role of lender and arms supplier to Israel.

Incidentally, he had been furious when news had reached him that Israel had resorted to war (in 1967). He would continue to regard this decision as a great mistake all his life.

Death

Johnson died of cardiac arrest on January 22, 1973. He was 64 years old. Johnson's widow, Lady Bird Johnson, died 34 years later.

37. Richard Nixon (1969-1974)

Republican party | Vice presidents: Spiro Agnew and Gerald Ford

*"Always remember, others may hate you, but those
who hate you don't win unless you hate them, and
then you destroy yourself."*

Richard Milhous Nixon (Yorba Linda, January 9, 1913 - New York,
April 22, 1994) was an American politician of the Republican Party. He
was the 37th president of the United States from 1969 to 1974.

Prior to that, Nixon served as Representative for California (12th
District) from 1947 to 1950 when he was elected as a Senator for
California. In 1952 he was chosen by Dwight D. Eisenhower as his
running mate for the 1952 presidential election which they also won.
Nixon resigned from the Senate to become the 36th Vice President of
the United States. After two terms as Eisenhower's vice president,
Nixon ran for the 1960 U.S. presidential election. He won the

nomination for the Republican Party but lost to Senator for Massachusetts John F. Kennedy. After a failed attempt in 1962 to become governor of California, Nixon retired from politics and resumed his old profession of law.

However, Nixon made a successful comeback in politics by winning the Republican Party's nomination for the 1968 U.S. presidential election. Together with *running mate* Spiro Agnew, he defeated the Democratic Party candidate, Vice President Hubert Humphrey. Nixon also won the 1972 U.S. presidential election, in which he defeated Democratic Party candidate George McGovern in one of the largest political victories in the U.S. presidential election ever.

Nixon's presidency was marked by the Vietnam War and the growing opposition to it in the United States, pursuing a policy of relaxation with the Soviet Union, and establishing relations with the People's Republic of China. Also during his presidency, the Environmental Protection Agency and the Drug Enforcement Administration were established and Apollo 11 performed the first moon landing.

Nixon resigned on August 9, 1974 when his position had become untenable due to the Watergate scandal. This made him the first president of the United States to voluntarily resign. He was succeeded by his second vice president, Gerald Ford.

Biography

Youth and early career

Nixon was born into a poor family in Yorba Linda, California. His father owned a grocery store and a gas station. He grew up with the rules and customs of the conservative, Christian Quaker community. During his political career, he often referred to his simple origins.

Nixon was a talented boy, but his family could not financially afford to put him through an expensive university. Instead, he took classes at a local Quaker school, Whittier College, where he graduated in 1934. He was then offered a scholarship to law school at Harvard University, which he had to refuse because he could not be missed at home. Later he went, on scholarship, to the newly established (and now prestigious) law school at Duke University.

In 1946, he won a seat in the U.S. Congress. His campaigns at this stage of his career were characterized by an anti-communist tone and aggressive style.

In 1950, Nixon was elected senator, defeating actress and congresswoman Helen Gahagan, whom he had accused of having communist sympathies during the campaign.

Nixon became the 36th vice president in 1952, under Dwight D. Eisenhower.Noteworthy about his vice presidency is that he actually ran the country three times; in all cases Eisenhower was ill. Furthermore, as president of the Senate (one of the duties of the vice president), he openly supported Senator Joseph McCarthy and his pursuit of (alleged) communists.

The first time Nixon competed for the presidency was in 1960, against John F. Kennedy, a close friend and the first to congratulate him on his vice presidency in 1952. He narrowly lost this battle. One of the factors that played a role was the first American televised debate between presidential candidates. Nixon refused television makeup (despite his stubble) and felt bad because he was recovering from major knee surgery. He expected to win voters with his knowledge and experience in foreign affairs, but his appearance (sickly, pale and sweating) contrasted too much with that of the sun-tanned, charismatic Kennedy (although Kennedy also had poor health and his "healthy tan" was probably caused by Addison's Disease). In addition, many people did not see the opportunities of television, while Kennedy, like no one else, did see the advantages of the new medium and knew how to capitalize on them. Later research showed that people who had followed the debate on the radio largely indicated Nixon as the winner, while the television viewers had a clear preference for Kennedy.

In 1962 he lost the race for the governorship of California and in the ensuing speech declared that it would be his last press conference: "You won't have Nixon to kick around anymore".

Presidency

After this dip in Nixon's career, he made another bid for the presidency in 1968 after a stint as a lawyer in New York, defeating then-Vice President Hubert Humphrey.

The major issues from his tenure are:

- Normalization of diplomatic relations with the Communist People's Republic of China.

- Establishment of the Environmental Protection Agency, an agency to protect human health and the environment.

- Establishment of the Drug Enforcement Administration, an agency to combat the illegal distribution of narcotics.

- In 1971, he ended the exchange of U.S. dollars for gold. This put an end to the gold standard and the system of fixed exchange rates agreed upon at Bretton Woods in 1944. This action is also known as the Nixon shock.

- The withdrawal of U.S. troops from Vietnam.

- The start of the Spaceshuttle program.

Nixon reopened peace negotiations with North Vietnam, which had been extremely difficult. His Secretary of State, Henry Kissinger, played an important role in this. Simultaneously with the peace negotiations, ties with China and the Soviet Union were strengthened. This policy is also known as triangular diplomacy. In 1973, this led in part to the Paris Accords, which allowed the U.S. to stop its interference in the Vietnam War.

Nixon's foreign policy was characterized by a spirit of rapprochement. By strengthening relations with China, the end of the Cold War was in sight and the Vietnam War could slowly be ended, with the help of the so-called *Nixon doctrine*, which stated that America's Asian allies were once again responsible for their own military defense, to which end some loyal allies (such as Iran) were militarily strengthened. In 1973, through the CIA, he helped Augusto Pinochet in his successful coup in Chile, which deposed the socialist Salvador Allende.

That same year, when - on the Jewish holiday Yom Kippur - the Israeli army at the Suez Canal had been surprisingly attacked by the Egyptian army and driven back some distance into the Sinai Desert, Nixon came to Israel's aid via a major airlift with massive arms shipments (567 US Airforce airlifts, in addition El Al flights and shipments by sea). The Sinai had been conquered from Egypt in 1967 during the Six Day War.In the years that followed, it was US envoy Henry Kissinger who mediated between Israel and Egypt. By the press that followed him on his trips between the various capitals, this was called "shuttle diplomacy." His mediation concerned the separation of forces between, respectively, the armies of Israel and Egypt (on the Sinai Peninsula) and the armies of Israel and Syria (on the Golan Heights. For Syria too had attacked Israeli positions on the Golan Heights with the intention of recapturing this Syrian territory captured by Israel in 1967.

In his domestic policy, Nixon concentrated more on strict legislation and less on social programs for racial integration and against poverty than his predecessors. His domestic policies were of the right-wing persuasion, and it has been argued that his electoral victory was the result of the resentment allegedly aroused among much of the white American population in the southern states in the turbulent 1960s, as a result of the federal government's imposition of the abolition of racial segregation.

Watergate

As a result of the Watergate scandal, Nixon resigned on August 9, 1974 to avoid impeachment. His successor Gerald Ford pardoned him in advance, a controversial decision.

After the presidency

Nixon managed to restore his reputation somewhat and developed (as yet) into a respected statesman. He made some unofficial trips to China and the Soviet Union, among others.

In 1977, British television producer David Frost made a series of interviews with Nixon, covering different periods of his presidency. Nixon made excuses (in so many words) to the American people for the Watergate affair.

Nixon died of a stroke in New York in April 1994 at the age of 81. He was buried on the grounds of his presidential library, the *Richard Nixon Presidential Library and Museum* in Yorba Linda. His wife Pat Nixon, who had died ten months earlier, is also buried here.

38. Gerald Ford (1974-1977)

Republican party | Vice president: Nelson Rockefeller

---

*"The harder you work, the luckier you are, and I
worked like hell."*

Gerald Rudolph Ford Jr. (Omaha (Nebraska), July 14, 1913 - Rancho
Mirage (California), December 26, 2006) was the 38th president of the
United States. Before that, he was the 40th Vice President of the
United States, from 1973 to 1974 under President Richard Nixon. He
was a politician of the Republican Party.

Biography

Youth and early career

Ford was born *Leslie Lynch King Jr.* and raised in Grand Rapids, Michigan as the son of Leslie Lynch King Sr. and Dorothy Ayer Gardner Ford. He was renamed Gerald Rudolph Ford Jr. after being adopted as a child by his mother's second husband. He was a good American football player. His *University of Michigan* team was undefeated for two seasons. In 1934, Ford was chosen as the *most valuable player.* He then attended law school at Yale University.

During World War II, he served on an aircraft carrier, among others, which was involved in battles off Saipan and the Philippines. In December 1944, he nearly lost his life when his ship was caught in a hurricane. In 1946, he left the service as a lieutenant colonel and joined a law firm.

Ford chose a political career in 1948 and was elected to the House of Representatives for the Republican Party in 1949. During his first campaign, he visited many farmers and promised them that he would come and milk their cows if elected. He was a representative for Michigan's 5th district from 1949 to 1973. As a Congressman, he was the most active member of the Warren Commission that investigated the assassination of President Kennedy. From 1965 to 1973 he was group leader of the Republicans. During this period he was a declared opponent of Democratic President Lyndon Johnson; he thought his social plans went too far and the military commitment in Vietnam was not far enough.

Vice President

In 1973, Vice President Spiro Agnew resigned for corruption. Shortly before that, a provision had been added to the Constitution authorizing Congress to fill a vacancy of Vice President. Until then, the *Speaker* of the House of Representatives had been the interim successor to the President. Ford's appointment was smoothly approved, since it was already likely at that time that Nixon would have to resign sooner or later. Ford took the oath during a simple ceremony in the House of Representatives. As vice president, Ford defended Nixon as long as possible during the Watergate scandal, but eventually he too had to recognize that the president's position had become untenable.

President

Ford became president on August 9, 1974 after the resignation of President Richard Nixon due to the Watergate scandal. Ford is the only person in American history so far to become president without having been elected by the people in (vice) presidential elections. Previous deputies such as Johnson had been the *running-mate* of their predecessor.

Shortly after taking office, Ford pardoned Nixon. This decision was greatly resented by much of the American people. Ford continued the policy of relaxation with the then Soviet Union initiated by his predecessor. In 1975, he allowed the U.S. military to pull out of Vietnam for good. During Ford's tenure as president, the United States was still facing economic problems.

During his presidency, two assassination attempts were made on Ford. On September 5, 1975, a follower of Charles Manson managed to point a gun at his abdomen. Seventeen days later, a second attack was foiled.

Ford retained Henry Kissinger as a mediator. Anwar Sadat convinced him and Kissinger to push for a second agreement between Israel and Egypt on Sinai in 1975. However, the negotiations for this second agreement were much more challenging and lasted several months. After initial discussions with the Egyptians and Israelis, Ford concluded that the Israelis were not as cooperative as Egypt. In March, he called for a reassessment of U.S. policy toward Israel. This led to outrage in the U.S. Senate, and Ford moderated his tone during the early summer. Finally, by August, an agreement was in sight. Kissinger completed the second Egyptian-Israeli withdrawal agreement, known as the Sinai Interim Agreement or Sinai II, which Egypt and Israel signed on September 4. This agreement resulted in the withdrawal of Israeli forces further east in Sinai and the formation of a UN buffer zone in their place. With the agreement, the U.S. also committed funding to establish three manned stations and three unmanned electronic sensor fields in Sinai.

In the 1976 Republican primaries, Ford won only narrowly over opposing candidate Ronald Reagan, later president. As a Republican presidential candidate, Ford was surpassed by his Democratic opponent Jimmy Carter in the November 1976 presidential election. Major reasons for the loss were the impending economic slowdown and the gratification of his predecessor Richard Nixon.

After his presidency

By 1980, Ford had almost become Ronald Reagan's *running mate*, but he wanted some new powers as vice president, especially in the area of foreign policy. Therefore, Reagan ultimately chose George H.W. Bush. After his presidency, Ford developed somewhat as a spokesman for the left wing of the Republicans; for example, he repeatedly spoke out against a ban on abortion and in favor of equal rights for homosexuals. He was one of the few Republicans to oppose the impeachment (removal proceedings) of Democratic President Bill Clinton.

After his presidency, Ford became good friends with Jimmy Carter, the man who defeated him in 1976. Together, in 2000, they made an attempt to break the deadlock that developed during the presidential election.

In recent years, Ford has been struggling with his health. In 2000, he suffered a mild stroke twice, and in 2004, for the first time in his life, he was unable to attend the Republican Convention. He was later hospitalized three times, including for pneumonia.

On December 26, 2006, Gerald Ford died at the age of 93. As of December 30, 2006, there were six days of national mourning in the United States. On January 3, 2007, Ford was buried.

39. Jimmy Carter (1977-1981)

Democratic party | Vice president: Walter Mondale

"We must adjust to changing times and still hold to unchanging principles."

James Earl (Jimmy) Carter Jr. (Plains (Georgia), October 1, 1924) is an American former Democratic Party politician. He was the 39th president of the United States from 1977 to 1981.

Carter, a farmer by trade, owned a peanut plantation in Georgia and was governor of that state from 1971 to 1975. He ran for the 1976 U.S. presidential election and defeated the incumbent, Republican Gerald Ford. In the 1980 presidential election, Carter was defeated by Republican candidate Ronald Reagan.

After his presidency, Carter pursued activism and wrote more than twenty books. In 2002, Carter was awarded the Nobel Peace Prize for his commitment to human rights.

Since the death of George H.W. Bush on November 30, 2018, Jimmy Carter is the oldest living former president of the United States of America and, as of March 22, 2019, the oldest former president of the United States ever.

Biography

Presidency

Carter inherited gigantic economic and financial problems from his predecessors. The federation was deep in the red due to the Vietnam War, while the self-confidence of the population had been severely eroded. The interest burden combined with the oil crisis and the unwillingness of business to invest led to a new phenomenon in the economy: stagflation. During Carter's term, the answer to this problem was not found.

Carter had more success in his foreign policy. Within his tenure, he managed to mediate a peace treaty between Egyptian President Anwar Sadat and Israeli Prime Minister Menachem Begin. This resulted in the Camp David Accords. However, soon after this success, in Carter's last year in office, 52 American citizens and military personnel were taken hostage in Iran at the U.S. Embassy in Tehran. This hostage situation lasted 444 days.

In his foreign policy, Carter saw the importance of human rights. This went against the policies of Richard Nixon's administration, which often turned a blind eye to friendly regimes. The Carter administration ended support for the longtime U.S.-backed Nicaraguan dictator Somoza and gave the new administration millions in aid.

The main clash between the importance of human rights and U.S. self-interest arose from Carter's ties to the Shah of Iran. The Shah had, since World War II, been a strong Middle Eastern supporter of America. His regime, however, was brutal and oppressive. Although Carter praised the Shah as a wise and valuable leader, the U.S. did not intervene when a popular uprising broke out against the Shah's monarchy.

The Shah was removed from the throne and exiled. Many have since seen the declining American support for the Shah as the main cause of his rapid revolution. Carter was initially willing to acknowledge the revolutionary movement, but his efforts proved unsuccessful.

In 1979, the Shah was granted political asylum and medical treatment in the US. In response, Iranian militants besieged the U.S. Embassy in Tehran only to take 52 Americans hostage and demand the Shah's extradition to Iran for trial and execution. Despite the fact that the Shah would leave the U.S. later that year to die in Egypt, the hostage crisis continued. A failed liberation operation on April 25, 1980, made the

Revolutionary Guards even more stubborn, and the issue thus dominated the last year of Carter's presidency.

According to Carter's security adviser Zbigniew Brzeziński, the Soviet invasion of Afghanistan in December 1979 was a response to the U.S. military presence there. After the invasion, Carter announced the Carter Doctrine, which stated that the U.S. would not allow any other power to gain control of the Persian Gulf. Other responses by Carter included banning the participation of Americans in the 1980 Moscow Olympics and reinstating registration for military service.

To counter the Soviet occupation of Afghanistan, Carter and Zbigniew Brzeziński launched a $40 billion training program for Islamic fundamentalists in Pakistan and Afghanistan. In retrospect, it is well regarded as the cause of the instability of post-Soviet Afghan governments, which led to the rise of Islamic theocracy in the region.

In 1980, Jimmy Carter lost the presidential election to Ronald Reagan. He ingloriously disappeared from the scene, given lagging international tensions such as the hostage-taking of the U.S. Embassy in Iran. Ironically, on the day Carter left as president, the hostages in Iran were released. It was later claimed that the late release of the hostages was the result of a deal between Reagan's campaign and the government of Iran, but this theory was never proven.

After his presidency

After his presidential career, Carter was widely appreciated for his humanitarian work. In 1982, he founded the Carter Center dedicated to human rights, the spread of democracy, the resolution of international conflicts, and the fight against diseases such as dracunculiasis and river blindness. He became good friends with his predecessor Gerald Ford. Together, in 2000, they made an attempt to break the deadlock that arose during the presidential election.

In 2002, Carter was awarded the Nobel Peace Prize "for decades of unwavering commitment to finding peaceful solutions to international conflicts and promoting democracy, human rights, and economic and social development." He played a mediating role in the Ogaden dispute between Somalia and Ethiopia, in Bosnia and Herzegovina and oversaw many elections, among others.

Carter strongly opposed the 2003 Iraq War. In March 2004, he condemned George W. Bush and Tony Blair for waging an unnecessary war "based on lies and misinterpretations" in order to remove Saddam Hussein. He claimed that Blair had allowed his judgment to be clouded by Bush's desire to end a war that his father had started.

In April 2006, Carter, along with Bill Clinton and Bill Underwood, director of Mercer University, initiated the *New Baptist Covenant*. The goal of the movement is to show that Baptism is not identical to the socially and culturally conservative Southern Baptist Convention, the largest Protestant church in the United States with 16 million members. The *New Baptist Covenant* primarily calls attention to poverty alleviation, environmental issues and conflicts worldwide. It is also committed to the integration of Baptist churches, which are often still separated by race. The initiative is supported by approximately 20 million American Baptists. Carter's own roots are in the Southern Baptist Convention, but he has difficulty with its conservative direction. He has been a Sunday school teacher almost all his life and serves as a deacon at Maranatha Baptist Church in his hometown of Plains.

Book on Palestinian peace agreement

In November 2006, the book *Palestine: Peace not Apartheid* was published. According to Carter, "The ultimate goal of my book was to present facts about the Middle East that are largely unknown in [the U.S. of] America, initiate discussion and help reopen peace talks (...)."

Carter argues in his book that "Israel's continued control and colonization of Palestinian land are the first obstacles to a coherent peace agreement in the Holy Land." Carter is the one who made possible the peace agreement between Egypt and Israel in 1978, the Camp David Accords, a peace that has since proven to be sustainable. He faced criticism for his book, which critics said was selective in its use of historical data and interpreted it only to Israel's disadvantage.

On a visit to Israel in April 2015, Prime Minister Benjamin Netanyahu and President Reuven Rivlin refused to meet with Carter after consulting with the Foreign Ministry and Israel's National Security Council. An Israeli security source did not want to cooperate with his team regarding his visit to Gaza to gauge Hamas' chances for peace.

As of 2014

In 2014, Carter, now 90 years old, went on another campaign. This time not for himself, but for his grandson Jason. Jason was the Democratic candidate for governor of Georgia, but was not elected.

In August 2015, Carter announced that during surgery on his liver, he had been diagnosed with cancer with metastases to the brain and other areas. In early December 2015, he was found to be cancer-free again. Carter was treated with the drug pembrolizumab, developed in Oss. After February 2016, no more treatments were needed.

In October 2017, Carter told a South Korean professor that he would like to mediate the conflict with North Korea. He would be willing to go to Pyongyang to negotiate with North Korean leader Kim Jong-un for "final peace. Carter's stance runs counter to that of the U.S. government. In 2011, Carter, together with former presidents of Finland and Ireland and a former prime minister of Norway, already visited North Korea. On that occasion he spoke with Kim Jong-un's father Kim Jong-il, among others.

40. Ronald Reagan (1981-1989)

Republican party | Vice president: George H. W. Bush

"The greatest leader is not necessarily the one who does the greatest things. He is the one that gets the people to do the greatest things."

Ronald Wilson Reagan (Tampico (Illinois), February 6, 1911 - Los Angeles, June 5, 2004) was the 40th president of the United States from 1981 to 1989. Reagan, after a career as an actor, went into politics. A member of the Republican Party, he served as the 33rd Governor of California from 1967 to 1975, before becoming the 40th President of the United States as a successor to Democrat Jimmy Carter and ruling the United States for two terms in office - from 1981 to 1989.

Reagan's first term as president was characterized primarily by on-the-ground economic policies, later called *Reaganomics*, with an emphasis on tax cuts to stimulate economic growth, restrictions on the supply of money to reduce inflation, deregulation of the economy, a reduction in government spending, and a limitation on the power of labor unions. He was re-elected president in 1984. His second term was dominated by foreign events, such as the end of the Cold War, the 1986 bombing of Libya carried out by him, and the uncovering of the Iran-Contra affair that caused his government great image damage: it turned out that weapons had been secretly supplied to Iran, with the proceeds of which had financed insurgents in Nicaragua. Reagan publicly described the Soviet Union as "the empire of evil," and supported anti-communist movements worldwide. However, Reagan simultaneously sought a diplomatic way out of the arms race between the US and the Soviet Union; this resulted in the conclusion of the INF Treaty in which both countries agreed to destroy a large number of (nuclear) missiles.

Biography

Youth

Reagan was the son of shoe salesman and storyteller Jack Reagan (of Irish-Catholic descent) and Nelle Clyde Wilson Reagan (of Scottish-English descent). He was born in Tampico, but grew up in Dixon. His first job was as a lifeguard at the Rock River in Lowell Park, near Dixon, in 1927. He rescued 77 persons in this position, and he recorded each rescue attempt by making a mark on a piece of wood. He then enjoyed his education at Eureka College, where he earned degrees in economics and sociology. While in college, he excelled in politics, sports and theater and was a member of the soccer team and captain of the swim team. While in college, Reagan led a student revolt against the president of the college.

Acting career

After college, Reagan began his career at a regional radio station as a sportscaster. The film company Warner Bros offered him a contract in 1937; he spent the next few years in Hollywood as an actor in B-movies, where, as Reagan joked, the producers *didn't want them good, they wanted them Thursday*. Although his roles were often overshadowed by those of others, he received good reviews for his acting skills. Reagan's first major role was the lead in the film *Love is on the Air* (1937), and by the end of 1939 he had appeared in 19 films, including *Dark Victory*. Just before the film *Santa Fe Trail*, he played the role of George "The Gipper" Gipp in the feature film *Knute Rockne, all American*. This film later earned him the nickname "The Gipper". In 1941, he was voted the fifth most popular actor of the new generation in Hollywood. Reagan's favorite role was that of a man who was double amputee (*Kings Row*, 1942), in which he uttered the lines *Where's the rest of me?*; he later used these words as the title of his autobiography, which came out in 1965. Many critics today consider *Kings Row* to be one of Reagan's best films, although the film was cracked by New York Times critic Bosley Crowther, but nevertheless nominated for three Oscars.

Although Reagan called *Kings Row* the film that made him a star, he was unable to capitalize on the success because he was called into active duty by the U.S. Army at San Francisco; that was two months after the film was released. Nor would he regain star status in films in the future. In the postwar period, after nearly four years of service with the World War II stateside service in the first Motion Picture Unit, he resumed his film career with *The Voice of the Turtle*, *John loves Mary*, *The Hasty Heart*, *Bedtime for Bonzo*, *Cattle Queen of Montana*, *Tennessee's Partner*, *Hellcats of the Navy* and *The Killers* (his last film, a 1964 remake). During his film career, he often personally answered his fan mail.

Movies

Military service

Reagan's career, like that of many other actors in those years, was adversely affected by World War II. Just before its outbreak, he had signed a contract that made him one of the highest paid actors of the time. During the term of this contract, war broke out and he was called to active duty in the U.S. Army. He had taken 14 Army courses in the 1930s, during the time he was a reserve officer, and on April 29, 1937, was added as a private to troop B, 322nd cavalry in Des Moines. On May 25, 1937, he was promoted to second lieutenant in the reserve corps of cavalry officers. Because Reagan had bad eyes, he was not sent to Europe but deployed as a liaison officer at San Francisco Port with the Port and Transportation Office.

Reagan applied for transfer to the AAF on May 15, 1942 and was added to the AAF Public Relations and eventually placed with the First Motion Pictures Unit. Reagan returned to this unit upon completion of his tour of duty and was promoted to captain there on July 22, 1943. During this time he was a supporter of the Democratic Party. While serving with the First Motion Picture Unit in 1945 he was directly involved in the discovery of actress Marilyn Monroe. He then returned to Fort MacArthur, California, where he left active duty on December 9,

1945. By the end of the war, his unit had produced over 400 training films for the AAF.

After the war

At the end of the war, Reagan joined the HICCASP (*Hollywood Independent Citizens Committee of the Arts, Sciences and Professions*), a progressive association of Hollywood actors that defended the legacy of President Roosevelt's New Deal. Leading member Olivia de Havilland opposed the HICCASP's increasingly left-wing direction in 1946 and was supported by Reagan. When it became apparent that the organization had been infiltrated by members of the American Communist Party, De Havilland and Reagan resigned.

Work for the Screen Actors Guild

Reagan was first elected to the Board of Directors of the Screen Actors Guild in 1941. After World War II he resumed this work and in 1946 was elected third vice president. In 1947, the passage of a number of laws led to the resignation of the SAG president and six members of the board; Reagan was elected president in a special election; he was additionally elected to hold this position for seven more years, from 1947-1952 and in 1959. He led the SAG through difficult years, marked by a variety of squabbles, the *Taft-Hartley Act*, the *House Committee on Un-American Activities* (HUAC) hearings, and the era of the Black List. During the period of Mccarthyism, he arranged for the FBI to get names of actors he believed to be followers of communism. Reagan also testified about this before the House Un-American Activities Committee. He was a staunch anti-Communist and expressed support for democratic principles, about which he said, *I never as a citizen want to see our country become urged, by either fear or resentment of this group, that we ever compromise with any of our democratic principles through that fear or resentment.*

Career at General Electric

In 1950, in addition to his acting life, he went to work for the General Electric company (home appliances). He became the "advertising face" of GE and toured the country with a road show to promote its products. He also worked from time to time for television, then still a medium in its infancy. Ronald Reagan acted as "host" of a number of Saturday night programs, the most famous being GE Theater.

Marriages

In 1938, Reagan starred alongside actress Jane Wyman (1917-2007) in the film *Brother Rat*. They got engaged at the Chicago Theater and married on January 26, 1940 at the Wee Kirk o' the Heather church in Glendale. The couple had 2 children, Maureen (1941-2001) and Christine (1947, died after 1 day) and adopted a third child, Michael (1945). After a feud over Reagan's political aspirations, Wyman filed for divorce in 1948, citing Reagan's activities for the Screen Actors Guild as the reason, which had created an unbridgeable distance. Reagan was later the first and, until the election of Donald Trump in 2016, the only American president to be divorced.

Reagan met actress Nancy Davis (1921-2016) in 1949, after she approached him in his capacity as president of the Screen Actors Guild to help her with matters concerning her appearance on the Hollywood blacklist (on the list she had been mistaken for another Nancy Davis). They married quietly in the San Fernando Valley on March 4, 1952. The only guests were the actor William Holden and his wife Brenda Marshall. Ronald and Nancy had two children, Patti (1952) and Ron Jr. (1958).

41. George H. W. Bush (1989-1993)

Republican Party | Vice President: Dan Quayle

"I was offered a job on Wall Street by my uncle. But I wanted to get out. Make-it-on-my-own kinda thing."

George Herbert Walker Bush (Milton (Massachusetts), June 12, 1924 - Houston (Texas), November 30, 2018) was an American politician and diplomat of the Republican Party and the 41st president of the United States from 1989 to 1993.

An entrepreneur by trade, Bush previously served as a member of the House of Representatives for the 7th District of Texas from 1967 to 1971, ambassador to the United Nations under President Richard Nixon from 1971 to 1973, ambassador to China under President Gerald Ford from 1974 to 1975, and director of the Central Intelligence Agency (CIA) for President Ford from 1976 to 1977. During the 1980 presidential election, he was the *running mate* of presidential candidate

Ronald Reagan and then served as the 43rd Vice President of the United States from 1981 to 1989. For the 1988 presidential election, Bush was nominated as the presidential candidate for the Republican Party and defeated the candidate on behalf of the Democratic Party, Massachusetts Governor Michael Dukakis after which Bush was sworn in as the 41st President of the United States on January 20, 1989.

Biography

Youth

Bush was born into a political family. His father Prescott Bush was a banker and senator from Connecticut from 1952 to 1963. His mother, Dorothy Walker Bush, was the daughter of wealthy businessman and banker George Herbert Walker.

Bush attended high school at Phillips Academy in Andover, Massachusetts, where he became an early captain of the local baseball team.

In 1942, during World War II Bush joined U.S. Navy as a pilot of a Grumman TBF Avenger destroyer on an aircraft carrier. At the time, he was the youngest pilot ever. Bush distinguished himself several times. He was shot down by the Japanese during an attack on a radio station in the Pacific. After Bush jumped out of the plane, because the aircraft had become hopelessly uncontrollable, Bush hit the Grumman's tail with his head. Bush was not unconscious on impact and he managed to open his parachute. After floating in the sea for three hours on an inflatable raft, Bush was rescued by the U.S. submarine USS *Finback*.

After the war, he went to study commercial science at Yale, where he joined the Delta Kappa Epsilon sorority and the Skull and Bones secret society. On January 6, 1945, he married Barbara Pierce. Together they had six children, including George W. and John (Jeb) Bush. In 1948 Bush went to work in West Texas in the oil industry for Dresser Industries. Major shareholder of Dresser was Brown Brothers Harriman & Co. where Prescott Bush was a partner and actively involved in Dresser's management. The first job director Henry Neil Mallon gave him was for the International Derrick and Equipment Company (Ideco) in Odessa. Although coming from a well-to-do family, Bush made long days here with a lot of physical labor in order to learn about this side of the industry as well. In the first house, they shared the bathroom with two prostitutes, after which the family would move around Odessa two more times until Bush was able to work in California in 1949. In

California, the family lived in Ventura, Bakersfield and Compton until they returned to Texas and settled in Midland. In 1950, Bush and James Overby started the Bush-Overbey Oil Development Company. In 1953, the Liedtke brothers joined them in what would become the Zapata Petroleum Corporation. The following year the Zapata Off-Shore Company was formed of which Bush was president until 1966. Thus he established important contacts with the royal family of Saudi Arabia and the Bin Laden family.

Political career

In 1964 Bush ran for the U.S. Senate on behalf of Texas. In doing so, he challenged the incumbent Democratic senator Ralph Yarborough and focused his campaign on his support for the Civil Rights Act, which was intended to prevent any discrimination. This law was not at all popular with the Democrats, especially in the southern part of the US, which voted mainly Democrat. Yarborough was one of the few supporters of the law there. Bush played on this, but he still lost.

In 1966 and 1968 he had better luck and was elected as a delegate for Texas' 7th constituency to the House of Representatives. In 1970, he was urged by President Nixon to once again compete for a Senate seat. Again Bush lost, this time to Lloyd Bentsen. In 1971 Nixon appointed him ambassador to the United Nations. He retained this position until 1973. At the time of the Watergate scandal, Bush was asked by Nixon to chair the Republican National Committee (party leadership). After Nixon resigned as president, his successor Gerald Ford appointed Bush as U.S. ambassador to China, a position Bush held from 1974 to 1975. Bush was then nominated by President Ford to be the new director of the CIA. Bush held this position from 1976 until Jimmy Carter's presidency in 1977.

In 1980, Bush made his first bid for the presidency in the 1980 U.S. presidential election. He lost the Republican primaries to Ronald Reagan and became his running mate. Reagan chose George Bush over Gerald Ford for this. Together with Reagan, Bush defeated incumbent President Carter and his vice president Walter Mondale and thus became vice president of the United States. Four years later, in the 1984 U.S. presidential election, Reagan was re-elected president and Bush won a second term as vice president.

After eight years as vice president, Bush made another bid for the presidency in the 1988 presidential election. With Reagan's support, Bush won the Republican primaries by a wide margin. He continued that success against Democratic candidate Michael Dukakis and won the election along with running mate Dan Quayle. Bush was the first sitting vice president to be elected president since Martin Van Buren in 1836.

Presidency

As president, Bush tried to reconcile with the Democrats.

His first meeting with Soviet leader Mikhail Gorbachev, on a ship near Malta in December 1989, was seen as a new start for more relaxed relations between the United States and the Soviet Union.

In August 1990, Iraq, led by Saddam Hussein, conquered and occupied the neighboring country of Kuwait. Bush then, together with his Secretary of State James Baker and with the backing of the UN Security Council, organized an international coalition, which even included rival states such as Egypt and Syria, that liberated the country again in early 1991 during the brief Gulf War .

Now that he and his "coalition-of-the-willing" had won this Gulf War, he understood that a Middle East peace conference was necessary. To that end he committed himself - at the peak of his power now. The conference was held in Madrid. Israel sat down with its Arab enemies for the first time around the table. A delegation of (partyless!) Palestinians was accommodated by the Jordanian delegation. (Ultimately, however, it was through secret Israeli-Palestinian consultations in Oslo that the Oslo Accords came to a standstill.)With regard to the Israeli-Palestinian conflict, Bush proved able to show concrete "tough love" to both sides. In other words, to Israel as well. Israel needed a lot of money to accommodate the numerous Jews who were allowed to leave the Soviet Union. Bush made it a condition of cheap U.S. loans that Israel would not use them for the settlements planted/planned by Israel in Palestinian territory, which the U.S. considered illegal. Just before "Madrid" now, Israeli Prime Minister Yitzhak Shamir asked for a large loan and was infuriated by the condition. Shamir then believed he would get the loan through the US Congress by means of AIPAC. Bush stood his ground and Congress stood aloof, and when the loan was granted in the spring of 1992, it was with the clause that for every one billion dollars in loans to be guaranteed, the U.S. would deduct 200 million in proportion to Israel's planned illegal settlement construction.

Bush tried to reduce the huge budget deficit with severe austerity measures.

Presidential elections of 1992

In the 1992 presidential election, Bush ran for a second term. In doing so, he ran against his Democratic challenger Bill Clinton and his running mate Al Gore. About a year before the election, Bush's success in the Gulf War seemed to ensure that he would win the election easily, but the poor economy reduced his popularity. Despite his promise not to introduce new taxes (*Read my lips: no new taxes*), new taxes were imposed anyway. He lost the 1992 election by a clear margin of 168 to 370 electoral votes.

Later life

Bush left public life but remained active as a former president. For example, he was the only former president to exercise his right to receive CIA reports after his presidency ended.

His sons continued the political tradition: George W. Bush was the 46th governor of Texas from 1995 until he was elected as the 43rd president of the United States in 2000, a position he held from 2001 to 2009. Jeb Bush was the 43rd governor of Florida from 1999 to 2007 and made a (failed) bid for the candidacy in the 2016 U.S. presidential election.

In April 1993, an Iraqi attempt to assassinate Bush was foiled by Kuwaiti authorities through a series of car bombs. The Iraqi Security Service (Jihaz Al-Mukhabarat Al-A'ma) was allegedly involved in the attack. The attack, for which 17 people were arrested, was responded to two months later by President Clinton by firing 23 cruise missiles at the Mukhabarat headquarters. Son George W. Bush - in the run-up to the Iraq War - cited this incident in a September 2002 campaign speech as a personal motivation why the United States should depose Saddam Hussein with the words *After all, this is the guy who tried to kill my dad*.

On February 15, 2011, George H.W. Bush was awarded the Presidential Medal of Freedom by President Barack Obama.

In 2014, he celebrated his 90th birthday with a parachute jump. At the end of that year, he was admitted to a Houston hospital for shortness of breath. In July 2015, the 91-year-old Bush broke a cervical vertebra in a fall. In January 2017, he was again in a hospital with breathing problems due to pneumonia.

In Mark K. Updegrove's book *The Last Republicans,* published in 2017, Bush declared that he did not vote for Donald Trump in the 2016 U.S.

presidential election, but for his Democratic opponent candidate Hillary Clinton. About Trump, he said, "I don't like him. I don't know him, but I know he's a patsy. After his election victory, Bush sent congratulations to Donald Trump.

As of October 2017, Bush was in controversy because several women accused him of groping them lewdly, mainly at photo opportunities. His spokesperson responded by stating that on the one hand this was explained by the fact that Bush has been confined to a wheelchair for years and his arms reach at hip level as a result, but that on the other hand Bush apologized if he had offended anyone.

His wife Barbara Bush passed away on April 17, 2018.

Bush suffered from vascular parkinsonism, a form of Parkinson's disease that had forced him to use a scooter or motorized wheelchair since at least 2012. Bush died on November 30, 2018, at the age of 94, at his home in Houston.

42. Bill Clinton (1993-2001)

Democratic party | Vice president: Al Gore

William Jefferson (Bill) Clinton (Hope (Arkansas), August 19, 1946) is an American politician of the Democratic Party. He was the 42nd president of the United States from 1993 to 2001.

Clinton, a lawyer by profession, was a professor of constitutional law at the University of Arkansas from 1973 to 1976. He served as Arkansas' attorney general from 1977 to 1979 and as Arkansas' 40th and 42nd governor from 1979 to 1981 and 1983 to 1992, respectively.

In 1992, Clinton, along with running mate Al Gore, won the 1992 election, defeating incumbent President George H.W. Bush. In the 1996 election, he defeated Republican Bob Dole and was thus elected to a second term.

Clinton is married to former Secretary of State and former Senator Hillary Clinton. Together they have one daughter, Chelsea. Hillary Clinton was the presidential candidate on behalf of the Democratic Party for the 2016 presidential election, but lost the election to Donald Trump.

Biography

Youth and marriage

Clinton was born William Jefferson Blythe III on August 19, 1946 in Hope, Arkansas. His father, William Jefferson Blythe, Jr. died in a car accident three months before Clinton was born. When William was four years old, his mother remarried Roger Clinton of Hot Springs. That is also where William (Bill) grew up. During his time at the local high school, he took the last name Clinton.

When he met President John F. Kennedy during a visit to the White House in 1963 and gave Martin Luther King his historic "I Have a Dream" speech, Clinton decided to pursue a career in politics.

In 1968 he graduated from Georgetown University and won the prestigious Rhodes Scholarship to Oxford University. In 1973, he received the degree of "Juris Doctor" from Yale University.

While studying at Yale, he met Hillary Diane Rodham. They married in 1975. Five years later, in 1980, their only child was born, daughter Chelsea Victoria.

After the Lewinsky affair, he told them he was ashamed of the relationship he had had with Lewinsky, and especially of explicitly denying it to them when it was in the news.

Early career

After teaching law for several years as an associate professor at the University of Arkansas, Clinton became Attorney General (Attorney General) of Arkansas.

In 1978, Clinton was elected as the 40th governor of Arkansas, but lost to his Republican challenger Frank White in 1980. Clinton spent the next two years working on his comeback. In 1982, he succeeded in being re-elected as the 42nd governor. He held the position of governor of Arkansas for a total of three terms (in 1981, one term was for two years; afterwards, it was for four years), namely from 1979 to 1981, and from 1983 to 1992.

In 1992, Clinton ran for president. By winning the Gulf War, President George H.W. Bush seemed assured of re-election. Several prominent Democrats therefore did not run for office. In the primaries, Clinton competed against Jerry Brown and Paul Tsongas. Clinton won the primaries with a large majority and with it the nomination of the Democratic Party. He chose Senator Al Gore of Tennessee as his running mate.

Thanks in part to the poor economy (Clinton: "It's the economy, stupid!" - *transl.:* "It's the economy, stupid!"), a tax increase and - not to be underestimated - his exceptional charm and charisma, Clinton won the 1992 election along with Al Gore.According to commentators, however, Clinton's charisma also had a downside, which would be painfully expressed during his presidency.

Presidency

Clinton was the first Democrat since Franklin D. Roosevelt to complete two full terms as president.His election marked the end of an era of dominance by the Republicans, who had provided the president for the 12 years before and for 20 of the 24 years before that. This election gave the Democrats, for the first time since Jimmy Carter, back full control of the three main branches of the federal government namely both chambers of Congress and the presidency.

Immediately after taking office, Clinton fulfilled an election promise by signing the so-called "Family and Medical Leave Act" (1993), a law that required companies of a certain size to give their employees unpaid leave in the event of serious medical or family problems. This did more good for his popularity than his reluctance to fulfill another promise, that to increase acceptance of openly gay people in the military. From the left came criticism that his approach was too noncommittal, while the right believed that Clinton understood little about the military. After a long debate, Clinton and the Pentagon decided on a "Don't ask, don't tell" policy ("don't ask, don't tell"), which after a long discussion was abolished on December 22, 2010 under the presidency of Barack Obama.

Under Clinton, throughout the 1990s, there was sustained economic growth (which, according to the Office of Management and Budget, began as early as April 1991), declining unemployment, and increasing prosperity as a result of the Wall Street boom. To what extent this is due to Clinton is a much debated issue. Much positive influence also came from Congress and from Alan Greenspan, Clinton's reappointed head of the Federal Reserve. Also playing a role was the combination of positive technological developments and the favorable state of the global economy, things that Clinton had little influence over.

Between 1992 and 1994, the Democrats were able to make a big impact, but the so-called "mid-term" elections of 1994 became a tragedy for the party. They lost their majority in the House and Senate for the first time in 40 years. This was largely due to the failed attempt by his partner, Hillary Clinton, to create a comprehensive public health system.

After the 1994 election, the focus shifted mainly to the "Contract with America" ("Contract with America") promoted by "Speaker of the House" (Speaker) Newt Gingrich. The majority Republican Congress fought with Clinton over the budget. Clinton was re-elected in the 1996 election by a wide margin at the expense of Republican candidate Bob Dole. The Republicans kept their majority in Congress, but lost some seats.

Whitewater scandal, Paula Jones case, Lewinsky affair, impeachment and acquittal

Much of Clinton's presidency was overshadowed by scandals or fake scandals. Kenneth Starr was *Special Prosecutor* (*independent counsel*) investigating the Whitewater scandal, about a failed land deal years earlier, but this case expanded to include the suicide of Clinton's friend Vince Foster and "Troopergate," a case that revolved around an Arkansas State "Trooper" (security guard) who claimed to have arranged sexual encounters for Clinton, then governor. Later, the Trooper retracted those claims and claimed to have received money from the conservative magazine *American Spectator*. Something similar applied to Jones, who admitted to receiving money from conservative political groups. Starr's successor, Robert Ray, did not prosecute for any of the charges.

Starr's scope of work was successively further expanded to include the two cases mentioned below.

Paula Jones, an employee of the state of Arkansas, began a civil lawsuit against Clinton, over an incident of sexual harassment during the time Clinton was governor of Arkansas. This case was later settled for $850,000. A federal judge sentenced Clinton for contempt of court (lying in a deposition) to pay a $90,000 fine. To avoid proceedings to deprive him of his right to practice law, he surrendered this right himself.

In the context of this case, Clinton was forced to name any sexual relationships he had had at work, including those with mutual consent (this would be customary in a case like this). Clinton then stated under oath that he had not had any sexual relations at work. He was charged with perjury when he was found to have had a sexual relationship with intern Monica Lewinsky. He was further questioned about this (a *(discovery) deposition*) in January 1998, and in August 1998 at an interrogation in the White House which was followed live on video in the courthouse by the *grand jury* of this case. In January he still denied everything, including to his wife and daughter. The *grand jury's deliberations* included the definition of a sexual relationship. He had mainly received oral sex from Lewinsky (this appeared from statements by Lewinsky, he himself only said that it was inappropriate behavior), and that he did not think that fell under the definition presented to him. Incidentally, he had also groped her breasts, which at least fell under it.

Starr submitted the case to the U.S. House of Representatives in September 1998 for "impeachment" of Clinton (an impeachment proceeding) on suspicion of perjury and obstruction of justice (not the relationship itself, which was not formally an issue). The House of Representatives then decided on impeachment. However, the Senate decided on February 12, 1999, in a trial that began on January 7, 1999, not to convict Clinton, allowing him to finish his second term. The Senate needed 67 votes to impeach the president. The charge of perjury received 45 votes in favor and 55 against. On the charge of obstruction of justice, the votes were evenly divided: 50 to 50.

After impeachment

Clinton developed a close working relationship with Tony Blair, who had been elected British prime minister in 1997. He showed personal interest in the Northern Ireland issue and visited the area three times to promote peace. This led to talks between the two camps, which culminated in the Irish Republican Army promising, on October 23, 2001, to disarm.

In 1999, Clinton and the Republican-dominated Congress succeeded in balancing the budget for the first time since 1969.

43. George W. Bush (2001-2009)

Republican party | Vice president: Dick Cheney

---

*"I just want you to know that, when we talk about war,
we're really talking about peace."*

George Walker Bush (New Haven (Connecticut), July 6, 1946) is an American politician of the Republican Party. Between 2001 and 2009, he was the 43rd president of the United States. From 1995 to 2000, Bush was the 46th governor of Texas.

George W. Bush is the son of George and Barbara Bush. His father was the 41st president of the United States. Bush earned a bachelor's degree from Yale University in 1968 and a Master of Business Administration from Harvard Business School in 1975. Between those two studies, he was a pilot of an F-102, for the Texas National Guard.

Bush is a descendant of a family of politicians. Prescott Bush, Bush's grandfather, was a senator and his father was president from 1989 to 1993. His brother Jeb was governor of Florida from 1999 to 2007.

George W. Bush married Laura Welch in 1977, a former teacher and librarian. They have two daughters.

Early life

Bush was born in the state of Connecticut, the first child of George H.W. Bush and his wife Barbara Bush. When he was two years old they moved to the state of Texas. He was raised in Midland and Houston. The Bush couple had five more children after George, Jeb, Neil, Marvin, Dorothy and Robin. Robin died of leukemia in 1953 at the age of three.

Bush attended Phillips Academy and then became a student at Yale University, the university from which his father had also studied. In 1968, he became a Bachelor of Arts after studying history. During his time at Yale, he helped with several election campaigns for the Republicans. At Yale, Bush became a member of the private society Skull and Bones. According to Bush himself, he was an average student.

In 1968, Bush became a reserve officer pilot in the Texas National Guard. During the rest of his career, he would be criticized for his service there being too short and for his irregular attendance. In 1972, he was transferred to Alabama so that he could work on the Republican Senate campaign there. In 1974, he was granted permission to finish his six-year service six months early in order to study at Harvard.

During this time, Bush had an alcohol problem. Bush later admitted to drinking too much during this time and that he had an irresponsible childhood. On September 4, 1976, Bush was arrested for driving under the influence. He was found guilty and not allowed to drive until 1978. Bush managed to keep this a secret, during his years as governor of Texas, but it would later come out in the press.

After Bush got his MBA from Harvard, he went to work in the oil industry. In 1977, friends introduced him to Laura Welch, who was then a teacher and librarian. The spark was immediate and George and Laura were married three months later, on November 5, 1977 in Midland, Texas. They also went to live there and had twins in 1981: Jenna and Barbara.

In 1978, Bush ran for the House of Representatives, but lost to Democrat Kent Hance. Bush went back to work in the oil industry and worked for several energy companies. He said goodbye to alcohol for good in 1986 and began studying the Bible.

Bush moved with his family to Washington, D.C. in 1988, where he supported his father in his campaign for the presidency. Together with Lee Atwater, Doug Wead and Jimbo Oldhand, he designed a strategy to win over conservative voters.

When Bush returned to Texas he bought a stake in the baseball team the Texas Rangers. In 1993, he ran the Houston Marathon just before the gubernatorial election.

Governor of Texas

Simultaneously with his father's election to the presidency in 1988 came speculation that George W. Bush would run for governor in 1990. However, personal problems and the fact that he had just become co-owner of the Texas Rangers prevented this. Due in part to his success with the Rangers, George decided to run for governor of Texas in 1994. His brother Jeb also ran in the election, but in Florida. When Bush was quite easily chosen by the Republicans as the new candidate, he was up against then Governor Ann Richards.

Bush was aided in his campaign by a group of advisers, including Karen Hughes, John Allbaugh and Karl Rove. His team of advisers decided to focus the campaign on education, crime and deregulation of the economy. Bush developed a positive image during the election. The campaign was criticized for using controversial methods to attack Richards policies. Due to his impressive performance during the debates, Bush's popularity grew.

As governor, he improved the schools and reformed the legal system. During his governorship, 152 prisoners were executed, more than during any other governor's term.

In 1998, Bush was re-elected with a majority of 69% of the vote. This made him the first Texas governor to be elected to two four-year terms (prior to 1975 there were two-year terms).

Presidential Elections

Presidential Elections 2000

In the 2000 presidential election, Bush was elected president with a very narrow margin of victory over the Democratic candidate and incumbent Vice President Al Gore. Bush won 271 electoral votes compared to 266 for Gore. Due to the small difference, the vote counting process was particularly difficult in the state of Florida. There was an uproar in the state of Florida: some of the votes in some districts were declared invalid because the voters were said to be criminal (perpetrators of certain types of crimes lose their right to vote in the U.S.). It was also said that the voting forms in one county were unclear, which would have caused many people to vote incorrectly, and that elsewhere not all votes had been properly counted by the machines, requiring a manual recount. Gore went to the Florida Supreme Court to request such a recount, but for only four specific counties (namely counties where it was known that the majority of registered voters were Democrats), and this was granted.

Then Bush argued in a petition to the same court that recounting in only four selected counties is not allowed under Florida election law and thus the recount should stop, or at least take place in *all* counties. This argument was rejected and so Bush went to the United States Federal Supreme Court to stop the local recounts. (There was not enough time left for a general recount under Florida election law.) In a 5-4 decision, the Federal Supreme Court ruled in favor of Bush.

In the end, thanks to a 537-vote difference in Florida, Bush won an absolute majority of votes in the Electoral College and was thus elected the 43rd president of the United States. As in five other elections in the history of the United States, Bush did not obtain a majority of the votes, but still won the presidential election, because presidential elections are all about getting as many electoral votes behind him as possible.

Presidential Elections 2004

In the November 2, 2004 presidential election, Bush won by 286 electoral votes compared to 251 electoral votes for his opponent John Kerry (51% of the vote compared to 48%). The Republicans also strengthened their hold on Congress with both seat wins in the House of Representatives and the Senate. The political strategy for Bush's re-election was partly determined by Karl Rove who is seen as a key advisor to President Bush. Bush's second and final term ended on January 20, 2009.

As in the 2000 presidential election, there were noises of election fraud, this time it was supposed to have occurred in the state of Ohio. However, these noises were not as strong as in 2000. Moreover, unlike in 2000, the results were overwhelmingly in favor of the Republicans.

Presidency

Although Bush was elected on a program of most domestic policies such as tax cuts and other social and economic issues, it was the September 11, 2001 attacks that would come to define Bush's presidency more than any other event.

Foreign Policy and Security

One of the pillars of Bush's foreign policy is the so-called *Bush Doctrine* which states that the U.S. will not distinguish between terrorists and those who harbor terrorists.

Kyoto Protocol

During his first presidential visit to Europe in June 2001, Bush was criticized by European leaders for his rejection of the Kyoto Protocol, which seeks to reduce carbon dioxide emissions that contribute to global warming. While representatives of the United States and other countries were still negotiating the Kyoto Protocol, the U.S. Senate had demanded in a 95-0 vote in 1997 that the protocol include binding commitments for developing countries. Although the protocol was symbolically signed in 1998 by Peter Burleigh, the acting U.S. ambassador to the United Nations, it was never nominated to the Senate for ratification by then-President Bill Clinton. In 2002, Bush strongly protested the treaty would be harmful to economic growth: "My approach recognizes that economic growth is the solution, not the problem." The Bush administration also disputed the scientific basis for the treaty. In November 2004, Russia ratified the treaty, reaching the minimum number of countries required to make the protocol effective without the United States.

Steel

Bush's imposition of tariffs on imported steel was controversial given Bush's free market policies and was criticized by both fellow conservatives and the countries involved. The steel tariff was later repealed under pressure from the World Trade Organization.

Softwood

Canada and the United States have been in conflict over softwood lumber trade since the early 1980s. An agreement signed in 1996 expired in 2001 and the conflict flared up again when the two countries could not agree on a new deal. The Bush administration then imposed an import tariff on Canadian softwood lumber that was ruled illegal by NAFTA in 2003. In the same decision, moreover, NAFTA ruled that Canada was unfairly subsidizing its softwood industry. International organizations such as the GTO and NAFTA issued conflicting judgments and it was not until July 2006 that the Bush administration reached an agreement with the Canadian government in which Canada's wishes were partially met although the United States would not have to repay all of the import taxes levied.

Latin America

During his 2000 campaign, Bush's foreign policy platform included supporting a stronger economic and political relationship with Latin America, especially Mexico, and a reduction in involvement in civilian and small-scale military engagements. In Colombia, Bush sees a strong regional ally in the fight against terrorism while populist Venezuelan President Hugo Chávez, whom Bush addressed extremely undiplomatically at the United Nations, is seen as a disruptive influence. With several countries in Latin America, Bush is attempting to negotiate free trade agreements.

Afghanistan

After the terrorist attacks of September 11, 2001, which killed nearly 3,000 Americans, Bush's foreign policy focused much more on the Middle East. Shortly after the attacks, Bush launched a U.S. invasion of Afghanistan to overthrow the Taliban regime for harboring Osama bin Laden. The Taliban refused to unconditionally hand over bin Laden as well as to close terrorist group training camps, whereupon the U.S., along with its allies, intervened militarily. This action received strong international support and the Taliban fell soon after the invasion.

Reconstruction efforts under Afghan President Hamid Karzai in concert with the United Nations had mixed results; bin Laden was not found at the time. Ten years later, under the administration of President Barack Obama, America succeeded in tracking down bin Laden and killing him in the villa in Pakistan where he was then residing. A significant U.S. contingent of troops and advisers is in Afghanistan to this day, and part of the country remains unsettled.

Missile Treaty

On December 14, 2001, Bush withdrew his country from the 1972 antiballistic missile treaty, which had been a basis of nuclear stability between the U.S. and Soviet Union during the Cold War, which he no longer considered relevant. Bush has since concentrated resources on a ballistic missile defense system. The proposed system has been the subject of much scientific criticism. Testing in this area has been mixed, with both successes and failures. It is scheduled to begin deployment in 2005. A ballistic missile defense system will not stop cruise missiles or missiles carried by a boat or land vehicle. Therefore, critics of the system argue that it is an expensive mistake, being built for the least likely attack, a nuclear-armed ballistic missile. Bush also spends on military research and development and modernization of weapons systems, but canceled programs such as the Crusader motorized artillery system. Initially, research on bunker-infiltrating nuclear missiles also began.

Iraq

Since the policy setting in the 1998 Iraq Liberation Act, the U.S. declared it would strip Saddam Hussein of power in Iraq. After the terrorist attacks on September 11, 2001, the Bush administration stated that the situation in Iraq had now become dire. It stated that Saddam's regime had attempted to acquire nuclear material and had not properly accounted for biological and chemical material it might possess, including potential weapons of mass destruction in violation of U.N. sanctions. There remained a long-standing debate between proponents and opponents of the war as to what evidence the U.S. and its allies had that Iraq had weapons of mass destruction and ties to terrorist organizations.

Bush claimed that Saddam could provide weapons of mass destruction to terrorists such as al-Qaeda. Beginning in 2002 and with multiple degrees in the spring of 2003, Bush pressured the U.N. to act on its disarmament mandates to Iraq, leading to Iraq's disarmament crisis. He began by pushing for renewed U.N. weapons inspections in Iraq, which the U.N. instituted UN Security Council Resolution 1441. Hans Blix and Mohamed ElBaradei led the U.N. weapons inspectors in Iraq. There were some time lapses in cooperation and restrictions placed on inspections by the Iraqi government, which led to intense debate about the effectiveness of inspections. Increasing pressure from the United States in the spring of 2003 forced U.N. weapons inspectors to end inspections. After his arrest, Saddam still claimed that he had no weapons of mass destruction and that he would not let inspectors into presidential areas because of privacy concerns.

In the Bush administration, Secretary of State Colin Powell insisted that the United States would not go to war without U.N. approval. The administration explored the possibility of obtaining a U.N. Security

Council resolution authorizing the use of military force according to the United Nations Charter, but abandoned the idea because the majority of Security Council members opposed the idea and there was a public threat of a veto from France. Instead, the United States brought together a group of about forty countries, including the United Kingdom, Spain, Italy, Poland and the Netherlands in the "coalition of the willing."

The coalition invaded Iraq on March 20, 2003, citing many Security Council resolutions on Iraq (715, 778, 1060, 1150, 1205 and 1441), as well as current and past lack of Iraqi cooperation with those resolutions, Saddam's intermittent refusal to cooperate with U.N. weapons inspectors, the accusation that Saddam tried to assassinate former President George H.W. Bush in Kuwait and Saddam's violation of the 1991 cease-fire treaties. The coalition claimed that these resolutions authorized the use of force. Other world leaders, including United Nations Secretary General Kofi Annan, disagreed and called the war illegal. The primary stated goal of the war was to stop Iraq from fielding and developing weapons of mass destruction by removing Saddam from power.

The coalition was highly successful against conventionally armed Iraqi forces and soon gained military superiority over the entire country. After the declared end of major combat operations on May 1, 2003, however, insurgents caused substantially more trouble than U.S. leaders had predicted. U.S. public support for Bush's policy in Iraq declined as the fighting continued. Moreover, a report by people from both political parties of the intelligence community found no credible evidence that Saddam Hussein possessed weapons of mass destruction, although the report did conclude that Hussein's government was actively trying to acquire technology that would allow Iraq to produce weapons of mass destruction once U.N. sanctions were lifted.

The report also found "no partnership" between Saddam Hussein and al-Qaeda. Bush nevertheless continued to defend his decision, arguing that the "world is safer today." Questions remained, however, about biased formation or distortion of prewar intelligence reports, democratization of the Middle East, its relationship to the "fight against terrorism," the relationship of the United States to European powers and the role and function of the United Nations, the reconstruction of Iraq, and the effect on nearby countries such as Iran, Syria, Lebanon, and Turkey. In December 2006, Bush admitted for the first time that he was not winning in Iraq.

In response to the continuously deteriorating situation in Iraq, Bush announced on January 10, 2007, a sharp increase in the number of

U.S. troops in Iraq, known as the *Troop surge*. After the troop surge was completed, in the summer of 2007, violence in Iraq began to decline sharply. Critics of Bush cited the lack of political progress and continued to protest his Iraq policy.

Second Inaugural Address

Bush used his second inaugural address in 2005 to give his vision for the spread of Democracy in the world. He stated that it would become U.S. policy to promote the spread of democratic values with the goal of "ending tyranny in the world." He further stated that maintaining "freedom in our country increasingly relies on the success of freedom in other countries." Critics called the speech too idealistic and vague, while supporters praised Bush's vision.

Israel and Palestine

During the first years of his presidency, Bush devoted relatively little time to the Israeli-Palestinian conflict. He categorically refused to deal with former PLO leader Yasser Arafat and waited for new Palestinian leadership.

In May 2003, The Quartet (US, EU, Russia and UN) presented the Roadmap for Peace. This had the goal of reaching a solution to the conflict by 2005. In 2006, following elections, Hamas came to power. After failed negotiations with Fatah, Hamas formed the government (PNA). Because Hamas was seen as a terror organization, the quartet began a boycott of the Palestinian National Authority. Hamas refused to recognize Israel, acknowledge the agreements made and renounce violence against Israel.

In 2005, Bush became the first U.S. president to openly express support for a "Democratic Palestinian state existing peacefully side by side with a secure Israel." In November 2007, Bush convened a conference in Annapolis, Maryland that was attended by Israel, the Palestinians as well as other Arab countries. Bush said his goal was to reach a final peace agreement between Israel and the Palestinians by the end of 2008.

Military expenditure

Of the $2.4 trillion in the 2005 budget, about $401 billion are earmarked for defense (16.7%) Adjusted for inflation, this military budget is higher than in the 1990s, but roughly comparable to the average during the Cold War.

Political ideology

Bush is generally described as conservative or "compassionate conservative"; the latter is a term he has used in reference to himself. Conservatives have criticized Bush for his willingness to maintain large budget deficits. In his first policy paper of 2005, he outlined his new foreign policy as the "National Security Strategy." Bush's supporters see the rejection of "balance of power" policies and a redefinition of America's role in the international forum as a necessary policy. Critics of Bush see it as a withdrawal of America from the international forum.

Domestic Policy

Religion-based initiatives

In early 2001, Bush, with the help of Republicans in Congress, changed the law that governs the manner of control, taxation, and funding by the federal government of charitable and nonprofit initiatives from religious organizations. Although it was possible for these organizations to receive federal aid even before the legislation, the new legislation no longer requires these organizations to separate their charitable functions from their religious functions. Bush provided a position within the White House for faith-based initiatives and communities. Several organizations such as the American Civil Liberties Union (ACLU) criticized Bush's faith-based initiatives program, finding it a violation of the principle of separation of church and state.

Diversity

Bush opposed most forms of affirmative action, but expressed approval of a federal Supreme Court ruling that allowed the continued selection of college applicants on the basis of diversity. Bush has met with the National Urban League as president. In 2000, he spoke in Baltimore as a presidential candidate to the annual conference of the NAACP

Colin Powell became the first black Secretary of State in Bush's first term in office. In 2005, Powell was succeeded by Condoleezza Rice, the first black woman in the same position.

Bush opposes same-sex marriage and supported a proposal to amend the United States Constitution so that marriage would be defined as the union of a man and a woman. This should make it impossible for individual states to legalize same-sex marriage in their laws. However, Bush does want to leave room for the states to recognize civil cohabitation contracts.

During Bush's first term, Michael Guest became the first openly gay ambassador (to Romania). (The first openly gay ambassador, James Hormel, had received a recess appointment from Bill Clinton when the Senate failed to confirm).

Economy

During his first term as president, Bush obtained Congressional approval for three substantial tax cuts that increased the income tax cut for married couples, eliminated the property tax, and also lowered other marginal tax rates. These tax cuts will expire in their current form after the expiration of a decade. Bush has asked Congress to make these tax cuts permanent. According to the Center on Budget and Policy Priorities, these tax cuts had reduced total federal revenues for 2003 as a percentage of gross domestic product (GDP) to the lowest level since 1959.

The effect of these tax cuts, combined with simultaneous increases in spending, did have to create budget deficits. In the last year of Clinton's presidency, the federal budget showed an annual surplus of more than $230 billion. Under Bush, the budget deficit returned. The annual deficit reached record levels of $374 billion in 2003 (adjusted for inflation) and $413 billion in 2004. Yet as a percentage of GDP, these deficits were lower than the post-World War II record set as a result of Ronald Reagan's fiscal policies in the 1980s. In an open letter in 2004, more than 100 professors of finance and economics attributed the 'fiscal turnaround' to Bush's policies of *tax cuts that primarily benefit the top of the income pyramid."*

Bush supporters countered that primarily as a result of doubling the value of the child tax credit, *"7.8 million low- and middle-income families saw their entire income tax liability canceled as a result of the tax cuts."* In addition, the Bush administration had to deal with a unique combination of negative factors including the end of the Internet hype, several accounting scandals, the aftermath of the Asia crisis, and shocked consumer confidence after 9/11, all of which had severely damaged the global economy. Bush's policies kept U.S. consumption up. This benefited both the U.S. economy and the rest of the world.

According to the "baseline" forecast of federal revenues and spending by the Congressional Budget Office (CBO; in its January 2005 Baseline Budget Projections), the trend of rising deficits during Bush's first term would change to shrinking deficits during his second term. According to this projection, the deficit will be $368 billion in 2005, $261 billion in 2007, and $207 billion in 2009, with a small surplus in the year 2012.

However, the CBO noted that this projection *"excludes a significant portion of this year's expenditures-and perhaps in future years-for U.S. military actions in Iraq and Afghanistan and for other activities related to the global 'fight against terrorism.'"* The projection also assumes that Bush's tax cuts will expire on December 31, 2010 as provided by law. However, if-as Bush announced-the tax cuts are continued, then the "2015 budget projections will change from a surplus of $141 billion to a deficit of $282 billion."

After the last jobs report was released before the 2004 election, Kerry supporters continued to criticize Bush as the first U.S. president after Herbert Hoover during whose term there had been a net loss of jobs. By including the November and December numbers, Bush managed to arrive at net job growth during his first term.

Social Services

Bush has proposed significant changes to the Social Security Administration of the United States (Social Security), an issue he identifies as a priority for his second term. In 2005, Bush made a proposal to progressively reduce tax breaks for Social Security taxes and include partial privatization in the retirement plan by allowing individual workers to invest a portion of their Social Security taxes in personal retirement accounts. Most Democrats and many Republicans are critical of such ideas, in part because of the required cost of the plan ($1 trillion or more) to pay for the transition and because of the problems that arose in funding the privatized pension plan in the United Kingdom.

Health

Bush signed The Medicare Prescription Drug, Improvement, and Modernization Act of 2003, which added prescription drug coverage to the United States Medicare program, subsidized pharmaceutical companies, and hindered the Federal Government from negotiating discounts with pharmaceutical companies.

Bush is pro-life (for the protectiveness of human life from conception). His goal, he says, is to promote the culture of life.

Education

In January 2002, Bush signed the No Child Left Behind Act, which focuses on supporting early learning. The Act regulates the measurement of student achievement, provides policy options for addressing failing schools, and secures more resources for schools. Critics, including Senator Kerry and the National Education Association, say schools are not getting the resources to meet the new standards, even though the House of Representatives Education Committee said in June 2003 that in three years under the Bush administration the Department of Education's budget has been increased by $13.2 billion. The governments of some U.S. states refuse to implement provisions of the Act until they receive sufficient funds.

Science

On December 19, 2002, Bush signed H. R. 4664, the far-reaching legislation to give the National Science Foundation (NSF) a push toward doubling its budget over five years and creating new initiatives for math and science, both at the pre-university and undergraduate levels.

Some scientists are upset about immigration restrictions that stemmed from national security considerations, with the unintended consequence of declining immigration of foreign scientists.

Bush opposes embryonic stem cell research and makes only limited funds available for it. Federal funding for embryonic stem cell research was introduced under the Clinton administration (on January 19, 1999), but no money could be spent until guidelines were released. The guidelines were released under Clinton (on August 23, 2000). They allowed the use of unused, frozen embryos. On August 9, 2001, before any funding had been granted, Bush announced changes to the guidelines that would only allow the use of existing lines of stem cells.

Although Bush claimed that more than 60 privately funded lines of embryonic stem cells already existed for research, scientists said in 2003 that there were only 11 usable lines; this was followed in 2005 by the announcement that all the lines with approved, federal funding were contaminated and unusable. Funding for research on adult stem cells was not restricted.

In February 2004, more than 5,000 scientists - including 48 Nobel laureates - from the Union of Concerned Scientists signed a statement "opposing the Bush administration's use of government scientific advice." They argued that "the Bush administration has ignored unbiased scientific advice in the policy-making that is so important to our collective well-being."

On January 14, 2004, Bush announced a major increase in NASA's budget in his "vision for space exploration." In it, he called for a return to the moon by 2020, completion of the International Space Station (ISS) by 2010, and eventually sending astronauts to Mars. Although the plan received a generally lukewarm reception, the budget was approved with a few minor changes after the November election. In January 2005, the White House issued a new document outlining the administration's space policy and tying the development of space transportation capabilities to national security requirements.

Environment

The Bush administration's environmental policies have been criticized by most environmentalists, who argued that Bush's policies gave in to industry demands to weaken environmental protections. However, two major laws met with little resistance in 2002: the Great Lakes Legacy Act that authorizes the federal government to begin cleaning up pollution and contaminated sediments in the Great Lakes, and the Brownfields Legislation that speeds up the cleanup of abandoned industrial sites and "brownfields" (abandoned hazardous materials storage facilities, gas stations, and the like).

In December of 2003, Bush signed laws to implement key points of his "Healthy Forests Initiative." Environmental groups argued that this plan simply amounted to giving away coppice to sawmills. For his part, Bush insisted on extracting petroleum from large deposits in the ecologically sensitive Arctic National Wildlife Refuge, a nature reserve above the Arctic Circle. This area is widely regarded as the last pristine wilderness in the United States. Most of the oil extracted here is shipped to other countries, such as Japan, where U.S. oil companies can earn larger profits. The foreign sale of this oil increased the controversy as it was previously argued that drilling in this area would reduce U.S. dependence on foreign fossil energy. Another controversial topic was the "Clean Air Initiative"; opponents said that the initiative would allow utilities to actually increase the level of their polluting emissions.

Bush opposed the Kyoto Protocol because he believed it would harm the United States economy. Environmental groups noted, however, that many officials in the Bush administration, in addition to Bush and Cheney themselves, had ties to the energy industry, the automobile industry, and other groups that fought against environmental protection. Bush himself said that his reason for not supporting the Kyoto Protocol was that it was excessively strict on the U.S. but at the same time left other major countries such as China and India virtually untouched.

Bush stated that China is the second largest producer of greenhouse gases. Yet China was completely exempted from requirements in the Kyoto Protocol." He also expressed doubt about the scientific basis of anthropogenic global warming and called for more research to determine its validity.

In early 2005, the White House announced that the Bush administration was now convinced of the existence of the greenhouse effect. The Bush administration stated that it wanted to "look for technological solutions to combat pollution without curtailing industry".

Immigration

Bush, who generally favored open borders, made liberalizing U.S. immigration policy one of the priorities of his second term. He proposed immigration legislation that would greatly expand the use of guest worker visas. His proposal would link employers to foreign workers for a period of up to 6 years. During this period, the immigrants could then apply for permanent residency, which could often take years. Bush opposed a blanket amnesty for illegally residing aliens. He felt that it disadvantaged immigrants who were trying to enter the country in an honest way.

Trade

Bush's tariff levies on imported steel and on Canadian softwood lumber were controversial given his formally professed ideology of free market policies and drew criticism from fellow conservatives and influenced countries alike. The steel tariff was later rescinded under pressure from the World Trade Organization.

President Bush has refused to act against the theft of intellectual property by companies in China, as allowed by provisions in the World Trade Organization's "Agreement on Commercial Aspects of Intellectual Property Law."

Public Debt

The national debt increased sharply in the period 2000-2008. This is mainly due to the budget deficit. In 2008, for example, the Bush administration faced a deficit of 277 billion euros ($410 billion). This budget deficit was mainly due to the wars in Iraq and Afghanistan. The Bush administration filled the budget deficit by increasing the national debt, China and other new economies bought many of those government bonds.

Katrina

In 2005, Hurricane Katrina ravaged the coasts of Louisiana, Mississippi and Alabama, causing considerable damage. The city of New Orleans was particularly hard hit. President Bush then declared a state of emergency for the area which automatically released funds from the federal government for the affected areas as well as allowing agencies such as *FEMA to* come into action. There was much criticism of the federal government's response to the disaster and Bush took full responsibility for it.

Important appointments

Cabinet

Bush's cabinet included the largest number of members drawn from ethnic minorities of any federal cabinet in the United States, including the first ever female Asian-American minister, Secretary of Labor Elaine Chao. The diversity of his cabinet prompted an entry in the Guinness Book of Records.

There was one non-Republican in Bush's last cabinet: Secretary of Transportation Norman Mineta. This Democrat became the first Asian-American cabinet member in U.S. history to serve as Secretary of Commerce before Bill Clinton.

Bush appointed many individuals with long records of service in the U.S. government, including Colin Powell, who served as National Security Advisor under Ronald Reagan and as Chief of the General Staff under George H.W. Bush and Bill Clinton, and Secretary of Defense Donald Rumsfeld, who also served as Secretary of Defense under Gerald Ford, becoming both the youngest and oldest U.S. Secretary of Defense. Bush's vice president, Dick Cheney, was secretary of defense under George H.W. Bush.

44. Barack Obama (2009-2017)

Democratic party | Vice president: Joe Biden

"The best way to not feel hopeless is to get up and do something. Don't wait for good things to happen to you. If you go out and make some good things happen, you will fill the world with hope, you will fill yourself with hope."

Barack Hussein Obama II (Honolulu, August 4, 1961) is an American politician, lawyer, and author. He was the 44th President of the United States, in office from January 20, 2009 to January 20, 2017 for two terms in office. He was the first American president of (partially) African descent.

Between January 3, 2005 and November 16, 2008, Obama was a senator for Illinois and before that he was a state senator in the legislative assembly of his home state. After defeating Republican candidate John McCain in the 2008 U.S. presidential election, he was sworn in as president on January 20, 2009 during the inauguration at the Capitol. On October 9, 2009, Obama was awarded the Nobel Peace Prize. He was re-elected in the 2012 U.S. presidential election by defeating Republican candidate Mitt Romney by a margin in terms of electoral votes, but less delineated in terms of vote count and by a smaller margin than in his 2008 victory.

Biography

Obama's father, Barack Obama Sr. was a Luo from Kenya. His mother, Ann Dunham, was an American from Kansas. His parents divorced in 1964 when Obama was two years old. His father returned to Kenya. Obama saw him only once after that. After the divorce, his mother remarried Lolo Soetoro, an Indonesian student studying in Hawaii. In 1967, the family moved to Jakarta. During this period, Barry Soetoro, as he was then called, attended a Catholic elementary school for two years. He was enrolled there as a Muslim. He then continued his primary schooling at the State Elementary School Menteng 01, which Janssen describes as an "elite Muslim school." Four years later, Obama was then ten, he returned to Honolulu and went to live with his mother's parents. Here he attended high school until 1979. When Obama was 21, his father was killed in a car accident in Kenya. His mother also returned to Hawaii briefly, but eventually went back to Indonesia. She died of cancer in 1995, a few months after the publication of Obama's book *Dreams from My Father*.

Study

After high school, Obama moved to Los Angeles, where he studied for two years at Occidental College. He continued his studies at Columbia University in New York, where he graduated in 1983 in political science with a specialization in international relations. After college, he worked as a researcher at the New York Public Interest Group. In 1985 he moved to Chicago where he did projects in poorer neighborhoods. From 1985 to 1988 he was head of the Developing Communities Project (DCP). DCP was an aid program set up by the Catholic Church. To conclude this period, Obama visited Europe and Kenya. In Kenya, he met with family members.

In 1988, Barack Obama began studying law at Harvard University. In 1990, he made headlines when he became the first African American to be named president of the Harvard Law Review. In this capacity, he provided a political and ideological balance to the journal's content; he himself anonymously published an article on the right of the child to sue its own mother for neglect during pregnancy. He graduated cum laude in 1991, after which he returned to Chicago and began working as an attorney. Obama taught law part-time at the University of Chicago between 1993 and 2004. From 1992 to 2002, he also worked at the law firm of Davis, Miner, Barnhill & Galland.His activities as a lawyer in human rights cases was the decisive step that led him to political activities.

Family

Obama's wife Michelle Robinson also studied at Harvard. The two met in 1989 while working for a law firm and married in 1992. They have two daughters, *Malia Ann* (July 4, 1998) and *Natasha "Sasha"* (June 10, 2001). Michelle Obama is currently vice president for community affairs at the University of Chicago Hospitals. She came into controversy when her salary tripled after Obama became a senator. However, the reason for this was a promotion and her full job with overtime when she was no longer campaigning for her husband.

Obama is a Christian, but not by birth. He was baptized into the United Church of Christ in 1988.

Barack Obama is a descendant of the Protestant "Pilgrim Fathers," namely the Blossom family, who had fled from England to Leiden in the early 17th century due to religious persecution and sailed from there to America in 1629 for a life of religious freedom. Most remarkable about this find, which was announced by the city of Leiden on December 5, 2008 and confirmed by the New England Historic Genealogical Society in Boston, is that Obama is descended from Elizabeth Blossom, whose brother Peter is a distant ancestor of Obama's predecessor in office George W. Bush.

The vice president of the US during Bush's administration, Dick Cheney, is also distant relatives of Obama. Half-brother Malik Obama competed in Kenya's Siaya district gubernatorial election and came in third.

Political

In the 2004 Illinois Senate election, he competed for an open seat against Republican Alan Keyes. The winner became at least the fifth African-American in Senate history, following Hiram Revels, Blanche Bruce, Edward Brooke and Carol Moseley Braun. Obama won the election with 70% of the vote compared to 27% for Keyes.

In the Senate, Obama championed education, immigration, and greater government transparency through *e-government*, among other issues. Obama was also active in foreign affairs. His trip to Africa, in which he visited South Africa, Kenya, Djibouti, Ethiopia, and Chad, attracted considerable attention from media in the United States and the countries visited. Obama was the third African-American to give a "keynote address" at a Democratic National Convention (in 2004). This was a landmark speech, introducing himself to American voters as a political pledge, with the most quoted words being:

There is no leftist America and no conservative America; there is the United States of America. There are not a black America and a white America and a Latino America and an Asian America; there is the United States of America.

Presidential election 2008

On January 16, 2007, Barack Obama announced that he had formed an exploratory committee in preparation for his participation in the Democratic primaries for the 2008 U.S. presidential election. On February 10, 2007, he made his candidacy official in Springfield, Illinois. His main opposing candidate in the Democratic primaries became Hillary Clinton.

The first primary took place in Iowa on January 3, 2008. Obama won this state by a wide margin over John Edwards (second) and Clinton (third). In the second primary, in New Hampshire, Clinton stayed narrowly ahead of him. After that, Obama and Clinton went at it evenly for quite some time. *Super Tuesday*, when 24 states cast their votes, also failed to bring a decision. Obama then took the lead by winning ten states in a row. Clinton could not catch up with this performance, although she had managed to get key states such as Florida, Pennsylvania and California behind her. Obama eventually won by far the most primaries and caucuses. After the final primaries on June 3, Obama had enough delegates behind him to claim the Democratic nomination for the election. Clinton officially withdrew from the electoral race on June 7.

Since becoming the Democratic presidential candidate, Obama campaigned in so-called swing states. His campaign team set records with registering new voters for the Democratic Party, much of it using the Internet. Obama's speeches brought thousands of people to their feet and he used slogans like *Yes we can* and *Change we can believe in*. On August 23, 2008, it was announced that Obama had chosen 65-year-old Senator Joe Biden as his *running mate*.

Obama was supported in the campaign by a number of well-known American politicians, including Jimmy Carter, John Kerry, Ted Kennedy and Colin Powell, as well as celebrities such as Caroline Kennedy, Robert De Niro, Stevie Wonder, Oprah Winfrey, Jennifer Aniston and Will Smith.

Obama debated three times with his Republican opponent John McCain.

However, during the campaign period, some Americans had also developed doubts about Obama's sincerity. Doubts were raised as to whether Obama was born in America and is an American citizen, which is a prerequisite for being president of America. A lawyer in Philadelphia (and supporter of Hillary Clinton), Philip J. Berg, believed that Obama was born in Africa and therefore took legal action to have him removed from the electoral roll in November. This sowing of doubt was adopted by the Republicans, such as his later successor Donald Trump. It did not even stop once Obama had produced his birth certificate.

In terms of content, there were concerns about what Obama's economic policies would mean for the U.S. and about his promise to talk with America's hostile world leaders like Hugo Chávez and Mahmoud Ahmadinejad without preconditions.

Five days before the election, Obama interrupted his campaign to visit his grandmother, who lived in Hawaii. She was on her deathbed and passed away two days before the election.

On November 4, 2008, Obama won the election, after which he gave his victory speech at Grant Park in hometown Chicago.

Presidential Elections 2012

During the Democratic primaries, Obama had no serious opposition. Obama again chose Joe Biden as his running mate, despite rumors that the choice would fall to Hillary Clinton. In the general election, Obama took on the Republican Mitt Romney. Romney did better than McCain four years earlier, but still ended up with 206 electoral votes compared to 332 for the Obama-Biden duo.

Presidency

Inauguration and first days

Barack Obama was sworn in as the 44th President of the United States on Tuesday, January 20, 2009 at 12:05 p.m. (local time) in Washington, DC. The oath was administered to him by Chief Justice Roberts using the same Bible used at Abraham Lincoln's inauguration in 1861. Judge Roberts made a mistake in the oath, pronouncing the word faithfully later than the text of the oath in the Constitution requires. The correct text is: *I will faithfully execute the office of President of the United States*, Roberts said: *I will faithfully execute the office of President of the United States*. Obama noticed the error, faltered for a moment, but spoke after Roberts anyway. To be on the safe side, Obama was sworn in again the following day - privately - in accordance with the correct text.

In his first days as president, he issued *executive orders* to withdraw U.S. troops from Iraq. He ordered the closure of the Guantanamo Bay detention center "as soon as possible, but no later than January 2010," He limited the secrecy given to the presidential administration and changed the procedures of the *Freedom of Information Act*. He also lifted the ban on federal funding for foreign organizations that facilitate abortion provocatus, followed in March 2009 by lifting the ban on federal grants for embryonic stem cell research.

Obama was president for two terms in office. He began his presidency with a Democratic majority both in the House of Representatives and the Senate, but lost the House in the first midterm election in 2010. In his second midterm election in 2014, he also lost the Senate.

Domestic Policy

Economy

Obama became president while the economic crisis - also known as the credit crunch - was at its height. Obama signed the *American Recovery and Reinvestment Act of 2009* on February 17. This was a $787 billion economic package that consisted of various measures related to education, health care, infrastructure and various tax breaks. It was intended to stimulate the American economy, which was at a low point.

Obama's Treasury Secretary Timothy Geithner announced in February 2009 that he wanted to create a public-private fund to buy up banks' risky products. In June 2009, Obama used government aid to prop up U.S. automobile conglomerates General Motors and Chrysler.

The total budget deficit for 2010 was 10.6 percent of gross domestic product (GDP). For 2011, the expectation is much lower, but the total national debt will have risen to about 8.53 trillion dollars, 80 percent of U.S. GDP. Unemployment rose to 10.1 percent in October 2009, but then began to fall again.

Health care reform

In the first year of his administration, Obama committed heavily to American health care reform. His plan provided health insurance for some 32 million previously uninsured Americans. Basic health insurance became mandatory for the vast majority of Americans. Insurance companies would no longer be allowed to turn away sick Americans.

A major criticism of the Republicans was the high cost of the plans. Approximately 1 trillion dollars (700 billion euros) were needed. prolife organizations and the religious right also strongly opposed the plans. In particular, the possibility of taxpayer-funded abortion met with fierce protests. Obama gave assurances that no federal funds would be used to finance abortion. However, individual states retained the option of making public funds available for abortion.

Thanks to a large majority of his party in the Senate, Obama was able to realize his plans. On March 23, 2010, he signed the so-called Patient Protection and Affordable Care Act.

Oil spill Gulf of Mexico

On April 20, 2010, an underwater explosion occurred on the Deepwater Horizon drilling platform in the Gulf of Mexico. As a result, a gigantic amount of oil spilled into the sea. BP, leaser of the drilling rig, tried to plug the hole, but did not succeed for a long time. President Obama visited the disaster region for the first time on May 2, and later on May 28 and June 4. He ordered a federal investigation and established an independent commission to investigate new safety measures. Obama declared a state of emergency and on May 27 announced a moratorium on offshore drilling in deep water. The leak was not plugged until July 15. The Obama administration subsequently sued BP for failing to comply with required safety measures.

Foreign Policy

Iraq War

During the presidential transition period, Obama announced that he would retain Robert Gates, already Secretary of Defense under President George W.H. Bush, as Secretary of State. On February 27, 2009, he announced that the military combat mission in Iraq was to end on August 31, 2010. He reduced the force from 142,000 troops to a number between 35,000 and 50,000. These will remain until the end of 2011 and will help train Iraqi soldiers. On August 31, Obama also actually announced the end of the combat mission in Iraq.

Afghanistan

Early in his presidency, Obama announced his intention to send additional troops to Afghanistan. On December 1, he announced sending 30,000 troops to reinforce the 71,000 troops present. He also proposed to begin withdrawing troops from Afghanistan within 18 months. In June 2010, Obama replaced Stanley McChrystal, the military commander in Afghanistan, after the commander sharply criticized the White House in an interview. The new commander became David Petraeus.

Nobel Peace Prize

In 2009, he received the Nobel Peace Prize for "his outstanding efforts to strengthen international diplomacy and cooperation among peoples." There was surprise and criticism of the Nobel Prize committee's choice, claiming that Obama had achieved little as president. Obama himself indicated "not feeling that I belong in the company of those who have won the prize before." The former director of the Norwegian Nobel Institute, Geir Lundestad, stated in 2015 that he was sorry that the Peace Prize had gone to Barack Obama in 2009.

Libya

Massive protests broke out in Libya in February 2011 against the long-serving dictator Moammar al-Qadhafi. A civil war subsequently broke out. The rebels called on the international community to establish a no-fly zone. On March 17, 2011, the UN Security Council adopted United Nations Security Council Resolution 1973, which imposed a no-fly zone on Syria. After it became clear that Libya was violating this ban, the U.S., Canada, France and Britain decided to intervene militarily. Later, the military actions took place under the banner of NATO. This intervention eventually contributed to the fall of al-Qadhafi. After his death, the country became embroiled in a civil war. In September 2012, there was a storming of the U.S. consulate in Benghazi, in which U.S. Ambassador Christopher Stevens lost his life.

Death of Osama bin Laden

On May 2, 2011, Obama authorized a unit of Navy SEALs to raid a villa in Abbottabad, Pakistan, where Osama bin Laden was holed up. In the raid, the al-Qaeda leader was killed.

Cuba

In March 2016, Obama was the first U.S. president in 88 years to visit Cuba. In late 2014, Obama had already announced with Cuban leader Raul Castro that ties between the two countries would be restored. Thus, the United States would open an embassy in Havana and Cuba vice versa in Washington D.C.. This happened in the summer of 2015.

Iran

Obama was the initiator behind the nuclear deal struck with Iran, known as the *Joint Comprehensive Plan of Action*. The treaty agreed that Iran would abide by agreements that would make it impossible for the country to produce a nuclear bomb. In return, international sanctions would be slowly lifted. Obama's successor Donald Trump canceled the deal. Iran and the other signatories to the deal (Britain, France, Germany, Russia and China) indicated that they did want to abide by the agreements.

Israel/Palestine

Obama gave an important speech in Cairo on June 4, 2009 about his vision for the relationship between the US and the world of Islam . In it he showed an eye for the difficult situation of the Palestinians and pleaded for a viable Palestinian state. Hamas had to stop violence and Israel with its illegal settlements. In 2014, he made an unsuccessful attempt, through his Secretary of State John Kerry, to get the stalled peace talks going. The following year, Netanyahu passed him and directly addressed the U.S. Congress about the danger he believed was posed by Iran's nuclear program .In 2016, Obama signed off on a military aid package for Israel worth $38 billion for the period 2018-2028.On December 23, 2016, the U.S. abstained - to Israel's anger - during the U.N. Security Council vote on Resolution 2334 , which passed. The Council condemned any attempt to "change the demographic composition, character and status of the Palestinian Territory occupied since 1967" (including East Jerusalem).

45. Donald Trump (2017-2021)

Republican party | Vice president: Mike Pence

"Watch, listen, and learn. You can't know it all yourself. Anyone who thinks they do is destined for mediocrity."

Donald John Trump (New York, June 14, 1946) was the 45th president of the United States from January 20, 2017 to January 20, 2021. Trump belongs to the Republican Party. Before his presidency, he had never held political office. By profession, he was an entrepreneur, mainly in real estate. Furthermore, he is known as a television personality.

Donald Trump is the son of Fred Trump, a New York real estate developer. When Donald Trump attended the Wharton School at the University of Pennsylvania, he was already working for his father and grandmother's company, Elizabeth Trump & Son, the forerunner of The Trump Organization. In 1968, he officially joined his father's company. He gained control of the company in 1971 and changed the name to The Trump Organization. Through his promotional efforts, career, appearances in media and books (often written by ghostwriters), he became a media personality in the United States. Trump hosted *The Apprentice*, an American television program on NBC.

On June 16, 2015, Trump officially declared his candidacy for the 2016 presidential election as a Republican. From the first stage of his campaign, he proved to be very popular, much to the dismay of the top Republican Party. As of late July 2015, he was at the top of the polls for the Republican nomination, and in July 2016 he became the presidential candidate for the Republican Party. On November 8, 2016, he won the presidential election and became President-Elect of the United States. On January 6, 2017, he was confirmed as president by the United States Congress and was sworn in on January 20, 2017. On January 20, 2021, his presidency ended and he was succeeded by Joe Biden.

Origin

Trump's paternal grandparents were German immigrants from Kallstadt. Grandfather Friedrich Trumpf emigrated to New York in 1885 at the age of 16 after which he unified his German name to Frederick Trump.

Trump's mother, Mary Anne MacLeod (1912-2000), was born in 1912 in the village of Tong on the Isle of Lewis, on the west coast of Scotland. In 1930, when she was eighteen years old, she met Fred Trump (1905-1999) while on vacation in New York. They married in 1936.

Youth and education

Donald Trump was born on June 14, 1946 in Queens, one of the five boroughs (boroughs) of New York. His parents were real estate developer Fred Trump (1905-1999) and Mary Anne MacLeod Trump (1912-2000). He grew up with two brothers and two sisters: Maryanne, Fred Jr., Elizabeth and Robert. Fred Jr. died in 1981 at the age of 43 as a result of alcohol abuse. In several interviews, Donald said that this event made him a teetotaler himself. Maryanne was a judge on the Court of Appeals for the 3rd Circuit until 2011.

During the time the Trump family lived in Jamaica Estates, he attended *The Kew-Forest School* in Forest Hills, where his father was a member of the school board. Several siblings also attended that school. At thirteen, Trump was suspended by his school for bad behavior. He was then sent by his parents to the New York Military Academy so that he could put his energy to good use. At the age of 17, he attained the rank of captain.

In August 1964, Trump began studies at Fordham University in The Bronx. Two years later he switched to the Wharton School at the University of Pennsylvania, which was one of the few in the U.S. to offer a real estate degree. He graduated in 1968 with a Bachelor of Science in economics.

Although Trump was of draft age during the Vietnam War, he was never actually drafted and deployed to Vietnam. During his college years (1964-1968), he was granted four deferments from military service. In 1968, he was granted another deferment on medical grounds due to a heel spur. When the government began to determine through lotteries who would be deployed to Vietnam, Trump was initially ineligible because of his medical deferment. Apparently by chance, he had been given a very high number for the lottery, so he was ultimately never called up.

Business life

Start in real estate

Trump began his career with the family's real estate firm, Elizabeth Trump & Son. This focused on middle-class rental properties in the New York boroughs of Brooklyn, Queens and Staten Island. Still in college, Trump's first project was to revitalize an apartment complex, Swifton Village in Cincinnati, which his father purchased in 1962 for $5.7 million. After the company became involved in the project, the complex of 1,200 apartments went from 66% vacancy to full occupancy within two years with a $500,000 investment. The company eventually sold Swifton Village in 1972 for $6.75 million.

In 1971, Trump moved to Manhattan. According to Trump, the margins in social and middle-class rentals were too small, and that sector was too laborious in terms of management. This sector has many customers, who pay relatively little per person, but who proportionally often have payment problems, according to Trump. For this reason he focused on Manhattan, where there were fewer, but more capital-rich clients, with higher margins. He took on larger projects, using attractive, eye-catching and sometimes controversial designs to achieve public interest, and thus commercial success. A typical example is the Grand Hyatt Hotel, where the masonry facade was converted to a glass facade.

The Trump Organization

The Trump Organization was founded in 1923 by his father and grandmother. In 2016, around 250 companies were part of the organization. After becoming president, he stepped down as chief executive. Since his presidency, the company has been led by his two sons Donald Jr. and Eric, and CFO Allan Weisselberg. The company focuses primarily on construction projects and building operations. In addition, there are interests in other sectors.

Some of the most notable and large construction projects in Manhattan include the Trump Tower, the Trump World Tower and the Grand Hyatt Hotel. He also owned 50% of the Empire State Building from 1994 to 2002. Outside Manhattan, his holdings include the Trump Tai Mahal Hotel in Atlantic City and the Trump International Hotel and Tower in Chicago. Outside the U.S., he also has holdings, such as the Turnberry Hotel in Scotland.

In purchasing and remodeling the Commodore Hotel in Manhattan in the late 1970s, now the Grand Hyatt, some say he received tax breaks that competitors did not. According to Trump himself, it was the other way around: his competitors received tax breaks that he did not, and he had to file a lawsuit to get those same breaks. In 1981, Trump borrowed a sum of 17.5 million from his father to pay off some of his debts. Due to high business debts, Trump had to sell his share of the property in 1996 to pay it off.

In the early 1980s, the city of New York wanted to build the Jacob K. Javits Convention Center on land on which Trump had an option to buy. Trump estimated that his company could do the project for $110 million. The city rejected his offer, but Trump did receive a brokerage fee. After the New York City Council took over the project, construction stalled for several years, the budget was exceeded by about $50 million, and when it was completed the operation was done by the mob. Trump has mentioned this a number of times as an example of what he sees as often incompetent and corrupt politicians.

In 1980, the City of New York began renovating the Wollman Rink, a 1955 ice skating rink, in Central Park. The renovation would take 2.5

years. Six years later and with a $12 million budget overrun, the project was not yet complete. Trump took over management of the project at no additional cost to the city. The renovation ended successfully three months later, for $1.95 million, $750,000 under budget. Trump received a lot of positive media attention because of this, and according to himself, this was a breakthrough for him as a media personality.

In 1985, Trump offered $28 million for the Mar-a-Lago estate in Florida. The owner thought that amount was too low. Trump did not want to increase his bid. Instead, through an intermediary, he bought the strip of land between the estate and the beach. After this, he threatened to erect a large and ugly building there, blocking the view of the beach. This threat scared away other possible buyers. In the end, Trump was able to buy the estate for $5 million with an additional $2 million for the inventory. Trump himself gives another explanation for the relatively low price, namely that he has a nose for undervalued real estate.

Bankruptcies

Trump has never personally gone bankrupt, although he did have to temporarily relinquish control of his personal finances to the banks once in the late 1980s. His casinos and hotels have gone bankrupt a total of six times. These were so-called "technical bankruptcies": the debts were restructured, but the businesses continued to exist. After negotiating new terms for the loans with interested banks, the businesses continued to exist. Lenders did not want Trump to get out of the casinos: that would result in a lot of loss because a new casino license would have to be applied for and the casino would be shut down. This allowed Trump to command a majority stake of 50.5% in the casinos, while the other shares went to creditors. The Taj Mahal emerged from bankruptcy on October 5, 1991.

Aircraft company Trump Shuttle could not pay off the interest on its loans, so the management was taken over by the banks. In 1992, the airline was sold to US Airways. On November 2, 1992, the Plaza Hotel filed a plan of reorganization as part of a bankruptcy filing (and thus protection from creditors). In the plan, Trump agreed to give a 49% stake in the hotel to Citibank and five other lenders. In return, Trump would get better terms on the remaining debt amount of over $550 million that he still owed to the lenders. In return, he was also allowed to keep his position as chief executive, although he would no longer have a role in the company's day-to-day affairs. Plaza Hotel in New York also went bankrupt. This was Trump's fourth bankruptcy in a short time after the three casinos went bankrupt.

According to *Forbes*, Trump's first bankruptcy was the only bankruptcy that affected his personal wealth. However, according to *Time,* the 2004 bankruptcy also involved $72 million of Trump's own money.

Trump said years later about the bankruptcies:

I've used the laws of this country to pare debt. ...We'll have the company. We'll throw it into a chapter. We'll negotiate with the banks. We'll make a fantastic deal. You know, it's like on 'The Apprentice'. It's not personal. It's just business."

He indicated that other "important entrepreneurs" were doing the same.

Real estate revival

In 2001, Trump opened World Tower, a 72-story apartment complex near the United Nations Headquarters in New York. Trump also began construction of Trump Place, a project consisting of several buildings along the Hudson River. He additionally owns business space in Trump International Hotel and Tower, a 44-story multipurpose building (hotel and apartment complex) on Columbus Circle. In total, Trump owns hundreds of thousands of square feet of real estate in Manhattan.

Trump has started a large number of real estate projects, including Trump International Hotel and Tower (Honolulu), Trump International Hotel and Tower (Chicago), Trump International Hotel and Tower (Toronto) and Trump Tower (Tampa (Florida)). In Fort Lauderdale, one of Trump's projects (Trump International Hotel and Tower) was halted due to money problems. At the same time, Trump Towers Atlanta One was being developed.

In 2015, *Forbes* magazine estimated his net worth at $4.1 billion. In June 2015, *Business Insider* published a financial report from Trump, which stated that his assets were $8.7 billion. Of that, $3.3 billion fell under "licensing agreements on real estate, his brand and developments of his brand."

Name Licenses

After starting the television program The Apprentice, Trump began selling name licenses, in which companies were allowed to attach the Trump name to their products for large sums of money. For some licenses, Trump participated in advertising campaigns. With name licenses, Trump does not run any financial risk and does not invest in the companies. In 2016, he had income from 25 licenses. For several licenses of real estate projects, there were confidentiality obligations regarding the existence of the licenses. Products under the name license "Trump" include: Trump Financial (mortgages), Trump Sales and Leasing (residential sales), Trump Restaurants (located in Trump Tower), GoTrump (travel website), Donald J. Trump Signature College (line of men's clothing, accessories and watches).

Net power

In April 2011, when Trump was considering running for president in 2012, *Politico* quoted a source close to Trump who stated that if Trump were to become a presidential candidate, his financial statement would show that his wealth exceeded $7 billion, that he had $250 million in cash, and that he had virtually no debt. Although Trump did not run for president, he did publish his finances in a book of his. He claimed that his wealth was $7 billion.

Estimates of Trump's wealth have fluctuated over the years along with the value of his real estate. In 2015, *Forbes* estimated his wealth at $4.1 billion. On June 16, 2015, Trump published his financial report just before his candidacy for the presidential election. This stated that his wealth was about $9 billion. In July 2015, election supervisors released new details about Trump's assets: his assets had a value of over $1.4 billion, including at least $70 million in stocks, and he had debt of at least $265 million.

Trump Tower

Trump owns Trump Tower, a 58-story skyscraper in Midtown Manhattan, at 725 Fifth Avenue at the corner with East 56th Street. The architect was Der Scutt of the architectural firm *Swanke Hayden Connell Architects*. The land was originally owned by the *Equitable Life Assurance Society*, which transferred the land to Trump in exchange for a 50% stake in the new building.

Scholarship Investments

In 2011, Trump invested in the stock market because he was disappointed with the U.S. real estate market, which was in a depression, and because he felt he was not getting enough interest from the bank. He said he was not a stock market person, but that it was difficult to get good real estate at good prices. Trump stated that he had bought shares of Bank of America, Citigroup, Caterpillar, Facebook, Intel, Johnson & Johnson and Procter & Gamble, among others. When he sold his shares in 2014, he had a profit of $27 million and 40 of the total 45 different stocks he had bought had increased in value.

Sport

In 1983, Trump purchased the New Jersey Generals for the first season of the United States Football League. The sports team hired Walt Michaels, former coach of the New York Jets, as head coach. However, Trump sold the team to Oklahoma oil tycoon J. Walter Duncan prior to the start of the first season. After the first season, Duncan sold the team back to Trump.

The United States Football League planned to host the 1986 season in the fall, at the same time as the National Football League. That decision was made largely thanks to Trump's efforts. Two years earlier, Trump had persuaded his co-owners to move the timing of the season because he thought that would eventually cause a merger of the United States Football League and the National Football League. As a result, the owners of all the teams in the league would see their investments double.

The New Jersey Generals merged with the Houston Gamblers in the offseason, giving the team quarterback Jim Kelly and wide receiver Ricky Sanders, among others. Michaels, the coach, was fired and replaced by Jack Pardee, the former coach of the Houston Gamblers, who planned to use Houston Gamblers tactics. However, the new team never played because of the cancellation of the season in 1986: an antitrust case by the United States Football League against the National Football League did not favor the USFL. Although it was vindicated by the jury on many points, it did not receive the large compensation it had hoped for. The league finally disappeared shortly thereafter.

When Trump hosted a fight between Mike Tyson and Michael Spinks in Atlantic City, New Jersey, in 1988, he was Tyson's financial advisor for the occasion.

The Trump Organization manages a number of golf courses and resorts in the United States and around the world. On February 11, 2014, it was announced that Trump had purchased the Doonbeg Golf Club in Ireland. The golf course would be renamed the Trump International Golf Links. In 2006, Trump bought the Menie estate in the Scottish town of Balmedie in Aberdeenshire to build a controversial golf resort. In June 2015, Trump's appeal was rejected, in which he objected to a wind farm that would be visible from that golf resort. In April 2014, Trump purchased the Turnberry hotel and golf resort in Scotland, which regularly features on The Open Championship roster.

Beauty pageants

Trump has been the owner of the Miss USA and Miss Universe beauty pageants since 1996. Miss Universe is one of the most recognized beauty pageants in the world.

In 2015, NBC and Univision both ended their partnership with the Miss Universe Organization following Trump's speech at the beginning of his 2016 presidential election campaign on June 16, in which he spoke negatively about Mexicans and U.S. immigration policy.

Trump responded by filing a $500 million lawsuit against Univison for breach of contract and defamation. The television station Reelz then bought the exclusive rights to broadcast Miss USA.

Entertainment Media

In the media, Trump gained fame for his two Emmy Award nominations, for his appearances in films and television series as a caricature of himself (for example, in Home Alone 2: Lost in New York, The Nanny, The Fresh Prince of Bel-Air, Days of our Lives and Wall Street: Money Never Sleeps) and for his role in the film The Little Rascals. He has also been the subject of comedians, flash animation creators and online caricature makers. Trump additionally had his own daily talk show on the radio called *Trumped*!

In March 2011, Trump was the subject of the *Comedy Central Roast* television program. The special episode was hosted by Seth MacFarlane and Trump was roasted by Larry King, Snoop Dogg and Anthony Jeselnik, among others. In April 2011, Trump attended the White House Correspondents' Association dinner. President Barack Obama made a number of pre-prepared mocking jokes about Trump during this occasion.

For an overview of Trump's film and television appearances, see the article Filmography of Donald Trump.

The Apprentice

In 2003, Trump became the executive producer and host of an NBC reality series called *The Apprentice*. In that television series, a group of contestants competed for an important job in one of Trump's companies.

World Wrestling Entertainment

Trump is known as a fan of World Wrestling Entertainment (WWE) and is friends with that company's president, Vince McMahon. He has presented two WrestleMania events at Trump Plaza and has been an active participant in several shows. In 1991, the World Bodybuilding Federation championship, which was owned by the WWE (then called the World Wrestling Federation), was held at Trump Taj Mahal in Atlantic City. Trump was interviewed at ringside by Jesse Ventura during WrestleMania XX in 2004.

He also appeared at WrestleMania 23 in 2007 in a match called *The Battle of the Billionaires*, a fight between Bobby Lashley and Umaga. Trump was on Lashley's side and Vince McMahon was on Umaga's side. Stone Cold Steve Austin was the referee for the occasion in the so-called "hair versus hair" fight. This involved shaving off Trump's hair if Umaga won and McMahon's hair if Lashley won. Lashley eventually won, after which Trump shaved McMahon bald.

On June 15, 2009, McMahon announced on the wrestling show *Monday Night Raw* that he had "sold" the program to Trump. Trump stated in the program that he would appear in the next ad-free episode and that he would reimburse the tickets of all the people who had purchased a ticket to that show. The following week, *Monday Night Raw* was supposedly "bought back" by McMahon for double the price.

In 2013, Trump was inducted into the celebrity wing of the WWE Hall of Fame at New York's Madison Square Garden for his contributions to the promotion of WWE. The following night, he appeared at WrestleMania for the fifth time.

Political

Political activities through 2015

Trump has been a member of multiple parties, the Democrats, the Reform Party, and since 2009 the Republicans. He has donated to Democrats and Republicans, and sometimes to both simultaneously. In total, he has donated $1.4 million since 1989 (adjusted for inflation). As of 2009, he stopped donating to Democrats and has only donated to Republicans. He has often participated in public debate, voicing his opinions on a wide range of social issues, such as trade and climate, but until his presidency he held no official positions.

In April 2011, he questioned President Barack Obama's U.S. citizenship. On April 25, 2011, he called on President Obama to release the long version of his birth certificate. Two days later, the White House published the long version of Obama's birth certificate. Trump revealed in a subsequent press conference that he was proud of his role in the publication of the birth certificate.

Trump considered running for president in 1988, 2004 and 2012 and for the office of governor of New York in 2006 and 2014, but ultimately renounced it. He did run for the Reform Party in the 2000 presidential election and won the primary in California. He wrote the book *The America We Deserve* to outline his program points for his candidacy in 2000.

Presidential campaign 2015-2016

On June 16, 2015, Trump officially ran for the office of President of the United States on behalf of the Republican Party. On Twitter, he put his personal slogan: *Make America Great Again*. Throughout his subsequent political career, his almost daily tweets played a major role in the perception of him as a politician.

Pre-elections

On July 9, 2015, the results of the first major national poll were released, which showed that Trump had the largest following among the Republican candidates at that time. The poll had been conducted by *The Economist* and YouGov. A poll by Suffolk University and *USA Today* five days later showed that 17% of Republican voters supported Trump and 14% supported Jeb Bush. A poll by *The Washington Post* and ABC News conducted between July 16 and July 19 found that 24% of Republican voters adhered to Trump and Scott Walker, the poll's number two, had a 13% following. A CNN and ORC poll of Republican voters found that Trump had the largest support with 18%. In doing so, he defeated Jeb Bush, who received a percentage of 15%. In the August 4 CBS News poll, Trump was again in first place with 24% support. Second was Bush with 13% support and third was Walker with 10% support. In September 2015, a group of forty pastors met at Trump's New York headquarters, including Paula White of New Destiny Christian Center, Robert Jeffress of First Baptist Dallas, and David Jeremiah of Shadow Mountain Community Church.

In response to a shooting in California's San Bernardino in December 2015, Trump called for a complete halt to Muslim immigration to the United States "until our members of Congress have been able to investigate what is going on."

In February 2016, Trump won two Republican primaries in a row, in the states of New Hampshire and South Carolina. In Iowa, he came in second, behind Ted Cruz.

On May 3, Trump won the primary in Indiana, knocking out his opponent Ted Cruz. After Cruz and Kasich dropped out of the race for the nomination in early May 2016, Trump was the only remaining candidate on behalf of the Republicans. On May 9, Trump appointed Chris Christie, the governor of New Jersey, as the one to put together a team in case Trump won the upcoming election. Trump officially announced his candidacy on June 16, 2015, from his headquarters at Trump Tower in New York. During the start of his campaign, he played *Rockin' in the free world*, against the wishes of its singer-songwriter, Neil Young. He opened with the slogan "We are going to make our country great again." In doing so, he pledged to become the "best jobs president God ever made." On June 20, he fired his campaign manager, Corey Lewandowski.

On July 18, 2016, Trump's wife Melania delivered a speech at the Republican Party Convention with passages that bore remarkable similarities to a 2008 speech by Michelle Obama. This led to much controversy; it was primarily thought to be a blunder by the speechwriters.

Nomination

On July 20, Trump was officially nominated as a presidential candidate on behalf of the Republicans, and the next day he accepted the nomination.

In mid-August, Trump temporarily made a marked fall in the polls and lost many supporters in key states. At this, he reorganized his campaign and appointed Steve Bannon as the new chief. A few weeks later, Trump had largely caught up again with his Democratic opponent Hillary Clinton.

Scandals

On October 1, 2016, *The New York Times broke* the news that Trump may have paid little or no federal income tax for 18 years, offsetting a

$916 million loss - made as a result of bad deals in the early 1990s - with it in an entirely legal manner. A week earlier, Clinton had urged Trump to disclose his tax returns during their first live election debate, suggesting that he did not want to disclose them because it might turn out that he had paid hardly any taxes for years.

On October 7, exactly one month before the election, Trump became discredited when *The Washington Post* released a 2005 video excerpt in which he spoke in a sexist and derogatory manner about "groupies. "Following this, more than 150 prominent Republicans withdrew their support from the presidential candidate, including John McCain. Trump apologized on TV, in writing and on Facebook. On October 10, Paul Ryan, the leading Republican in Congress, also said in a telephone interview with party colleagues that he would no longer support Trump. In the days that followed, a number of women went public with statements that they had once been groped unwisely by Trump. Among them were the 2001 winner of Miss Arizona USA, a former model and a woman who had participated in *The Apprentice* in 2007.

After the aforementioned video became public, Trump made a free fall in the polls. On October 14, he completely discontinued his campaign in the state of Virginia. His deficit to Clinton here had become so large that Trump's team no longer gave him a chance.

Election to President

Shortly before the election, Clinton was still ahead in most polls. However, on November 8, Trump won, against general expectations, in the important states of Florida, Ohio, Pennsylvania and North Carolina, among others. In doing so, he achieved victory. Trump won 30 states, compared to 20 and the District of Columbia for Clinton, but won a smaller share of the "popular vote," the total number of votes: Clinton got 65,853,514 votes (48.18%), Trump got 62,984,828 (46.09%). Because of the way the U.S. electoral system works, Trump more than met the threshold of 270 members of the Electoral College, by 304 to 227.

Presidency

Oaths

On January 20, 2017, Trump took the presidential oath of office. In his first speech as president, he emphasized that from that moment on, the United States would come first in everything.

Almost immediately after taking office as president, Trump caused a stir internationally by making controversial decisions. As early as January 25, for example, he signed the executive order for the wall to be built along the Mexican-American border. A week after his inauguration, he instituted an entry ban that would apply to seven Muslim countries. However, this ban was suspended by several federal courts, as was a modified version of it in March.

Immigration

Immigration policy, and in particular illegal immigration to the United States, was one of the main themes of President Donald Trump's election campaign. His proposals for reform and statements on the subject caused a great deal of publicity. Official estimates of the number of illegal immigrants in the U.S. range from 11 to 12 million.

According to Trump, crime is one of the problems resulting from illegal immigration. Statistics show that illegals are proportionately 4 times more likely to end up in prison than U.S. citizens, not including those incarcerated solely for being illegal. Other problems include creating a shadow economy, making it harder to enforce the law, and illegals competing in the labor market with legal immigrants and US citizens.

A crucial promise from Trump's campaign was to build a "solid wall" on the U.S.-Mexico border. Trump has further expressed support for several variants of "restricting legal immigration and visas for foreign workers," including a "pause" for issuance of Green Cards, which Trump says will "reduce record-high levels of immigration to more modest historical averages."

As president, Trump issued an entry ban, specifically a ban on issuing visas to residents of seven largely Muslim countries. Responding to court rulings, he revised the *ban* twice, while his third version was approved by the Supreme Court in June 2018. He sought to end the *Deferred Action for Childhood Arrivals* (DACA) program, but a court order allowed the policy in question to continue while the case is under trial.

Trump further announced a zero-tolerance order to arrest and detain all illegal immigrants when crossing the border. This also led to children being separated from their parents, as the US does not want to incarcerate children in an adult prison. A possible underlying argument for this policy was its intended deterrent effect. Key architects of this approach were top counselor Stephen Miller and Attorney General Jeff

Sessions.Interior Secretary Nielsen was charged with the difficult task of reuniting children scattered across the U.S. with their parents.

In his first State of the Union on January 30, 2018, Trump laid out his administration's four pillars for immigration policy reform: 1. a pathway for naturalization of *DREAMers*, 2. funding for border security improvements, 3. ending the various visa lotteries, and 4. restricting immigration based on family relationships.These four pillars reinforce Trump's campaign promise of *Buy American, Hire American* and also the 2017 executive order of the same name, tracks with the immigration policy priorities previously laid out.

After the November 6, 2018 midterm election, Democrats regained the majority in, and thus control of, the House of Representatives. This made it more difficult for Trump to implement his desired immigration policy. In particular, the budget for the border wall was a point of contention. This led to the temporary government shutdown at the beginning of 2019. To get the budget anyway, Trump declared a state of emergency (delineated for the Mexican-American border) in early 2019, which gave him more control over the budget temporarily.

COVID-19 pandemic

As of December 2019, a global outbreak of the infectious disease COVID-19 occurred, first identified in the Chinese city of Wuhan. The first infection in the U.S. was detected on January 20, 2020. On January 31, Health Minister Alex Azar announced a partial entry ban versus non-Americans, who wanted to travel to the U.S. from China. This ban became effective on February 2.

President Trump was slow to respond to the pandemic. He waved away the initial alarm signals from official health experts and his Secretary of Health Azar.Warnings about public health he ignored, focusing instead on the economic and political consequences of the outbreak.He continued to claim that a vaccine could be expected within months, despite official agencies, such as the Department of Health (HHS) and Center for Disease Control (CDC) repeatedly assuring him that it would take a year to a year and a half to develop a safe vaccine.Also, Trump knocked the availability of testing materials for the virus - against his better judgment - claiming that "anyone who wants a test can get a test," when the presence of testing materials was grossly inadequate.

On March 6, 2020, Trump signed the *Coronavirus Preparedness and Response Supplemental Appropriations Act*, which provided $8.3 billion for an emergency fund to benefit federal agencies. On March 13, his partial entry ban became effective for travelers from most of Europe.He also addressed the American people for the first time in a serious speech from the *Oval office* about the "terrible" virus.

In mid-March, Trump held press conferences accompanied by medical experts and White House staff, some of whom were forced to contradict him when he touted unvalidated treatments or medications. During these conferences, he frequently praised his own handling of the pandemic and criticized his rival presidential candidate Joe Biden and members of the White House press corps.

On March 16, the president acknowledged for the first time that the pandemic was not under control and that months of disruption to daily life and a recession could be on the horizon.On April 3, Trump announced that the federal government was going to use budgets from the *CARES Act* to pay hospitals for uninsured patients infected by the coronavirus. He drew much criticism from the media, health experts, the World Health Organization (WHO), and the Chinese government for his repeated use of the terms "Chinese virus" and "China virus."

In early April, as the pandemic worsened and he came under pressure over his administration's handling of the situation, Trump refused to admit mistakes. Instead, he faulted the media, Democratic governors, the Obama administration, China and the WHO.

In mid-April 2020, some national news networks began to limit their live coverage of the press conferences. The *Washington Post* reported that "propagandistic and inaccurate" statements made by Trump differed from factual statements made by members of the *Coronavirus Task Force*, particularly coronavirus coordinator Deborah Birx and top expert Dr. Anthony Fauci.

The Task Force's daily briefings stopped in late April, after Trump made the dangerous suggestion to his audience that they inject themselves with bleach to combat the coronavirus, an idea that met with sharp condemnation from medical professionals.

On April 22, Trump signed an executive order restricting some forms of immigration to the United States. In April 2020, some Republican Party affiliated groups organized anti-lockdown protests against the government's measures against the pandemic. Trump encouraged these protests on Twitter, despite the fact that the states he targeted did not themselves comply with the Trump administration's regulations for relaxation.

Initially, he supported Georgia Governor Brian Kemp's later-criticized plan to reopen a number of nonvital businesses. Throughout the spring, he continued to press for restrictions to be lifted to reduce the damage to the country's economy. Despite the simultaneous intensification of the spread of the pandemic in the U.S., Trump's priority for the economy led to a sharp decline in *Coronavirus Task Force* meetings in late May.

For months, Trump refused to wear a mouthguard during his press conferences and public appearances, in violation of his cabinet's April 2020 consensus that all Americans should wear mouthguards in public. Around June, Trump claimed that masks were a "two-edged sword," ridiculed presidential candidate Joe Biden for wearing one, and continually reiterated that wearing a mouthguard was only "an option." In the superlative, he went on to suggest that wearing a mouth mask was a "political signal against him" personally.

In July, Trump wore a mouth mask in public for the first time - on camera - himself when visiting *Walter Reed National Military Medical Center*. As the numbers of infections and deaths continued to rise, he chose the strategy of shifting the blame for his administration's failures to the states.

In July 2020, Trump announced the formal withdrawal of the US from the WHO as of July 2021, after accusing the UN organization - without any evidence - of "enabling the Chinese government to conceal the origin of the pandemic."

In defiance of record numbers of infections in the U.S. as of mid-July and a rising rate of positive tests, Trump continued to downplay the pandemic. He claimed that 99% of infections were "quite harmless," a claim that contradicted statements from medical authorities.A spike in the July 2020 infection rate of more than 160,000 corona deaths in the U.S. did not stop Trump from pressuring all states to reopen schools to physical education in the fall. As the U.S. passed the unsurpassed 200,000 corona deaths mark in September, President Trump continued to fail to take or promote preventative measures. Instead, for electoral reasons - in contradiction to unanimous statements by medical experts - he continued to suggest that a vaccine against SARS-CoV-2 will be available for general use by early November.

On October 2, 2020, it was announced that Donald Trump and his wife Melania had themselves become infected with SARS-CoV-2, the virus that causes COVID-19. Several of his confidants were also found to be infected. On October 5, Trump was released from the hospital.

International Trade

As he had already announced during his election campaign, from the start of his term as president, Trump, in line with his "America First" agenda, showed a preference for a protectionist approach over the global trend of free trade. For example, he called for a renegotiation of the terms of NAFTA a free trade agreement between the U.S., Canada and Mexico, which went into effect in 1994.Trump showed himself to be an opponent of the Trans-Pacific Partnership (TPP), a free trade agreement of several countries bordering the Pacific Ocean. Shortly after taking office, he signed an executive order withdrawing the US from it.

In April 2017, he imposed higher import duties on the Canadian timber industry to address complaints from dairy producers in the state of Wisconsin about Canada's dairy product pricing policy.

In May 2017, the Trump administration announced a deal with China that would see China increase imports of U.S. beef. China would also accelerate the approval of genetically modified products.In return, the U.S. will allow the import of cooked poultry, encourage the export of liquefied natural gas to China, and tacitly support China's geopolitical and economic plan to revive the Silk Road.Initially, the Trump administration called the deal "gigantic and unprecedented" while considering it a gesture of rapprochement with China. However, research by the *Financial Times revealed* that most of the Chinese commitments were already part of pre-existing policies.

At the G7 Summit in Quebec on June 10, 2018, Trump surprised ministers of the other countries by calling for the elimination of all import duties between member states. Donald Tusk, the EU president, expressed concern that Trump was thereby undermining the regulated international order.Trump's suggestions came after increasing threats of countermeasures by his allies if the Trump administration pushes through the increase in import duties on steel and aluminum, announced earlier this year, by 25% and 10% respectively. At the time of Trump's remarks, import duties between the U.S., Canada and the EU were a percentage in the range of 3%. Canadian Prime Minister Justin Trudeau called Trump's threats "almost insulting." Trump then rescinded his agreement on the final declaration, prompting disapproval at home and abroad.

Foreign Policy

In terms of foreign policy, President Trump breaks with both the style and substance of his predecessors and Western allies. In terms of style, his instincts and impulses and especially the spearheads from his election campaign take precedence over prior policies and diplomatic policy preparation.Further, he dismantles policy acts and treaties in which his predecessor President Obama had a hand. One example is the unilateral cancellation by the U.S. of the 2015 anti-nuclear treaty with Iran shared with other major powers. In keeping with his "America First" slogan, a key takeaway is that he believes his predecessors allowed other nations, particularly his Western allies and China, to "benefit financially unilaterally and excessively from the US." Trump wants to put an end to that.

Trump gave a speech at the United Nations General Assembly in both 2017 and 2018. The first time, he threatened to destroy North Korea and called North Korean state leader Kim Jong-un "Rocketman." In the September 25, 2018 meeting, he spoke warm, praising words about Kim, claiming that he and his Secretary of State Mike Pompeo had taken fruitful steps toward denuclearization. He has now assigned the role of Trump's and America's greatest foreign enemy to Iran.In his second appearance before the UN, Trump showed himself to be an isolationist. All heads of state present would be wise to persiflate his slogan *America First*: "America respects everyone's sovereignty, but counts on other states to respect America's sovereignty as well."

North Korea

On March 9, 2018, the White House confirmed that a meeting was planned between Donald Trump and Kim Jong-un, the leader of North Korea. The invitation came from the North Korean side. This meeting would be the first in 70 years between a U.S. president and the leader of North Korea.

The establishment of the North Korean invitation was in line with the spectacular rapprochement, which had developed between the two Koreas starting with the 2018 Winter Olympics. Both in the latter and in the opening to the U.S., South Korean President Moon Jae-in played an important role. Ahead of the summit, U.S. Secretary of State Mike Pompeo visited the North Korean leader twice. This culminated in a proposed meeting between Kim and Trump scheduled for June 12 in Singapore.

On May 24, President Trump decided to cancel the meeting for the time being. He cited recent hostile statements from the North Korean side as arguments. These included calling Vice President Mike Pence a "dummy" after he had confirmed the U.S. objective for the summit envisioned by national security adviser John Bolton, namely the realization of the *Lybian model*, or *complete dismantling of nuclear capabilities* on the Korean Peninsula.

In a letter to the leader Kim Jong-un, in which he once again threatened him with the incomparably greater nuclear power of the U.S., President Trump kept open the option that Kim might change his mind, so that the summit could go ahead at a later date. On June 1, he said that as far as he was concerned, the summit could go ahead after all, on the previously set date of June 12.

After several rounds of preparatory staff meetings, Trump and Kim Jong-un met for a bilateral summit on June 12 at the Hotel Capella, Resort (Singapore) in Singapore. In a joint statement, the two countries solemnly pledged to unite their "efforts to establish a stable and lasting peace regime on the Korean Peninsula," while Kim reiterated his April 2018 pledge to "continue working toward the complete denuclearization of the Korean Peninsula."

Trump and Kim met for a second time at a specially convened summit in Hanoi, Vietnam, on February 27-28, 2019. No agreement was reached and the summit ended prematurely.

During the G20 summit in Osaka, Trump tweeted an invitation to Kim on June 28, 2019, to meet at the North Korean border on the sidelines of Trump's visit to South Korea. On June 30, 2019, Trump became the first sitting U.S. president to set foot on North Korean soil.

Israeli-Palestinian conflict

Regarding the conflict between Israel and the Palestinian Authority, Trump initially stressed the importance of impartiality during any negotiations. He called on Israeli Prime Minister Netanyahu several times for restraint regarding the construction of new Israeli settlements in the West Bank of Palestine.

Jerusalem

On December 6, 2017, Trump officially recognized Jerusalem as the capital of Israel and initiated the relocation of his embassy in Tel Aviv to Jerusalem, despite calls from several world leaders (including Antonio Guterres and Pope Francis) not to do so (independent of peace negotiations).

The United Nations General Assembly condemned this move. It adopted a resolution at a special session ("emergency session") on December 20, 2017, which also cited UN Security Council Resolution 2334 (2016) and called on all states *to distinguish between the territory of Israel and the territories occupied (by that state) since early June 1967 in their relevant political actions and decisions.*On May 14, 2018, during the celebrations due to 70 years of Israel, the U.S. Embassy in Jerusalem was solemnly opened.In the demonstrations that began after this in the Gaza Strip on the "border" with Israel, 58 people were killed on the same day. For the Palestinians and for their political leader Abbas, Trump had crossed a red line with this, they did not want to have anything more to do with the American-Trump administration. They wanted to negotiate only with a larger international forum. They no longer trusted Trump as an impartial and "honest peace broker." Also Mike Pence, US vice president, was later not received by the Palestinians during his trip to Israel (and as was his intention the Palestinian territories).

Deal of the Century

Announcement of Peace Plan

On May 22, 2017, Trump - in private - visited the Wailing Wall in Jerusalem and met with Netanyahu and later Palestinian leader Mahmoud Abbas in Bethlehem. According to him, the *"ultimate deal"* was possible. Trump announced that he would come up with a peace plan. In late August 2017, Jared Kushner, Trump's Jewish son-in-law, also visited Abbas as head of a peace delegation along with Trump's special envoy Greenblatt. Some 20 talks had been held by then. Abbas demanded that Kushner, within 45 days, publicly reaffirm his commitment to the two-state solution and also his commitment to bringing an immediate halt to illegal Jewish settlement construction. However, this was met with an unequivocal "no" from the Trump administration. In doing so, the Trump administration effectively abandoned decades of U.S. support for a two-state model as part of the peace process.

Peace Plan Presentation

In June 2019, Kushner presented in Bahrain part of his "peace plan for Israel and the Palestinians," which he called the "opportunity of the century" for the Palestinians. It included only an economic component of the plan and mirrored major investments in the region with thriving international businesses and economic prosperity for the Palestinian territories. A political solution to the conflict was not discussed. Neither Israeli nor Palestinian leaders were present at the presentation.

On January 27, 2020, Trump officially presented his "Peace to Prosperity" or "Deal of the Century" plan as a peace plan at the White House, just months before Israel's re-election and impeachment proceedings against Trump himself. In it, however, Israeli settlements in occupied Palestinian territory were earmarked as legal. The Palestinians were again not present, but Israeli Prime Minister Netanyahu and opposition leader Benny Gantz were. The Palestinians had rejected the plan in advance, but Netanyahu was praising it and Gantz also accepted it. The Arab League rejected the plan, saying it involved "a great waste of legitimate rights of Palestinians."

Peaceful Israeli figures turned against the plan. In Europe, 50 former government leaders and foreign ministers judged, in a letter to European government leaders, that "Trump's peace plan is reminiscent of apartheid.

Abraham chords

In September and October 2020, the White House reached a series of agreements between Israel on the one hand and the United Arab Emirates and Bahrain on the other. These agreements are called the Abraham Accords, after the patriarch Abraham, who appears in both the Torah, and the Quran. Trump signed on behalf of the United States on September 15, 2020. The declaration between Israel and the United Arab Emirates marked the first public normalization of relations between an Arab country and Israel since those of Egypt in 1979 (Camp David Accords) and Jordan in 1994. Agreements with Morocco and Sudan followed in October and November 2020. These countries also normalized their relations with Israel.

UNRWA

In the second half of 2018, Trump took a series of measures, including cutting the U.S. grant to UNRWA, which provides basic services to over 5 million Palestinian refugees. The U.S. State Department called UNRWA's operations an *"irreparably flawed operation"* due to the *"endless and exponentially growing"* number of people claiming emergency aid. Palestinian President Mahmoud Abbas condemned the decision as a *"blatant attack"* on the Palestinian people. Netanyahu had personally sent Trump a secret message shortly before to cut all funds to UNRWA. Also, Trump cut $25 million worth of Palestinian hospitals in East Jerusalem. Furthermore, he decided to close the PLO's diplomatic representation to the US, which had functioned for more than 20 years. Finally, his national security adviser, John Bolton, let it be known that the U.S. threatened to step into the International

Criminal Court if it went ahead with, among other things, the case brought to the International Criminal Court by Palestine against Israel for possible war crimes committed by that country in the Gaza Strip. In September 2019 in New York, where he had addressed the United Nations General Assembly, and after a conversation with Benjamin Netanyahu whom he had invited there, Trump expressed for the first time his opinion that a two-state model would be the best solution to the conflict. This also appeared in Trump's January 28, 2020 plan.

Golan Heights

On March 25, 2019, President Trump signed a statement that the United States recognizes the occupied Golan Heights as part of Israel. In doing so, Trump broke with U.S. policy of the past half century. Prime Minister Netanyahu of Israel attended the event. In 2013, the Israeli government had already issued a license to the American company Genie Energy with exclusive rights to drill oil and gas there, which after prior analysis is present in large quantities. Around that year, there were about 30 Israeli settlements with 20,000 settlers in the Golan Heights. Trump's decision went against the judgment of the United Nations, which has never recognized annexation by Israel of occupied territory. The United Nations, European and Arab states declared that the Golan Heights are Syrian state territory, regardless of what the U.S. decided on the matter. On April 23, 2019, Netanyahu announced that he will submit a resolution for government approval to name a new community in the Golan Heights after Trump. On June 16, 2019, Israel announced the establishment of Trump Heights, a planned settlement in the Golan Heights

ISIS and foreign wars

In April 2017, Trump ordered a 59 cruise missile attack on a Syrian airfield in retaliation for the Assad regime's chemical weapons bombing of Khan Shaykuhn, a town in northwestern Syria.According to investigative journalist Bob Woodward, Trump had ordered his Defense Secretary James Mattis to execute Syrian President Bashar al-Assad after the chemical attack, but Mattis distanced himself from that order. Trump denied having given that order.In April 2018, the president repeated a punitive action with missile strikes against Assad's regime as a repercussion to an alleged Syrian use of chemical weapons near Damascus.In December 2018, Trump claimed "we have defeated ISIS" and decreed the recall of all U.S. troops from Syria, completely thwarting the policies of the Department of Defense.Defense Secretary Jim Mattis resigned the next day due to conflicting views on foreign policy. He characterized the president's decision as abandoning

Kurdish allies, who play a key role in the ground battle against ISIS.A week later, Trump declared that he would not approve any expansion of U.S. deployments to Syria. On January 6, 2019, national security adviser John Bolton proclaimed that America would remain in Syria until ISIS is eradicated and as long as Turkey guarantees that it will refrain from attacking Kurdish fighters.

Trump actively supported the Saudi-led intervention in Yemen against the Houthis, and he signed a treaty to sell 110 billion worth of weapons to Saudi Arabia.Trump also praised his relationship with the powerful Saudi crown prince Mohammad bin Salman al-Saoed.Contrary to Trump's election promise, the number of U.S. troops in Afghanistan increased from 8,500 to 14,000 as of January 2017. U.S. diplomats said they were pressuring the Taliban to conclude a political agreement. However, President Trump spoke out against negotiations with the Taliban in January 2018.

In October 2019, following a telephone conversation between President Trump and Turkish President Erdogan, the White House confirmed that Turkey was about to launch a planned military offensive in northern Syria; assuming that U.S. troops would have departed from that region in order to avoid unintended and/or unwanted involvement in this Turkish offensive.The statement further transferred responsibility for the captured ISIS fighters to Turkey.Members of Congress from both parties disapproved of the action, including, among others, Trump's Republican supporter Senator Lindsey Graham and Senate Republican leader Mitch McConnell.They argued that the action represented a betrayal of U.S. allies, the Kurdish fighters. That it will favor the resurrection of the ISIS remnants, and further that this move will be welcomed by Russia, Iran and the Syrian regime of Bashar al-Assad.Trump defended the action by citing the high cost of supporting the Kurdish fighters and the lack of support from the Kurds in past U.S. wars. He also informed that if Turkey were to act disproportionately aggressively against Kurdish fighters they consider terrorists, hi, the economy of that country would be completely destroyed with the use of sanctions, boycotts, etc.Soon after the exit of the U.S. troops, the Turkish air force started bombing the Kurdish fighters occupied territory in northern Syria.

U.S.-Saudi Arabia Relations

The intense strategic and economic relationship between the United States and Saudi Arabia dates back to the end of World War II. The attacks on September 11, 2001, in which 12 hijackers had Saudi nationality, cooled it for a time. Nevertheless, mutual engagement in the areas of security, trade, and energy has steadily increased again. After two visits by President George W. Bush to Saudi Arabia in 2008 and three visits by King Abdoellahs to the U.S. (2002, 2005 and 2008), the relationship reached a peak. Both nations have prioritized their mutual relationship over petroleum and counterterrorism interests. King Abdullah, for example, has floated funds to allow young Saudis to study in the US. Main reasons are to give them Western perspectives and to let them establish a positive impression of Saudi Arabia among the American people.

The Bush administration took the Saudis very seriously because of their prevailing economic and defense presence in the region and their large media influence on the Islamic world. Broadly speaking, the two leaders made numerous decisions that dealt with security, economic, and business aspects of the relationship, which are the most important part of the fandom. In addition, since the late 20th century, Saudi Arabia has been viewed by successive U.S. cabinets as an important strategic ally against the threat of archenemy Iran. This has only increased following President Trump's decision in mid-2018 to make the US the only one of the six world powers to withdraw from the 2015 nuclear treaty with that country.

Arms deal Saudi Arabia

At the start of his first foreign tour, Trump signed a nearly $110 billion arms deal with Saudi Arabia on May 20, 2017, worth $300 billion over 10 years, including training and close cooperation with Saudi Arabia's military. The signed documents contain statements of principle and not actual contracts.

Murder of Jamal Khashoggi

In early October 2018, the relationship came under strain when Turkish authorities announced that Saudi-American NYT journalist Jamal Khashoggi had disappeared without a trace after entering the Saudi embassy in Istanbul for marriage formalities. In the following weeks, the Turkish side released further investigative details partly for legal reasons and partly for tactical diplomatic considerations. These led to Saudi authorities, after initially categorically denying having anything to do with it, admitting that an assassination commando from their country had eliminated Khashoggi in the embassy. Although some members of the commando were closely linked to him, it was strongly suggested that strongman and Crown Prince Mohammad bin Salman al-Saoed (MBS) was the principal.

President Trump initially reacted with restraint at the urging of his Turkish counterpart Erdogan, who seized his opportunity to play the human rights card, both against his Arab rival power and NATO ally the US. Trump sent his head of the CIA Gina Haspel to the sites of the disaster and wanted to await the investigation activities. In late November, nearly two months after the assassination and before the CIA report was released, Trump made it clear that based on his "America First" motto, trade interests (the Saudi's big arms order of early 2017) and alliance (anti-Iran) should prevail. He said he was left in the dark whether or not the Saudi crown prince had ordered Khashoggi's murder, and called the world "a dangerous place."

On November 22, 2018, Trump reiterated that the CIA's investigation did not conclude that Mohammad Bin Salman had ordered the assassination. Trump's assertions were criticized by members of Congress from both parties, who pledged to investigate. Adam Schiff, top Democrat and member of the House Intelligence Committee, who was briefed by the CIA, accused President Trump of lying about what the CIA had determined.On December 13, the Senate - contradicting the White House's position - unanimously passed a resolution declaring that Saudi Crown Prince Mohammad bin Salman was personally responsible for Khashoggi's death. On the same day, the Senate voted 56-41 in favor of legislation to cease military support for - the Saudi-led intervention in Yemen. A decision attributed to senators who want to punish Saudi Arabia for Khashoggi's murder and for the humanitarian crisis in Yemen, which is plagued by famine and human rights violations.

This was the first time ever that the Senate gave application to the War Powers Act.The House of Representatives then narrowly blocked consideration of any War Powers resolution to consider U.S. military action in Yemen for one year.

Climate Change

Before and after the election he won, Trump called climate change a "hoax," a fabrication sent into the world by the Chinese to undermine American interests. Consequently, during the election campaign he had promised to withdraw from the Paris Climate Agreement, and he kept that election promise as well. The U.S. is still only an observer "at Paris." Later in his presidency, he denied the hoax story again, stating that "something" is going on. The cause of that something, the measured warming, is unclear according to him: it came naturally and it will come naturally. Some time after he took office, the website of the US Department of the Environment (the US EPA), the Unites States

Environmental Protection Agency, changed. When it comes to climate change, it's not about combating it, but about "adaptation": adapting to its consequences.

However, many cities and states continued to take action on climate change after the announcement of the withdrawal from the agreement, forming what is known as the United States Climate Alliance.

#MeToo

The issue of unwelcome sexual approaches to women by Donald Trump (see #Scandals), also flared up after the global #MeToo wave of exposures, which followed that of film producer Harvey Weinstein in October 2017. Numerous top executives from various sectors of society, such as media, sports, science, etc., were confronted with the fact that female colleagues no longer tolerated their cross-border harassment and abuse of power and did, for the first time, dare to make it public. In almost all cases this resulted in the resignation or immediate dismissal of these high-ranking authorities.

In addition to many times unexpectedly intruding into locker rooms at "his" mass elections, at least 13 individual accusations by women of sexually transgressive behavior are pending against Trump, dating back to before he took office as president. He threatened to sue these women, but has yet to put that into action. Through his White House spokeswoman Sarah Huckabee Sanders, Trump continues to deny everything.Prior to the midterm election to fill the vacancy of Senator for the state of Alabama, President Trump - after initial hesitation due to great distaste from Senate Republicans - fully promoted the candidacy of Republican Roy Moore. Numerous allegations have been made against this radical Christian former judge for engaging in cross-border sexual behavior with teenage girls when he himself was in his early thirties. In addition to his other extreme views, this was a reason for Republicans in the Capitol to declare Moore persona non grata at first. However, he won the Republican primary over his moderate Republican counter-candidate in Alabama. After the narrow victory of Democratic candidate Doug Jones on December 12, 2017, Trump immediately congratulated the latter on his victory without paying any attention to Moore's claim for a recount. This first Democratic electoral win in Alabama after more than two decades was explained by researchers as a result of the turnout of women and African-American voters in particular.

In January 2018, the American newspaper *The New York Times* revealed that Stephanie Clifford, aka Stormy Daniels, allegedly had a sexual affair with Donald Trump in 2006. His former personal lawyer Michael Cohen acknowledged about a month later shortly before the 2016 presidential election to have paid $130,000 in hush money to Clifford. The #MeToo movement saw this as yet another incident by a president who had previously been under scrutiny for his treatment of women: Daniels has always refused to link her to the movement.

During his tenure, Trump pushed Brett Kavanaugh forward as a Supreme Court nominee. During the nomination process, Kavanaugh was accused by Christine Blasey Ford of sexual assault during a small party at the *high school*. She testified about this in the Senate Judiciary Committee. After Trump's initial short-lived positive reaction to Ford's testimony, he characterized her story a few days later at a rally in Mississippi as "hole-in-the-wall": "She didn't know what and where her story was about." In doing so, he sided with Kavanaugh, the (alleged) perpetrator. A repetition of a pattern he already showed in previous issues of sexual transgression by candidate Senator Roy Moore and staff secretary Rob Porter. In a press briefing on the Blasey-Ford issue, the president also cited his own problem about sexually harassing several women. He used that opportunity to reduce the recorded number of complaining women from at least twelve to four.

Relationship with the media

Ever since his candidacy, Trump has had a moderate to poor relationship with much of the media, especially what is often called the "mainstream media." He has accused the press of spreading *fake news*. He has also called certain specific media outlets "the enemy of the people." For example, on February 17, 2017, Trump tweeted "The FAKE NEWS media (the failing @nytimes, @NBCNews, @ABC, @CBS, @CNN) are not my enemies, they are the enemies of the American people." On August 16, 2018, the Senate unanimously passed a resolution "that the press is not the enemy of the people."

In March, a number of leading television networks refused to air a paid commercial for the Trump 2020 campaign, which conveyed the message that the mainstream media did not want to showcase his successes, and en passant referred to these media as "fake news." In a statement, CNN explained the refusal, arguing that it went against their policy of spreading falsehoods. Trump's daughter-in-law and campaign adviser, Lara Trump, called the rejection a "shocking precedent in the obstruction of the right to speech."

Twitter usage

Trump continued his frequent use of Twitter after his inauguration, which had also characterized his presidential campaign. He himself continued with the personal @realDonaldTrump, his personal account, while his staff tweeted for him through the official @POTUS account.His use of Twitter to communicate directly with the American people, without the intervention of more traditional mass media such as newspapers and TV stations, has not been seen before by a U.S. president. The Trump administration describes Trump's tweets as "official statements from the President of the United States." For Trump, Twitter is a media channel to share his views in his own words, without the risk of his words being twisted, which he believes is a risk.

The president uses Twitter for a variety of purposes: including to share policy proposals, express his opinion on a variety of issues, criticize other politicians, and garner political support for passing legislation.

He has used disparaging nicknames on Twitter a number of times for political opponents, such as "Little Marco (Rubio)," "Lying' Ted (Cruz)," and "Crooked Hillary (Clinton)" for his opponents during the campaign. A practice also continued after his election, such as "Sneaky Dianne Feinstein" and "Dicky Durbin". He used the nickname "Little Rocket Man" for head of state Kim Jong-un of North Korea, both in tweets and in a speech at the United Nations General Assembly.

He has also used the medium to criticize top officials in his own cabinet, including former Secretary of State Rex Tillerson, former national security adviser Herbert McMaster, Deputy Attorney General Rod Rosenstein and numerous times Attorney General Jeff Sessions. Tillerson was finally fired by Trump by tweet. Trump also tweeted that "his" Justice Department was part of the U.S. "deep state"; that there was "a terrible leaking, lying and corruption" going on at the highest levels of the FBI, the Departments of Justice & State, as well as that Special Prosecutor Robert Mueller's investigation would be a witch hunt.

Some other notable tweets were as follows: Criticism of a judge's ruling that had blocked a Trump decree regarding entry restrictions. That decree was later reinstated in amended form. Comments that Secretary Jeff Sessions should "immediately stop" the Special Prosecutor's investigation; that it was "rigged," and that the investigators were biased.

A federal judge ruled in May 2018 that Trump's blocking of other Twitter users because of opposing political views violates *First Amendment* of the Constitution. However, it did not include a specific order to unblock people. Trump has appealed.

Trump wrote the non-existent word *covfefe* in a tweet on May 31, 2017. The tweet read, *"Despite the constant negative press covfefe"*. The internet then reacted with amazement. Twitter flooded with people wondering what exactly Trump meant. #covfefe was temporarily the most used hashtag. The tweet in question was deleted by Trump, who wondered if anyone could figure out its true meaning. Democratic member of the House of Representatives Mike Quigly filed an amendment, Communications Over Various Feeds Electronically for Engagement Act (C.O.V.F.E.F.E Act), to include statements made via social media by the president to be covered by the Presidential Records Act and thus preserved. "Covfefe" turned out to be a typo when writing *news coverage*

Following the Trump-inspired storming of the U.S. Capitol by Trump supporters in Washington D.C. on January 6, 2021, Twitter and Facebook decided to temporarily block the president's account. A day later, Facebook CEO Mark Zuckerberg announced that the blockade would be extended indefinitely....

On January 8, 2021, Twitter announced it was permanently suspending Trump's account due to the risk of further incitement to violence.

Reaction to police brutality against George Floyd

In response to the mass protests - some of them violent - and the civil unrest resulting from the deadly arrest of African-American George Floyd by police, Trump publicly raised the possibility of enacting the *Insurrection Act* and deploying the military in certain U.S. cities, given the need to maintain authority and order.

A few days later, Trump stated that everyone deserves equal, fair treatment from the security forces and that what happened to Floyd is not permissible. In the same speech, he posited that something great is happening in the U.S., that it was a great day, for Floyd and for everyone regarding equality. Moreover, he claimed that no one ever did more for the black community than himself. His statements came in for criticism.

Elections 2020

In the 2020 U.S. presidential election, Donald Trump was the Republican candidate for a second term. His Democratic opponent was

Joe Biden, who was vice president under Trump's predecessor Obama. Because of the corona crisis, it was clear in advance that there would be a lot more voting by mail, especially by Democratic voters, who generally expressed more concern about the pandemic (Biden stood for strict corona measures and called for voting by mail, Trump favored few restrictive measures). Trump had warned before the election that voting by mail would be susceptible to fraud, even though most experts contradicted that it was widespread.

Shortly after the election, while the counting was still in full swing, Trump already proclaimed that he had won, as Biden was behind in many crucial states. The media labeled this as premature. Trump claimed to know about massive fraud in the counting of votes and called for an end to it in some states. However, the counting went on as usual and a few days later it appeared that Biden had gathered more electoral votes behind him than Trump and had thus won the election. Contrary to prevailing norms, Trump did not admit defeat. He would not help Biden take over, and lawsuits were filed by his team in several states to challenge the results and recounts were requested. Recounts and lawsuits always turned against Trump, who then initiated further proceedings.

According to preliminary figures from CNN, Trump garnered approximately 72.7 million votes, more in absolute terms than any other candidate for the presidency ever, however, the record was held by Joe Biden who garnered approximately 78 million votes according to the same figures.

On November 23, the General Services Administration (GSA) granted Joe Biden the facilities due to a President-Elect. However, Trump did not yet accept his loss and tried with lawsuits and recounts to change the result in his favor.

On November 25, Thanksgiving, Trump pardoned his former National Security Advisor Michael Flynn. That he did so when it became clear that he would most likely not get a second term as president immediately evoked criticism of abuse of power.

On January 3, 2021, an audio recording leaked in which Trump pressured officials in the state of Georgia to commit large-scale election fraud. He then went on to pressure Vice President Mike Pence to deny some results during the Electoral College vote count on January 6, but Pence did not relent.

After the Electoral College votes were confirmed following the tumultuous session (see below), Trump promised an orderly transfer of power on January 20. Earlier, Biden had accused Trump of working against him.

Riots at the Capitol

On January 6, 2021, at the Capitol, the Electoral College votes were officially counted by the House of Representatives and Congress. That same day, elections also took place in Georgia, where two seats for Congress were filled and where the Democrats appeared to be heading for a narrow win. That win gave the Democrats half of Congress, which represents a narrow majority, since the vice president (as of Joe Biden's swearing-in on January 20, that's Democratic Kamala Harris) provides a crucial extra vote in this case. Trump called on his supporters to come to Washington D.C. that day to protest what he still saw as a fraudulent result. He addressed his supporters there. Later, they demonstrated at the Capitol and some of the supporters stormed the building, during the session. They hit after the congressmen had left the conference room and been taken to safety, among other things, as far as the chair of that room, and also in the office of House Speaker Nancy Pelosi. Some offices were vandalized and looted. Shots were fired, with one person fatally hit. Trump called via Twitter to keep the peace, while his daughter Ivanka on the same medium praised the (peaceful) protesters as "American patriots." After three hours, he sent a video message into the world in which he once again and repeatedly stressed that the election was stolen from him, but he also called for people to go back home. By 6 p.m. local time and after the intervention of the National Guard, the building was evacuated.

At the demonstrations, one person died from a bullet, three others died from "medical complications" and one officer died a day after the demonstrations. 52 people were detained. Criticism of the Capitol's security soon reverberated. Elected officials from both major parties disapproved of the storming of the Capitol and pointed to the responsibility of Trump's words.

Trumpism

This is a term for the political ideology, style of governance, political movement, and set of mechanisms for acquiring and maintaining power that is associated with Donald Trump and his political base. It is an American political version of the right to far-right, national-populist sentiment seen in multiple countries worldwide in the late 2010s and includes aspects of illiberal democracy.

Impeachment

Attempts at indictment

Since Trump was sworn in as president, there have been several attempts to start impeachment proceedings ("impeachment") against him by filing one or more so-called *Articles of Impeachment* in the House of Representatives. These attempts were initially hopeless as long as the Republican faction in the House of Representatives, which had the majority there through 2018, remained behind the president.

- May 17, 2017: Al Green, a member of the House of Representatives for the Democratic Party, accused Trump of obstruction of justice. As justification, he cited Trump's firing of FBI boss James Comey and Trump's statement in connection with the FBI investigation into Russian state influence on the presidential election. The motion was not put to a vote.

- July 2017: Brad Sherman, member of the House of Representatives for the Democratic Party, accused him of obstructing justice by firing James Comey.

- November 2017: Al Green, member of the House of Representatives for the Democratic Party, with five supporters of the motion, also Democrats accused President Trump of violating the Constitution, according to them. Firing FBI Director James Comey and violating the so-called Emoluments Clause (the prohibition on government officials accepting gifts from foreign governments) were two arguments made by the Congressmen to initiate impeachment proceedings. Democrats also pointed to Trump's "undermining" of the independence of the judiciary and freedom of the press. Green indicated that he definitely wanted a (purely symbolic) vote on the motion, which had no real chance of passing. The motion eventually received 58 votes in the House of Representatives, which had 435 members, 193 of whom were Democrats.

During most of President Trump's presidency, Democrats were divided on the issue of impeachment of the president. Fewer than 20 delegates in the House of Representatives supported impeachment around January 2019, but this number increased to around 140 delegates after the Mueller report came out in April and after special prosecutor Robert Mueller testified in July.

Initial impeachment proceedings, process, acquittal

The first impeachment proceedings against Trump were formally announced on September 24, 2019 by the Speaker of the House of Representatives of the Democrats, Nancy Pelosi. The trigger was a telephone conversation of Trump with Volodymyr Zelensky, President of Ukraine. In doing so, Trump allegedly said on behalf of the United States that he would not provide the promised military aid to Ukraine until there was a corruption investigation in Ukraine into Joe Biden and his son Hunter's company, with which Trump was allegedly guilty of quid pro quo. At the time, former Vice President Biden was one of the Democratic Party's main contenders to become Trump's opponent in the 2020 U.S. presidential election.

Throughout October 2019, several State Department staffers testified behind closed doors in sessions of Congressional Committees on Ukrainian issue - Resolution 31-10-2019. On October 22, U.S. diplomat William B. Taylor Jr. stated that soon after arriving in June 2019, he discovered that Zelensky was being pressured by a private initiative led by Trump and directed by Rudy Giuliani, Trump's private lawyer.The intent was to force Zelensky to reach a public agreement on, on the one hand, a corruption investigation at the company that employed Hunter Biden, and on the other hand, into rumors of Ukrainian influence on the 2016 U.S. presidential election. He made it clear that until Zelensky made such an announcement, the U.S. Cabinet would not transfer the already budgeted military aid to Ukraine, nor would it send Zelensky the coveted invitation to visit the White House.As part of the impeachment investigation, the House of Representatives legal committee requested access to the Grand Jury information that had been used in the summary of the Mueller report. The Department of Justice (DOJ) refused to turn over that information, arguing that the secrecy of this material must be maintained and that the impeachment investigation is not sound.On October 25, 2019, federal Judge Beryl A. Howell ruled that the latter investigation is sound and that the DOJ must provide information to the committee within a week.On October 31, the House passed a resolution by 232 to 196 votes setting the rules for the next phase of the investigation, which includes public hearings.

On Wednesday, November 13, 2019, the official, public investigation into President Trump's impeachment over the Ukraine issue began with the questioning of top diplomats William B. Taylor Jr. and George Kent, who were working in the capital, Kiev. The Congressional Intelligence Committee meeting was led by Democratic Chairman Adam Schiff.The impeachment investigation stemmed from the unanticipated complaint of an anonymous whistleblower, who called Trump's phone call an abuse of power, and added other charges, viz. that the White House had intended to archive the file of the phone call in a secret digital system, and that the phone call was part of a broad campaign by Rudy Giuliani and the Trump administration to pressure Ukraine into launching a corruption investigation into the Bidens.The whistleblower further expressed suspicion that Trump's cancellation of Vice President Mike Pence's May 2019 visit to Kiev, and the President's withholding of financial aid to Ukraine, were part of the campaign to pressure Ukraine. President Trump confirmed that he had indeed temporarily stopped military aid to Ukraine, for which he gave conflicting reasons

On December 18, 2019, Trump was indicted for abuse of power and obstruction of Congress in the so-called Ukraine affair.after the House of Representatives passed articles of impeachment for abuse of power and obstruction of Congress.

The investigation mentions that Trump stopped military aid to Ukraine, as well as inviting that country's president to the White House, in order to achieve that side's public proclamation of a corruption investigation into Trump's political rivals and the disputed claim that Ukraine had interfered in the 2016 U.S. presidential election.The Senate then had to rule on this. Six committees of the House of Representatives began to conduct preliminary investigations. Later it was decided to hold public hearings. The *Articles of Impeachment* were transferred to the Senate on January 15, 2020.On January 31, 2020, Senate voted against calling witnesses, which had been strongly urged by the Democratic minority after being blocked by the White House. This made this the first impeachment trial in U.S. history in which no witnesses were heard.

On February 5, 2020, Trump was acquitted of both charges, almost entirely along party lines, by a majority vote of senators. All Democratic senators had voted for impeachment, almost all Republican senators had voted against. The exception was Utah's Republican senator, Mitt Romney, the only - and only senator ever - to declare the president of his own party guilty of either charge.

Second impeachment proceedings, trial, acquittal

On January 11, 2021, a second impeachment trial of Donald Trump was filed, following the storming of the Capitol on January 6 of that year. Trump is the first U.S. president against whom such proceedings were initiated twice. He was accused of "inciting an insurrection." On January 13, 2021, a majority of 232 to 197 members of the House of Representatives voted in favor of the procedure to depose President Trump. Those voting in favor included ten delegates from Trump's own Republican Party. The official impeachment proceedings were delivered to the Senate by the House of Representatives on January 25, 2021 (local time). This is after the end of Trump's regular term in office.

On February 9, 2021, a majority in the U.S. Senate, in a vote, declared the impeachment process against Donald Trump constitutional. The procedure was approved by 56 votes to 44. The trial in the Senate took place when his successor Biden was already president. While Trump's departure was no longer an issue at that time, it could still be decided that he could not run for president again in the future. Many Republicans voted against conviction on the grounds that the Constitution does not allow an ex-president to be deposed. As a result, there was no two-thirds majority for impeachment.

25th Amendment to the Constitution

Apart from *impeachment*, the U.S. Constitution has a second procedure for removing a sitting president from office, which is through the application of the 25th Amendment to the Constitution. This can be applied in the event that "he/she is unable to exercise the powers and duties of his office." His (alleged) mental state was hinted at several times during Trump's presidency to allow him to be removed from office, but in practice it was not used.

In mid-February 2019, then-Deputy Director of the FBI Andrew McCabe revealed that he and other top FBI and Justice officials had seriously discussed the option of applying the 25th Amendment following the unexpected resignation of FBI Director James Comey. This was in connection with the growing evidence of a Russian connection between President Trump and his entourage in May 2017.

After the storming of the Capitol by Trump supporters promoted by him on January 6, 2021, some officeholders again called for invoking the 25th Amendment to depose Trump, considering him responsible for the riots and therefore unfit to hold office.

Surveys

General

Starting in early 2019, with the Democratic majority in the House of Representatives, a variety of issues from the first half of the Trump administration's term, such as the election campaign, the transition process, the inauguration, as well as in parallel the relationship between government and private interests, private taxes and charitable funds will be subject to detailed scrutiny. The relevant House committees may subpoena witnesses and hear them under oath.

Russiagate

The allegations of collusion with "the Russians" are often referred to simply as *Russia-gate*. Special Prosecutor Robert Mueller's final report states that there is no evidence that the Trump campaign or any individuals or organizations affiliated with it colluded with Russia to influence the 2016 U.S. presidential election.

In the first two years of Donald Trump's presidency, much media attention was focused on the suspicion that his election win in November 2016 was partly due to collusion between his campaign team and high-ranking Russian authorities.The first weeks of the Trump administration did not help to weaken this suspicion. National security adviser Michael Flynn had to step down, due to lies about Russian contacts. Attorney General Jeff Sessions was forced to stay out of the Special Prosecutor's investigation into alleged Russian interference. The President distrusted his own Intelligence agencies and placed more value on President Vladimir Putin's denial. Fighting the digital media that the Russians have exploited was not Trump's interest.When, after several months, the president demanded personal loyalty from FBI Director James Comey over his professional integrity and then fired him headlong for investigating that "Russia-thing," Trump unleashed a scenario that would be directed by a Special Prosecutor, and may rival the drama of the Watergate scandal under the presidency of Richard Nixon.

Back in January 2017, the joint U.S. intelligence agencies, the CIA, FBI and NSA, claimed with "high confidentiality" that the Russian government interfered in the 2016 U.S. presidential election to favor Trump's election. In March 2017, FBI Director James Comey told Congress that "as part of our counterintelligence mission, it is the FBI's job to investigate the Russian government's attempts to influence the presidential election." That includes investigating the nature of the ties between individuals associated with the Trump campaign and the Russian government, and whether there was any coordination between the campaign and Russian effort. "Later, in testimony at the Senate Intelligence Committee meeting on June 8, he confirmed that he did not have "the slightest doubt" that the Russian government had interfered in the 2016 election, adding that "they did it intentionally and cunningly."Trump's ties to Russia have been widely reported in the press.One of Trump's campaign managers, Paul Manafort, worked for pro-Russian politician Viktor Yanukovych for several years to win the presidency of Ukraine. Other allies of Trump, including former national security adviser Michael Flynn and political consultant Roger Stone, had ties to Russian authorities. During the campaign, Russian agents were told that they knew they could bring in Manafort and Flynn to influence Trump.Members of Trump's campaign and later his White House staff, particularly Flynn, were in contact with Russian authorities both before and after the November 6 election. On December 29, 2016, Flynn spoke with Russian Ambassador Sergei Kislyak (diplomat) about sanctions imposed the same day. Later, Trump fired Flynn for falsely claiming that he had not spoken about the sanctions.

Resignation of CIA Director James Comey

On May 9, 2017, Trump fired FBI Director James Comey. Initially, he attributed this action to recommendations from Attorney General Jeff Sessions and Deputy Secretary of State Rod Rosenstein, who criticized Comey's handling of the investigation into Hillary Clinton's emails. On May 11, Trump stated that he was concerned about "that continuing Russian thing" and that he had previously planned to fire Comey, regardless of advice from the Justice Department.

According to a Comey memo from a personal conversation with the president on February 14, 2017, Trump said he hoped Comey would drop the investigation into Michael Flynn. In March and April, Trump told Comey that the lingering suspicions formed a "dark cloud" that damaged his presidency, and asked him to publicly state that he personally was not an object of investigation.He also asked intelligence chiefs Dan Coats and Michael Rogers to issue statements to the effect that there was no evidence that his campaign colluded with the Russians during the 2016 presidential election. Both refused, considering it an inappropriate, if not illegal, request.Finally, Comey himself testified as director on June 8 that the FBI's investigation was not directed at Trump himself. In a Twitter message, Trump suggested that he had tape recordings of conversations with Comey, only to later proclaim that he did not in fact have such recordings.

Special Prosecutor

On May 17, 2017, Deputy Secretary of State Rod Rosenstein appointed Robert Mueller, a former director of the FBI as Special Prosecutor of the Department of Justice (DOJ). In this capacity, Mueller was given oversight of the investigation into "any ties and/or coordination of the Russian government with President Donald Trump's campaign, and any issues, already raised or potentially to be raised directly from the investigation." Trump has repeatedly refuted any collusion between the Trump campaign and the Russian government.A few days after Comey's firing, *The Washington Post* reported that the Special Prosecutor's Office was going to investigate whether Trump had obstructed justice. Trump's new lawyer Jay Sekulow said no notice of such an investigation had reached him. ABC News later reported that the Special Prosecutor had gathered information in advance about possible obstruction of justice, but was not yet launching a full-scale investigation.

In January 2018, *The New York Times* reported that Trump had ordered that Mueller be fired in June 2017, after Mueller was busy investigating possible obstruction of justice. However, Trump backed down after White House counsel Don McGahn threatened to resign; Trump called the report "fake news." *The New York Times* reported in April 2018 that Trump had again demanded in December 2017 that the investigation cease, but stopped after reading news reports on which he based that his decision was wrong. In April 2018, following the FBI's raid on the home and office of Trump's private attorney Michael Cohen, Trump hinted aloud about firing Mueller. In August 2018, Trump wrote that Secretary of State Jeff Sessions should "stop the Special Prosecutor's investigation immediately now"; the president also referred to the investigation as a "witch hunt" and "rigged."

In January 2018, it was announced that Mueller wants to question Trump about the removal of Flynn and Comey. For most of 2018, there was discussion between Mueller's office and White House lawyers about whether Trump would give Mueller a one-on-one interview or an answer in writing, and what topics should be covered. Trump himself said publicly that he was willing to be interviewed. In November 2018, he said he was preparing written answers to a set of questions, and in late November his legal team stated that he had provided answers to written questions from the Special Prosecutor on "topics concerning the Russia-related key points of the investigation."

The New York Times reported on January 11, 2019 that the FBI's counterintelligence division is increasingly concerned about Trump's ties to Russia during the 2016 election campaign, but refrained from opening an investigation because of uncertainty about how to operate on such a sensitive issue. Trump's behavior during the days immediately preceding Comey's firing prompted them to open an investigation into whether Trump had worked for the Russians and knowingly or unknowingly to the detriment of American interests. The FBI merged the counter-info with that from the investigation into possible obstruction of justice in the firing of James Comey. Mueller took over the latter investigation after his appointment, although it was not immediately clear that he had taken the counterintelligence angle.

Companions

On August 21, 2018, Trump's former campaign manager Paul Manafort was convicted of eight felony counts of tax and bank fraud. Trump said in a response that he felt for Manafort and praised him for not succumbing to prosecutors' pressure to reach a settlement, noting, "So much respect for a brave man!" According to his personal lawyer Giuliani, Trump had been advised of the possibility of pardoning Manafort but had been advised against it.

In September, Manafort faced trial for the second time on numerous charges, but managed to agree on a plea deal by admitting guilt to conspiracy and witness tampering, as well as pledging full cooperation with the Justice Department.

In November, Mueller's office published in an official statement that Manafort had repeatedly lied to his interrogators, violating the terms of the plea deal. It also disclosed that Manafort, through his lawyer, had informed White House lawyers of his interactions with the Special Prosecutor's office. Trump publicly hinted that he might grant Manafort a pardon, but the nominee for chair of the House Judiciary Committee warned that "putting a pardon in front of Manafort" could lead to charges of obstruction of justice.

On Nov. 29, Trump's former lawyer Michael Cohen acknowledged guilt for making lying statements to Congress about Trump's efforts in 2016 to reach a deal with Russian authorities to build a Trump Tower in Moscow. Cohen said he had made the false statements on behalf of Trump, who was referred to in court documents as "Individual-1."

Trump's five companions who have admitted guilt or been convicted as a result of Mueller's investigation or related matters are: Paul Manafort, Rick Gates, George Papadopoulos, Michael Flynn and Michael Cohen. The charges against them were not related to collusion with Russia.

Final Report Special Prosecutor Robert Mueller

On March 22, 2019, Special Prosecutor Robert Mueller released his final report to Attorney General William Barr after nearly two years.

Then, on March 24, he sent a four-page letter to Congress summarizing the findings of the Special Prosecutor's final report on Russian interference and obstruction of justice.Barr divided the letter into two sections: a. Russian attempts to influence the 2016 U.S. presidential election, and b. whether Trump influenced the course of justice.Regarding a., Barr stated that the Special Prosecutor found no evidence that the Trump campaign, or any comrade thereof, colluded or coordinated with Russia in its efforts to influence the 2016 U.S. presidential election. Barr added that the Special Prosecutor identified "two distinguished Russian attempts to influence said election."

As for b., obstruction of justice, Barr stated that Mueller did not reach a conclusion; he quoted the Special Prosecutor as saying: "while this report does not conclude that the President committed a crime, it also does not exonerate him."Barr writes: "The Special Prosecutor's decision to report the facts of his obstruction of justice investigation without reaching legal conclusions leaves it to the Attorney General to decide whether the conduct described in the report constitutes a crime, adding that he and Deputy Attorney General Rosenstein "concluded that the evidence accumulated during the investigation is insufficient to establish that the President committed a criminal act of obstruction of justice."

That the Mueller report concluded that the investigation initiated could not uncover evidence of the alleged conspiracy was not an adequate rebuttal, according to critics.

In May 2019, Republican Congressman Justin Amash stated, based on the results of the *Mueller Report* on Obstruction of Justice, that President Trump "has engaged in 'impeachable' conduct." He added that "few members of Congress have read that report."

Amash also said that Attorney General William Barr "intentionally mischaracterized" the report's findings and that prevailing partisan politics make it difficult to secure the maintenance of "checks and balances" in the American system. Amash is the first Republican Congressman to speak out in favor of impeachment of President Trump.In response, President Trump made Amash out to be a "loser" and further stated - falsely - that the *Mueller Report* had concluded that no obstruction of justice had occurred. Ronna McDaniel, chair of the *Republican National Committee* (RNC), accused Amash of "parroting the Democrats' hobbyhorses about the Russians."

She made no statement about immediate action against Amash, but tweeted to voters from Amash's district "to strongly support this president." Republican Senator Mitt Romney let it be known that he found Amash's statement "courageous," but himself judged the cited obstruction of justice as insufficient.

Investigations by the House of Representatives in 2019

In March 2019, the House of Representatives Legal Committee launched a broad investigation of President Trump for possible obstruction of justice, corruption and abuse of power. Committee Chairman Jerrold Nadler sent petitions to 81 individuals and organizations, either business or private, connected to Trump's presidency to produce documents, arguing that it is "absolutely clear" that the president obstructed justice. Three other committee chairmen sent requests to the White House and the State Department, seeking details of Trump's conversations with President Putin, including his attempts to conceal the contents of those discussions. The White House refused to comply with that request, claiming that the president's discussions with foreign leaders are confidential for security reasons.According to Senator Mark Warner, Vice Chairman of the Senate Intelligence Committee, there is "overwhelming" evidence of the Trump campaign's collusion with the Russians. Representative Adam Schiff, chairman of the House Intelligence Committee, stated that there is "unequivocal evidence" of collusion between the Trump campaign and Russia.

Legal affairs

Lawsuits

In 1973, the United States Department of Justice sued the company Trump Management Corporation, when Trump was the director of that company. His real estate company was sued for discriminating against black tenants. In 1975, a settlement was reached outside the courtroom. This did not require Donald and Fred Trump to admit guilt, but it did require the company to stop discriminating and to actively offer its properties to black home seekers.

Between 1986 and 2016, Trump and his companies had filed about 1,900 indictments and there were about 1,450 lawsuits suing Trump and his companies.

In March 1990, Trump threatened to sue the Janney Montgomery Scott company. A company analyst said Trump's Taj Mahal in Atlantic City would "break records," but would fail before the end of the year. Trump said he would sue the company unless the analyst was fired. The analyst refused to retract the statements and was eventually fired. In November 1990, the Taj Mahal filed for bankruptcy. The analyst then sued Trump for $2 million. The case was eventually settled. The analyst's statements about the Taj Mahal were later called "amazingly accurate."

During the credit crisis in 2008, Trump struggled to sell enough apartments at Trump International Hotel and Tower in Chicago. When he wanted to lower prices to increase sales, the borrower, Deutsche Bank, refused. Trump reasoned that the financial crisis and the resulting drop in the real estate market were not within his control, and used a clause in the contract to stop paying the loan. Trump then sued Deutsche Bank for loss of face, and Deutsche Bank also filed a lawsuit against Trump. Both parties eventually decided to drop their lawsuits and the sale of the apartments went ahead.

In September 2011, the final verdict in a lawsuit filed by Trump against author Timothy L. O'Brien was determined on appeal. The damage claim was primarily about Trump's estimation of net worth. Trump demanded $5 billion from O'Brien because O'Brien had written in his 2006 book *TrumpNation: The Art of Being The Donald* that Trump's net worth was actually between $150 million and $250 million, rather than the billions of dollars Trump had stated he had in 2005. Trump mentioned a value between 5 and 6 billion in interviews with O'Brien for the book, while an advertising leaflet from one of Trump's companies mentioned the value of 9.5 billion. Financial experts came up with between $150 million and $250 million. In addition, Deutsche Bank came up with a net value of 788 million. According to Trump, this underestimation, which he said the author had put in the book out of anger, had led to business deals failing and Trump losing face. At the official deposition for the lawsuit, Trump said, "*My net worth varies and rises and falls depending on the markets and opinions and my own feelings, even my own feelings, but I do the best I can. (...) So yes, my feelings also affect the value that I represent in my eyes.* " A New Jersey judge rejected Trump's money claim, and on appeal a judge decided to uphold the New Jersey judge's ruling because of the consistency of O'Brien's three confidential sources. In an interview with Kranish and Fisher, Trump claimed that he started the lawsuit because he thought the lawsuit *cost* O'Brien "*a lot of time and a lot of energy and a lot of money.* "

In 2013, Trump sued Bill Maher for $5 million after Trump showed his birth certificate. Maher had said on *The Tonight Show* that he would reward Trump with $5 million for charity if Trump, who had long questioned President Obama's American citizenship, proved that he was not the son of an orangutan. According to Trump, the offer was serious and not a joke. However, Trump withdrew the lawsuit eight weeks later.

On August 24, 2013, New York State Attorney General Eric
Schneiderman filed a lawsuit against Trump for deposing over 5,000
people for $40 million by teaching his real estate techniques in a for-
profit training program called Trump University. The Manhattan
Supreme Court had previously dismissed the suit. On January 30,
2014, the New York court also dismissed all charges except the
licensing part. In October 2014, the court found that Trump could only
be held liable for not having a license for his investment school. Of the
three lawsuits still pending, at least one was expected to go to trial
before the presidential election. On November 18, 2016, it was
announced that Trump had reached a $25 million settlement in this
case. For violating education laws, he also had to pay $1 million to the
state.

In August 2014, Trump reached a settlement with *Miss Pennsylvania*
Sheena Monnin, in which Monnin had to pay $5 million. She claimed
that the results of Miss USA 2012 were manipulated. Monnin wrote on
her Facebook page that another contestant had told her that during a
rehearsal she had seen a list of the five finalists in the final order.
Monnin subsequently relinquished her title of Miss Pennsylvania.
According to Trump's lawyer, a lucrative sponsorship deal with BP had
failed because of the allegations, and the allegations threatened to
discourage women from competing in the Miss USA pageants.
According to Monnin, testimony from the Miss Universe Organization
and Ernst & Young revealed that the fifteen first places in the beauty
pageant were determined not by the judges, but by the directors of the
beauty pageant. Under the terms of the settlement, Monnin did not
have to retract her statements. She said the following: "Standing on
truth has cost me much."

In 2015, Trump sued Palm Beach County for $100 million because,
according to him, officials had pressured the Federal Aviation
Administration to direct planes flying to Palm Beach International
Airport specifically over his property, Mar-A-Lago. The air traffic would
disrupt the building's construction and atmosphere. Trump had twice
previously also filed a lawsuit over noise pollution from the airport.

In 2015, Trump filed a $10 million lawsuit against José Andrés for
allegedly withdrawing from an agreement to open a restaurant in the
Old Post Office in Washington, D.C..

46. Joe Biden (2021-now)

Democratic party | Vice president: Kamala Harris

"True bravery is when there is very little chance of winning, but you keep fighting."

Joseph (Joe) Robinette Biden Jr. (Scranton (Pennsylvania), November 20, 1942) is an American politician and the 46th President of the United States since January 2021. Biden is a member of the Democratic Party and previously served as the 47th Vice President of the United States under President Barack Obama from 2009 to 2017 and before that as a Senator for the State of Delaware from 1973 to 2009.

Biden grew up in Scranton in the state of Pennsylvania and New Castle County in the state of Delaware and studied at the University of Delaware before earning a law degree from Syracuse University in 1968. After being elected to the council in New Castle County in 1970, he became the sixth youngest senator in U.S. history when he was elected to the Senate for Delaware in 1972. He served a long time on the U.S. Senate Foreign Affairs Committee and eventually chaired it. He was an opponent of the 1990-1991 Gulf War but supported NATO's expansion into Eastern Europe and its intervention in the Yugoslav wars in the 1990s. He supported a resolution authorizing the Iraq War in 2002 but opposed sending more troops in 2007. He also served as chairman of the U.S. Senate Committee on Justice from 1987 to 1995 where he worked on drug policy, crime prevention and civil liberties issues. He was one of the spiritual fathers of the Violent Crime Control and Law Enforcement Act and the Violence Against Women Act, and led the hearings of six U.S. Supreme Court justices, including the controversial Robert Bork and Clarence Thomas hearings. In 1988 and 2008, he was an unsuccessful candidate in the Democratic primaries for President.

Biden was re-elected as a senator six times and was the fourth longest-serving senator when he resigned in 2009 to serve as Barack Obama's vice president after they won the 2008 presidential election. Obama and Biden were re-elected in 2012. As vice president, he oversaw infrastructure investments to counter the credit crunch. His negotiations with Republicans in the U.S. Congress led to the passage of new legislation, including the 2010 Tax Relief Act, the Budget Control Act of 2011 in response to the 2011 U.S. sovereign debt crisis, and the American Taxpayer Relief Act of 2012. He also pushed for passage of the New Start Treaty with Russia and supported military intervention in Libya and the withdrawal of U.S. troops from Iraq in 2011. After the Sandy Hook Elementary School shooting on December 14, 2012, he led a task force against gun violence. In 2017, Obama awarded him the Presidential Medal of Freedom with distinction.

In April 2019, Biden announced his candidacy for the 2020 presidential election. After getting enough delegates behind him to win the Democratic nomination in June 2020, he announced in August 2020 that he had chosen Kamala Harris of California as his *running mate*. He then won the November 3, 2020 election over incumbent Republican President Donald Trump, who himself refused to recognize Biden's victory. On November 23, the General Services Administration (GSA) granted Biden the facilities due to a President-Elect. In a session begun on January 6 that had to be suspended after pro-Trump supporters stormed the Capitol in Washington D.C., in the continuation begun several hours later, the election results were ratified on January 7 at 4 a.m. EST by Congress, chaired by former Vice President Mike Pence. As a result, Biden was inaugurated as the 46th president of the United States on January 20, 2021.

Biography

Young Years (1942-1965)

Joseph Robinette Biden Jr. was born on November 20, 1942 at St. Mary's Hospital in Scranton, northeastern Pennsylvania, the son of Catherine Eugenia "Jean" Biden (born Finnegan) (1917-2010) and Joseph Robinette Biden Sr. (1915-2002). After him, a daughter and two more sons were born to this Catholic family. Jean was of Irish descent, with lineage dating back to County Louth and County Londonderry. Joe's father's parents were Mary Elizabeth (born Robinette) and Joseph H. Biden, a businessman from Baltimore, Maryland. They were of English, French and Irish descent.

Biden's father was initially wealthy but experienced financial difficulties during the period when Joe Biden was born. The family lived with Joe's maternal grandparents for several years. During the 1950s, Scranton fell into economic decline and Biden's father was unable to find steady work. In early 1953 his family moved to an apartment in Claymont, Delaware and later to a home in Wilmington, also in Delaware. There, Biden's father became a successful car salesman, allowing the family to maintain a middle-class lifestyle.

While attending school at Archmere Academy in Claymont, Biden was a member of the school football team. He graduated from there in 1961. He then studied at the University of Delaware in Newark, where he earned a Bachelor of Arts In 1965 with a major in history and political science and a minor in English. In the undergraduate point rankings, he was 506th out of 688 students.

As a child, Biden was a stutterer, but this improved in his early twenties. Biden himself said he was able to reduce his stutter by reciting poetry in front of the mirror.

Early career (1966-1972)

On August 27, 1966, Biden married Neilia Hunter (1942-1972), a student at Syracuse University, which was initially against the wishes of Hunter's parents because of Biden's Roman Catholic faith. The wedding ceremony took place at a Catholic church in Skaneateles, New York. Together they had three children: Joseph R. "Beau" Biden III (1969-2015), Robert Hunter Biden (born 1970), and Naomi Christina "Amy" Biden (1971-1972).

In 1968, Biden earned a law degree from Syracuse University. In the point rankings, he was 76th out of 85 students. He joined the Delaware Bar in 1969. During his undergraduate years, he was disqualified for military service because of his asthma.

In 1968, Biden went to work as an assistant in the law firm of prominent local Republican politician William Prickett in Wilmington. Later, Biden would indicate that he also felt like a Republican during this period. He disagreed with the conservative policies of then-Democratic Governor of Delaware Charles L. Terry Jr. He therefore supported the moderate Republican Russell W. Peterson, who managed to defeat Terry in the 1968 gubernatorial election. Biden was solicited by Republicans to register as a Republican but registered as an independent because he did not support then-Republican candidate for president Richard Nixon.

In 1969 he went to work as a lawyer in a law firm run by a local Democratic politician who was trying to revamp the local Democratic party. Biden also registered as a Democrat during this period. Later, he and a confrere started their own law firm, though he combined this with an income from managing property. Later that year, Biden was elected as a councilman in predominantly Republican New Castle County. He combined his term with his legal activities until 1972. During this time, he was an opponent of the construction of highways that would disrupt the tranquility of the Wilmington area.

Senator (1972-2009)

In 1972, Joe Biden was the Democratic candidate in the Delaware Senate election. He was the only Democrat to challenge incumbent Republican Senator J. Caleb Boggs.

Biden's campaign had few financial resources and, as a result, few opportunities were afforded him. The campaign was supported by Biden's family members, who bet on personal conversations with voters and distributing leaflets. These campaign techniques were possible in Delaware given the small size of this state. Biden was supported by the American Federation of Labor and Congress of Industrial Organizations, among others. His positions included the withdrawal of U.S. troops from Vietnam, as well as the environment, civil rights, fair taxation, and health care.

A few months before the election, Biden was trailing Boggs in the polls by nearly thirty percentage points, but his energy, his young age and young family, and his ability to respond to voter emotion worked out in his favor. Biden was elected senator on November 7, 1972, with 50.5 percent of the vote.

A few weeks after his election to the Senate but before he was sworn in, Biden's wife Neilia and their one-year-old daughter Amy were killed in a car accident in Hockessin, Delaware. His sons Beau and Hunter were also involved in the accident but survived with a broken leg and a minor skull fracture, respectively, and would make a full recovery. Biden considered giving up his Senate seat to care for his sons, but Senate Democratic majority leader Mike Mansfield was able to persuade him not to.

Biden was sworn in as a senator on January 5, 1973 by Secretary of the Senate Francis R. Valeo at a hospital in Wilmington and not at the Capitol in Washington D.C. because of the hospitalization of his sons. The ceremony was attended by Beau, Hunter and other family members. Biden was 30 years old at the time, making him the sixth youngest senator in the history of the United States. In order to see his sons every day, Senator Biden traveled daily by train between Delaware and Washington D.C., 90 minutes one way. He would maintain this habit of traveling by train daily throughout his entire 36-year career in the Senate. This also earned him the nickname "Amtrak Joe," a reference to railroad company Amtrak. In 2011, Wilmington's train station was renamed the Joseph R. Biden Jr. Railroad Station.

In 1975, Biden met his later second wife, teacher Jill Tracy Jacobs, during a so-called *blind date* organized by Biden's brother. They married in New York on June 17, 1977. Jill was also a Roman Catholic. From their marriage another daughter was born: Ashley Blazer (born 1981). Biden's eldest son, Beau Biden, later served in Iraq and was Secretary of Justice in Delaware. Beau died of brain cancer in 2015, leaving Joe Biden two of his four children. Son Hunter became a lawyer and lobbyist.

In 1988, Biden himself was hospitalized after a severe headache, where he was diagnosed with a brain aneurysm. After surgery, it took seven months for him to return to the Senate.

Joe Biden was a candidate for the Democratic nomination in the 1988 U.S. presidential election. During this campaign, he was discredited when it was revealed that he had plagiarized parts of a speech by British Labour Party leader Neil Kinnock. Biden then withdrew from the race, which was won by Michael Dukakis. The latter in turn lost the election to Republican candidate George H.W. Bush.

Biden remained in the Senate, where he was re-elected in 1990, in 1996 and in 2002, and where he held a number of important roles. From 2001 to 2009, he was chairman of the Foreign Affairs Committee, having already served as chairman of the Judiciary Committee from 1987 to 1987.

Biden was known in the Senate for his criticism of the Bush administration's Iraq policy. Biden was appreciated for his many legislative proposals and practical alternatives. His proposal to divide Iraq into three autonomous regions, a Kurdish, a Sunni, and a Shiite part, also received support in Republican circles. In the conflict between Israel and the Palestinians and in the context of the diplomatic conflict with Iran, Biden declared that he was a "staunch Zionist." In a 2007 interview, he said, "I am a Zionist. You don't have to be a Jew to be a Zionist". Biden considers Israel to be the United States' most important ally in the Middle East and is a staunch supporter of the massive financial-military aid that Washington transfers to the Jewish state each year. Biden argues that a militarily strong Israel is critical to U.S. ambitions in that region. After the September 11, 2001 attacks, Biden said, "Many Americans can now taste what it must feel like for Israeli parents when they send their child to school or put them on the bus." Later, as vice president under Barack Obama, he stood by the Obama administration's position. He warned Prime Minister Netanyahu that, according to the United States, he was leading Israel in the wrong direction with its illegal settlements.

Vice President (2009-2017)

Biden was one of the candidates for the Democratic nomination in the 2008 U.S. presidential election as of February 1, 2007. He dropped out of the race after getting less than 1% of the vote in the Iowa caucus on January 3, 2008.

On August 23, 2008, presidential candidate Barack Obama announced that he had chosen Biden as his running mate. Biden brought a great deal of foreign policy experience, something Obama would lack. In the presidential election on November 4, 2008, Biden was elected vice president. Although the United States had already had a Catholic president with John F. Kennedy, Biden was the first Catholic vice president in American history.

Biden was also re-elected as a senator from Delaware. Since a president or vice president of the United States may not hold other offices under the U.S. Constitution, he withdrew from the Senate before his installation on January 20, 2009. Delaware's Democratic governor,

Ruth Ann Minner, appointed Ted Kaufman, Biden's aide for many years, as his deputy in the Senate.

He also considered running for the 2016 U.S. presidential election but ultimately decided against it in October 2015. He himself attributed that choice to the recent death of his son Beau, which would have made it impossible for him to focus on a candidacy in time and with all his attention.

Presidential Candidate (2020)

Biden announced his candidacy for the 2020 U.S. presidential election in April 2019 and quickly emerged as the favorite in early polls, in a field of (initially) over 20 presidential candidates. His spearhead, even more than his program, was his belief that he would have the personality and experience to defeat President Trump.

That President Trump himself also saw Joe Biden as his biggest rival became clear when a whistleblower blurted out about a conversation President Trump had with the brand-new president of Ukraine, Volodymyr Zelensky. Trump asked him for a favor: the Eastern European country - highly dependent on the financial and political support of the United States - should launch a corruption investigation into the Bidens. Trump hinted that U.S. support for Ukraine depended on his request. The focus of the investigation was Joe Bidens second son, Hunter Biden. He had been appointed in 2014 for a very high salary (at least $50,000 a month) as a board member at the Ukrainian gas company Burisma, although he would have no qualifications for the position in that country. At the same time, his father, as then Vice President of the United States, manifested a politically profound presence in Ukraine by forcing the resignation of a corrupt Attorney General.

Trump's covert action, directed by his personal lawyer Rudy Giuliani, prompted the Democratic majority in Congress to prepare impeachment proceedings against Trump on the grounds of quid pro quo. With the exception of a single Republican, Trump was nevertheless defended by his party colleagues, mostly with the argument he used, "Why be so difficult? It was an excellent conversation!"

No evidence was presented of any corruption and/or violation of law by the Bidens in Ukraine. Nevertheless, in the impeachment proceedings against President Trump in January 2020, Trump's defense seriously exposed the fact that the vice president's son received millions in salary from a company in Ukraine known to be corrupt for work for which he had no special qualifications. During the impeachment proceedings, support for Biden's presidential campaign plummeted.

In the first primary election for the Democrat candidacy in February 2020, he finished a disappointing fourth place for him. In an attempt to turn the tide, Biden's campaign team released a derogatory video about rival Pete Buttigieg. He managed to win the primary in the state of South Carolina by a wide margin on February 29, 2020. He received strong support from African-American voters. After the South Carolina primary, Pete Buttigieg and Amy Klobuchar withdrew as candidates and indicated that they would support Biden's candidacy. On March 3, 2020, Super Tuesday, Biden made a remarkable electoral comeback by winning in ten of the fourteen states where primaries for the Democratic candidacy were held, including Texas and Minnesota. In doing so, he immediately became a "frontrunner" in the battle for the Democrats' nomination for the presidency. He displaced Bernie Sanders, who managed to win in the largest state of California, from first place. After Sanders withdrew as a candidate on April 8, 2020, Biden became the favorite for the Democratic nomination.

In April 2020, during the campaign, Biden was accused by a former staffer, Tara Reade, of improperly groping her in 1993. Biden vehemently denied the accusation. He indicated that "anyone who believed Reade should not vote for him." The Democrats and the news media were accused of maintaining a double standard in the way they handled the sexual assault allegations against Biden and Judge Kavanaugh.

During an appearance on the radio program *The Breakfast Club,* Biden hit a nerve in May 2020 for suggesting that black voters naturally vote for Democrats based on their ethnicity. Literally, he said, "If you have a hard time figuring out whether you're for me or for Trump, then you're not black. Later, Biden apologized for his remark, criticized as arrogant. He noted that no voter should vote for any party "based on his or her racial or religious background.

On August 11, Biden announced that California Senator Kamala Harris would be his "running mate" in the 2020 presidential election. At the conclusion of the Democratic Party's convention in Wilmington, which could be attended mainly digitally due to the corona crisis, Biden accepted his party's nomination for the presidency later that month with a speech marked by "hope" and "light" after the "dark" period for the United States under Trump.

On September 29, 2020, the first presidential debate between President Donald Trump and Joe Biden took place in Cleveland, Ohio. The debate had a chaotic flow. Biden was interrupted numerous times by Trump. Biden called Trump a clown and the worst president the United States had ever had. The debate is considered a low point in the history of American democracy. Still, Biden managed to hold his own and did not show the image raised by the Trump campaign that he was senile.

The elections took place on November 3, but in many states the results were delayed for days, partly because, due to the corona crisis, many voters made use of the option to vote early or by mail and the processing and counting of those votes often did not start until after election day. Because the Democratic Party had encouraged its supporters to vote that way, while Trump had urged his supporters not to vote by mail but on the day itself, Trump was still ahead in a number of states when the first intermediate tallies were reported. As soon as all the votes were counted, Biden appeared to have surpassed him there after all. Trump seized upon this state of affairs to speak of election fraud. After the news media pointed to Biden as the winner on November 7, four days after the ballot, his victory was rapidly recognized internationally. In addition to many statesmen, he was also called by Pope Francis, who offered his congratulations to the second Roman Catholic American president-elect in history.

President (2021-present)

President-elect

Biden immediately went to work as president-elect of the United States. He created a COVID-19 task force in response to what he saw as the Trump administration's failed policies in dealing with the pandemic. He appointed Ron Klain as White House chief of staff on November 11. He announced during the months of November, December and January the nomination of other key ministers and staffers. Among them is one of his opposing candidates in the primaries within the Democratic party, Pete Buttigieg as Secretary of Transportation. His cabinet, if all are confirmed by the Senate, will be the most diverse in the history of the United States. With a number of firsts, including the first openly gay minister, the first Native American minister, and the first woman as finance minister.

He was, especially in the beginning, greatly opposed by Trump and his administration who, without being able to provide evidence, continued to question the outcome of the election. On November 23, 2020, the

General Services Administrator finally gave Biden and his transition team the resources due a President-Elect. At the same time, the GSA recognized Biden as the presumptive winner of the election.

During the transition from January 6 to 7, 2021, after a storming of the Capitol by Trump supporters, Biden was officially declared the winner by a joint session of the House and Senate. The final result was read by Vice President Mike Pence around 4:00 a.m. local time and confirmed as 306 to 232 in favor of Joe Biden.

Conclusion

We hope you enjoyed reading about the 46 Presidents of America. The 46 Presidents of the USA is a factual and informative book that shows readers from the age of 12 and up some interesting facts about American presidents, including what they did before becoming president, how each one served as President, where they are now in life, etc.

We think you loved learning about these brave men who dared to be president of America.

This factual and informative book provides readers with an understanding of these brave men who dared to be president. Hopefully, you loved learning about some of the most important traits they possessed, such as bravery, intelligence, and determination in this book which should motivate you to make your own history (by reading it again)!